The Story of Folkestone

Ann Nevill M.A. (Oxon)

ANTONY ROWE
PUBLISHING

Published in 2009 by Antony Rowe Publishing
48-50 Birch Close
Eastbourne
East Sussex
BN23 6PE
arp@cpi-group.co.uk

A catalogue record for this book is available from the British Library

ISBN: 9781905200870

Printed and Bound in Great Britain by
CPI Antony Rowe, Chippenham and Eastbourne

Typesetting & Design by:
Istreets Limited
01303 237399

FSC
Mixed Sources
Product group from well-managed
forests and other controlled sources
Cert no. SGS-COC-2953
www.fsc.org
© 1996 Forest Stewardship Council

FOR JOHN AND THE FAMILY

This book began as a study of the transformation of a small smuggling and fishing town, to its position as the smartest and most aristocratic seaside resort in the South East, with knowledge drawn primarily from reading local newspapers. Henry Stock, editor of the Folkestone Chronicle observed in 1886,future local historians will find recorded controversies, reports of meetings and information of every character upon which much of the future history of Folkestone will depend.

Of course this had to be supplemented from a variety of other sources, school logs, council minutes, poor law records and railway information. However there has not been a history of the town since 1973. Now with the extra knowledge provided by the Channel Tunnel excavations, it seemed the right time to extend the scope of Folkestone's history.

I would like to thank John Eveleigh and Dr. John Whyman for their encouragement at the beginning, the librarians, C.P. Davies, Janet Adamson, Brian Boreham, Maureen Criddle, Peter Bloomfield and Maureen Shaw, and the local historians who have shared their knowledge: Dr. Esme Stuart, Eamonn Rooney, Martin Easdown, Chris Philips, Linda Rene Martin, Paul Harris, Nicholas Reed, Jane Elder of the Canterbury Archaeological Trust and the People's History Centre. Christopher Nevill sorted out computer problems. Edwyn James and Paul Harris for proof reading and for the illustrations: there have been generous loans from Alan Taylor's wide collection of local images, Philip Rutt, Paul Harris and the Canterbury Archeological Trust (CAT).

CONTENTS

1

THE PAST UNEARTHED

The early history of the area which we now know as Folkestone is powerfully illumined by the excavations which took place on Dollands Moor, now the site of the Channel Tunnel Freight Yard, some two miles west of the tunnel portal. These excavations, including 700 trenches, were conducted under the supervision of the Canterbury Archaeological Trust before the building of the Channel Tunnel, which was the largest privately funded engineering venture in Europe. They revealed that, after the last Ice Age 13,000 years ago, plants and animals re-colonised Britain and the country became thickly forested. The first farmers would have been active four to five thousand years ago. Later investigations show that they exhausted the soil with intensive farming of crops and cattle and that there was a continuous pattern of soil erosion and re-occupation when fertility improved.

A BRONZE SWORD FOUND AT EAST WEAR BAY FOLKESTONE IN APRIL 1951. IT DATES FROM 700 B.C.

A Bronze Age settlement was found at Holywell Combe at the foot of Sugar Loaf Hill, about a mile to the north. Here there is a line of small streams, including the Pent Stream a little to the West. There were trackways, marks from an ancient form of plough, and evidence of timber-framed round huts. Pottery found in three burial mounds was of the Beaker type. Looking from Castle Hill over the broad level plain which

stretches to the sea one can imagine prehistoric trackways and scattered settlements. Worked flints 5,000 years old have been found. There were ditches and burial mounds from the Neolithic to the late Bronze Age and domestic occupation with bones and pottery through to the various stages of the Iron Age, covering in all about 2,500 years. From the seventh century B.C. there were successive waves of immigrants from Northern Gaul with their iron weapons and implements. They lived in squalid conditions, in round huts built of wood or wattle-and-daub which were smoky and dark, roofed with wood or thatch. They also built hill forts and it is possible there was one in the Bayle area. Pottery seems to have been made as required in separate households and not by a village potter. There were farms and evidences of animal

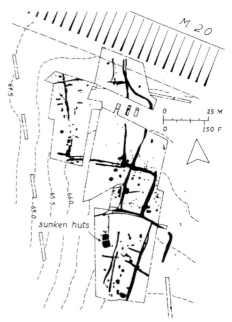

DOLLANDS MOOR - PLAN OF EXCAVATED FEATURES. (C.A.T.)

1

AN ANGLO SAXON FAMILY (RUTT)

husbandry, which continued during the Roman period and was little influenced by the conquest. Many sites seem to have been abandoned because of over-cropping and soil erosion.

There came to be an increasing amount of trade with Gaul, the British providing agricultural produce, slaves and oysters in exchange for fine pottery, jewellery, coins, wine and fish sauce. After his battles in Germany and Gaul, Julius Caesar decided to subdue the potentially hostile tribes in Britain, which would give him prestige at home. In 55 BC he did no more than effect a landing in Kent. The following year with more troops he was able to cross the Thames but was driven out by strong resistance and the British war chariots. The project was renewed a hundred years later when the Emperor Claudius sent Aulus Plautius, who landed successfully further North in Kent at Richborough, after which there was a visit from the Emperor himself. With the conquest Britain was now the northernmost portion of the mighty Empire, with all that this implied in the way of government,

THE ROMAN VILLA, EAST CLIFF

trade, religion, artefacts and the gradual integration of many members of the army into British and government life. Eventually all freeborn men and women became Roman citizens. Towns, that essential element of Mediterranean life, were established, with their temples, forums and basilicas. Houses were rectangular and brick built, often incorporating baths heated by hypocausts. An ordered and civilised life was possible with roads communicating with all corners of the country. There were occasional revolts but the Roman grip on the country seemed firm. In 1923 S.E. Winbolt, a schoolmaster on holiday, was attracted to Folkestone's East Cliff by rumours of finds of Samian ware.

In a hectic eight-week dig, he discovered a large Roman villa with another smaller villa built at right angles to it, possibly used for slaves and officials. This may have

REMAINS OF THE ROMAN VILLA. EAST CLIFF

formed the largest building in the area up to the nineteenth century. Under the villa were the remains of another building, giving a clue to a strong Romanising influence before the conquest. It posed fascinating questions of ownership. Was it a private dwelling or, on the evidence of twenty tiles stamped CL BR, (Classis Britannicus), the residence of the commander of the British fleet? This is now disputed though the site lay in a strategic position as a fine look-out between Dover and Boulogne, (Dubris and Gessoriacum), bases both for the ships which were necessary for transport and to protect the shores from the marauding Saxons.

At the time these villas were built, the sea would have been several hundred metres away. The main villa was some 69 ft. long and had 53 rooms with a central entrance and

two-story wing at each corner. One room, showing many fragments of gaily painted wall plaster, had a mosaic floor patterned with white and blue/black tesserae. Water from springs in the chalk was abundant allowing each villa to have a hypocaust and bath.

Valuable finds were few: a quantity of coins, some pottery and articles of bronze, bone, silver and iron. The

AN IMPRESSION OF THE ROMAN VILLA

foundations were of sandstone, quarried from what is now the sea bed at Copt Point.

There were twenty quern stones (stones used for hand-milling) and over a hundred more were found on the beach below, which must have been produced for export. These quarries were for centuries a valuable asset to the town. One can imagine a civilised Roman life in a comfortable home with fine furniture and good food, served by slaves. The dates of occupation are put at 100 to 353 AD. A fresh excavation in 1989 revealed that 10m. of masonry had slid into the sea at East Wear Bay. Apart from the villa, other traces of Rome had been described by Canon Jenkins in 1875, a church or

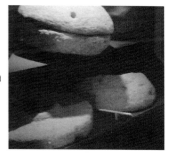

QUERN STONES

chapel apparently of Romano-British origin and the pillars of a hypocaust.

But all was not well. Barbarian tribes (amongst whom the British would at one time have been counted) were massing on the borders of the Empire and at the gates of the city of Rome itself. The British, according to Gildas writing two centuries later, appealed for help to Rome three times - the "groans of the Britons"- but Rome itself was in peril and they were told they had to defend themselves. From the middle of the fifth century a great blankness descends upon the historical record. The Roman army left, the buildings of Canterbury were abandoned and black earth covered the crumbling ruins. The roads which had

THE RUINS OF CANTERBURY (C.A.T)

provided access to all parts of England were scarcely used. The post holes of an Anglo Saxon hut were visible on the crossroads in the centre of Canterbury Even pottery making declined drastically. The inhabitants of the East Cliff Villa departed, and most of the valuables must have been removed or stolen. There is again only archaeological evidence for the succeeding centuries. The invaders became settlers. They, and the inhabitants of the farmsteads descended from Iron Age dwellings, had already existed side by side and were to form the basis of the succeeding Anglo-Saxon kingdoms.

The Gildas account has been questioned by Stuart Laycock in his book 'Britannia, The Failed State'. How could an established Roman population be overrun by a far smaller number of Germanic immigrants? The Roman invasion may not have been as complete as imagined, perhaps being no more than an intervention in the tangled affairs of the indigenous tribes who had different languages and coinages. They would have been seen as powerful allies in the struggle for power. Could this also have been a deep-seated suspicion of Europe and its customs which has lasted even into the twenty first century and the establishment of the European Union?

When the Dover Hill road was being widened in 1907, an ancient burial ground was discovered. It contained skeletons (one of which was female), together with a sword and daggers, shield bosses, amber beads and an elaborate brooch inlaid with gold and set with garnets. These were laid in the chalk in the fashion of the Jutes, who were Germanic invaders to Kent, and may have been warriors fallen in battle about 500 AD, with perhaps a camp follower. A complete skeleton from this site at one time formed the prize exhibit in Folkestone Museum.

SKELETON FROM THE JUTISH CEMETERY ON DOVER HILL

The year 597 was a watershed in English history, being the date of Augustine's mission to bring Christianity to Southern England. Aethelbert, King and lawgiver of Kent, had married Bertha, a Christian Frankish princess who came with a bishop and heard Mass in an existing ancient church in Canterbury. He was eventually converted. There had been Christians in Britain since Roman times but this marked the end of worship of the pagan gods. Britain was now incorporated into a wider European culture and the church was subject to orders from distant Rome. The parish churches and great monasteries unified social and intellectual life. According to the medieval historian John Capgrave, Aethelbert's granddaughter, Eanswythe, at the age of sixteen, founded the first nunnery in Britain on the West Cliff of the small town which had been built around the banks of the Pent stream. Her father, Eadbald, wished her to marry a Northumbrian prince but she had dedicated her life to the service of God as a virgin and refused the match. Her vocation and that of her sisters in Christ, whose lives were spent in singing the Divine Office and in manual work, must have made a deep impression on the inhabitants. This was the first of several nunneries in Kent founded for the benefit of a lady of royal rank. She was revered as a miracle worker, reputed to have restored sight to a blind man and cured someone possessed by the devil. The nunnery needed water so she struck a rock and commanded a stream to follow her uphill where it ended in a sizeable pond on the Bayle. Traces of a Roman or Anglo Saxon wooden aqueduct have been found and the miracle may have been due

THE WATER SUMMOUNED BY ST. EANSWYTHE IN THE BAYLE POND, 19TH CENTURY

to local ingenuity in conveying a strong current of water from the base of the chalk hills for the needs of the town. Through the centuries she has been the Patron of the town and is depicted on its seal.

After Eanswythe's death the nuns had to move to the church of SS. Peter and Paul, also built by Eadbald, as their original building was in danger of falling into the sea. The work carried on by the nuns was much appreciated and various bequests were made which added to the possessions and value of the nunnery until it was attacked and looted by the Danes. In 927 King Athelstan restored the church, giving the land to the monks of Christ Church, Canterbury, so that the services might once more be performed there. The relics of St. Eanswythe were transferred to the new church until Earl Godwin destroyed everything in 1052 in revenge. 43 years later Nigel de Muneville founded and endowed a new Priory for Benedictine monks, a cell of the house of Lully or Lonlay. The monks were moved to a new Priory and church built for them outside the Castle by William d'Averanches, Lord of the Manor, and dedicated to St. Mary and St. Eanswythe. This new church, for which a charter was granted in 1138 was the foundation of the present church. The relics of St. Eanswythe were carried there probably at the time of the consecration. Not yet could she rest peacefully – the church was destroyed in 1215 either by King John or by the French. It was rebuilt five years later.

The small settlement along the Pent was growing. After the refinements of Roman life, it was primitive and restricted but self sufficient, with small farms and a thriving fishing trade. It would also have been a place of pilgrimage to honour the saint's bones which had been so carefully carried from one church to another. A bewildering variety of names appeared in letters and charters from the seventh century onwards: Foulstone, Fulchestane, Foclestane, Folstone, Fulchestan and in 1586, Folkstone. It has been suggested that this could have been drawn from the name of a Celtic chieftain but more probably it referred to the stone quarries.

MEDIEVAL FOLKESTONE

With the Norman conquest, independent Saxon peasants became constrained by the obligations of the feudal system. A mass of information about Britain is provided with the compilation of the Domesday Book in 1086 at the command of William the Conqueror, anxious to list the possessions of his new kingdom for the purposes of taxation and legislation. The information, drawn from local juries, led to a chronicle unique in Europe, in which exactitude and order formed the key. All land now belonged to the king and its use was granted in exchange for services. Knights, who took an oath of fealty to their lord, had to give their services for a certain number of days, to be spent on call for the defence of the realm. The lower orders, the villeins and bondsmen, were tied to their land and were not free. They owed days of service on their lord's estate - digging, sowing, harvesting according to the season, often using their own equipment - and had to pay him on the marriage of their daughters. Their workdays could be increased at will or they could even be thrown off their land without any remedy from the courts. This is the reference to Folkestone in the Domesday Book:

"William d 'Arcy holds Fulchestan. In the reign of Edward it was rated at 40 sowlings; it is now rated at 39. The arable land is 120 carucates. In the demesne there are 209 villeins and 83 borderers (bondsmen). Between them all they have 45 carucates. There are five churches from which the archbishop has 55 shillings. There are three servants and seven mills of nine pounds twelve shillings. There are one hundred acres of meadow. Wood for the pannage of forty hogs. Earl Godwin holds this manor."

Ten sub-tenants are listed: seven, such as Hugh FitzWilliam and Walter de Appeville were probably Norman and three probably Saxon - Alured, Wesman and Alured Dapifer, the Purveyor. The five churches are a mystery. Later chroniclers suggest they were all carried away by the sea or even destroyed by the Vikings. Were it not for the archbishop's revenues, one might suspect this was a confusion with the five saints' altars described later as being in the parish church.

William made grants of land to his chief barons and at first the hundreds of Folkestone and Dover Castle were given to his brother Odo, Bishop of Bayeux, who was made Earl of Kent. In 1082 Odo was imprisoned because of his overriding ambitions and there was a new plan to defend Dover. Each baron was appointed to one of the towers of Dover Castle, the Baron of Folkestone holding responsibility for the d 'Averanches Tower. From the twelfth century onwards, feudal dues were gradually commuted into money payments and, with the growth of markets, the system became less regimented. In Folkestone the right to hold a market every Thursday was granted to Jeffrey FitzPeter in 1205 and further markets followed.

During the eleventh and twelfth centuries land in Newington and Normandy was inherited by the Lords of the Manor: William d'Arques, Nigel de Muneville (through his wife) and the d'Averanches family. Matilda d'Averanches married Hamo de Crevecoeur and they had four daughters. When Hamo died, a valuation of the manor was made in 1263 with its holdings and tenants. These details were attested by the local inhabitants: Sir Henry Hauereng, William the Reeve, Ralph the Reeve, Peter de Ecclesia and others. The Lord's Hall is described as a capital messuage (house with outbuildings and immediate ground), well built with a garden, a dovecote and stone-walled courtyard. A large deer park was enclosed by a hedge some 4-5 miles in circumference. It extended nearly to Sandgate, and would have afforded pasture for a hundred cattle. Fifty acres were covered with large oaks and great whitethorns. Twenty-two acres were a mowing meadow and the pig pasture was worth 40 shillings. The demesne lands comprised 815 acres of arable, pasture and meadowland, 710 acres in Folkestone and 115 acres in Newington. All this lasted as a unit till the sixteenth century. Reynden Wood comprised 150 acres, of which 40 could be sold each year, each acre being worth 4 shillings.

A RECONSTRUCTION OF THE PRIORY

The sub-tenants who paid knights' fees under the Barony also had to enclose a number of perches (an area of just over 30 square yards) of the property. Sir Nicholas de Crioll for example paid for five knights and enclosed 63 perches of parkland. Fourteen 'distinguished individuals' provided twelve knights in all. There were three very poor watermills and a windmill at Terlingham, between Folkestone and Hawkinge. Rents were various, such as 376 hens, 800 eggs at 3 pence per hundred, two-and-a-half pounds of pepper and two seams of fine white salt.

Stocks' Guide of 1865 put the location of the Hall as being near Park Farm (the present commercial estate in Folkestone) which meant it must have been moved from the Bayle. The foundations could be traced at that time and a portion of the moat was still remaining, though only partially filled with water. The spring which supplied it, crossed by a dilapidated stone bridge, ran down the Foord valley (the area of Folkestone around the viaduct) to the harbour. The Hall was allowed to decay from about 1578 and was never rebuilt.

Thirty-two shillings and ten pence was due for Peter's Pence or Romescot (the parish tax which had to be paid to Rome) which became a source of grievance. There were also tithes to pay, a tenth part of land and produce to be set aside for the upkeep of the church. The Lord of the Manor had the right of presentation to the living which was worth 40 shillings per annum. He held five courts for Folkestone and its dependencies and could collect the fees. Also, as the Priory was founded by the Lord of the Manor, he had the right to name a new Prior in case of death. The affairs of the Prior were to prove troublesome as he collected all the revenues of the parish church,

except for personal bequests, and was responsible for paying the Vicar's stipend. In the 1430s the Prior complained to the Chancellor of England that the townspeople had seized him from the altar and dragged him to the cliffs from which they threatened to hurl him into the sea. Within a few years they were again accused of harassment and refusing to pay their dues. A settlement was reached and the Vicar's salary fixed at ten marks a year.

PARK FARM

There was a new crisis in 1463. John Lord Clinton had chosen his brother-in-law Henry Ferrers as Prior. He had a rival, one Henry Banes, chaplain to a more powerful patron at Court, the Duchess of York, mother of Edward IV. Ferrers accused Banes of wandering about the world as a false monk, an apostate and sodomite, already excommunicated. Clinton wrote to the Mayor that he should keep Banes in custody. However Banes won and became both Prior of Folkestone and Vicar of Hawkinge and Appledore. Nothing more was heard till 1491, when Archbishop John Morton's campaign to reform religious houses was in progress. He charged Banes with absenteeism from his duties for thirty years while he was in Westminster, using the church and Priory receipts for his own purposes and incurring a debt of seven hundred marks. The monastic buildings were now in a state of disrepair and the monks wandered about the streets and fields of Folkestone unsupervised, with no regard for their rule of life. Banes was finally dismissed and Thomas Sudbury appointed Prior.

Money was left for candles to be lit or masses to be said, saving souls from the pains of Purgatory. These bequests were useful revenue for the parish church: Elizabeth Yocklett left the residue of her will to the Vicar Dom William Claybrook and the executor *"to dispose of my soul as they think best"*. William Gybbe in 1493 left six shillings and eight pence for lights on his burial day and every year for 8 years. John Gebon in 1558 willed a 1lb. wax taper to burn before the high altar on Sunday and *"master Vicar, my curate to be given six shillings and eight pence to pray for me"*. There are hundreds of wills leaving money for candles for various altars: St. James, St. John, St. Barbara, St. Anthony and St. Eanswythe. They must have been ablaze with lights on feast days.

Other bequests included William Foren's lodge by the sea (there were several of these mentioned in wills), which was to be sold to pay his debts. John Gebon's wife was to have his chamber for life, with free coming and going to the fire, half the crop of wheat, a cow and the goods she brought with her; but, if not content with these things, she was to take her jointure and go her ways.

Philippe Stret left to William Rigden, his kinsman, a quarter of each of his batelles (boats) called Peter, Gregory and Old Fortune.

In the reign of King John, for the first and only time in its history, the town became the stage for European politics. The king had enlisted a large number of mercenaries from the Low Countries to be lodged in Dover. As the town would be crowded, the King stayed in Folkestone in May 1216 on three occasions, remaining altogether about twelve days. The French Dauphin Louis, at the invitation of the Barons, invaded Thanet and took all of Kent save Dover. Folkestone was badly damaged and King John fled to Winchester. According to Hasted (see chapter 3), William d'Averanches, Lord of the Manor

KING JOHN

of Folkestone, took advantage of the confusion to deprive Hawkinge church of its tithes, by forcing his tenants to pay them to his Hall in Folkestone.

The Rev. Alan Gibson has given an account of the Norman castle on what is now known as Castle Hill, about a mile to the NW of Folkestone, formerly and erroneously named as Caesar's Camp. Excavations were made during the late nineteenth century by Augustus Lane Fox and others. He was at the School of Musketry in Hythe and later, known as General Pitt Rivers, became the father of British archaeology.

Fragments of medieval pottery and a coin of King Stephen were found. There was a motte and bailey castle which would have been constructed in or before the troubled reign of Stephen about 1135, a time when there were supporters of his wife Matilda in Boulogne and Dover and a civil war in progress. The Queen's

CASTLE HILL AS IT MAY HAVE LOOKED
ABOUT 800 YEARS AGO.

forces blockaded Dover. Stephen gave permission to the barons, amongst whom was the second William d' Averanches, to construct their own castles. The dangers here became obvious and Stephen's successor, Henry II, dismantled a thousand castles, amongst which was the one on Castle Hill.

The town was gaining a considerable amount of self government, a Mayor elected by the burgesses, a bailiff and twelve Jurats. The Mayor's election is described in the Folkestone Customal of 1327:

"They claim by usage of all times upon the day of the Nativity of Our Lady (September 8th) the Mayor and the Jurats shall upon the blowing of the horn hold a Common Assembly in the Churchyard and there shall be brought the common box with the common charter and all the other muniments of the town and shall charge the other Mayor that he shall be true and lawful unto the king of England and his heirs and lawfully shall maintain the franchise of the town rich and poor in one right so helping him God and his Saints, kissing the book. And all the XII Jurats shall do the same. Also a Bailiff to be appointed that shall be commissioned by the Lords of the Sea and the same shall be charged by the Mayor that he lawfully maintain the franchises." The Mayor also acted as Coroner of dead bodies and the Mayor and Jurats judged pleas, save those belonging to the Lord Warden.

THE REBUILT TOWN CROSS

The same ceremony of horn blowing to call together the townspeople is described in later elections and, to this day, Mayor Making continues on the same site. There is a record of a medieval house on the Bayle, built about 1400 and demolished in 1916 to

make way for the Folkestone Herald offices, it was evidently quite a good sized dwelling with large rooms. In Tudor times both a fireplace and a small new wing were added. There were traces of wall paintings and plaster figures of a hound pursuing a stag, also a quantity of clay pipes; eventually it was separated into two tenements. A row of small cottages on the Stade was demolished in 1935 due to a landslip and also because of a slum clearance programme. One can reasonably assume that

MEDIEVAL HOUSE STILL STANDING NEAR CHURCHYARD

there are no more medieval remains save for some sections of St. Eanswythe's, but Andrew Linklater of the Canterbury Archeological Trust has advised that there are areas of stone walling in the High Street shops, then as now, the crowded narrow passageway between the Bayle and the Stade. Also, there were two white weatherboarded houses abutting on the churchyard which have inside a crown post and blackened beams, indicating a large jettied hall house with an open fire and smoke escaping through a hole in the roof.

The Pent Stream was important. Rising in the vicinity of Castle Hill, it made its way to the sea, providing a convenient inlet where boats could be moored and unloaded, but it gradually became silted up. Perhaps it was used by the Romans and Anglo Saxons but there is no proof of this. Remnants of ash and sycamore have been found, together with twelve pieces of leather, some of these being the pointed toes of medieval shoes. The stream narrowed at two points where stone bridges were provided. In addition there were four-metre-long wooden posts and wood with carpenters' marks, implying more elaborate preparations for a harbour.

In 1313 Folkestone became a member of the Cinque Ports as a limb of Dover, supplying one boat to Dover's four. In the words of Mark Lower from Seaford (a Deputy in 1865), *"The fleet of the Cinque Ports was the flag and defence of our land and the first germ of our naval supremacy against England's enemies."* The ports provided 57 boats and crews who served for 15 days on warfare or defence. The portsmen in return enjoyed many privileges, being free from tax and tallage (tolls) and having the right of tol and team (self government), blodwit and fledwit (punishment) and others. One other important privilege was that of den and strond (regulating the herring fishery at Yarmouth), which led to many disputes. These were discussed at the courts of Brotherhood and Guestling which met to settle disputes and taxes. Folkestone did not always attend these. Here for example the fishermen of Folkestone complained that a debt was owed them by a Dover man. They were then empowered to seize any visitor from Dover until the debt was paid, the detention described as being 'in withernam'. The five original members were joined by the two ancient towns of Rye and Winchelsea and eventually a number of other towns and villages along the coast and inland. At the court of Shepway the Lord Warden was appointed. Apart from ports silting up and the Black Death, the practical value of the Cinque Ports finally disappeared with the foundation of the regular navy by Henry VII, but the meetings and ceremonial remain into the twenty first century. The office of Lord Warden has been filled by Sir Robert Menzies, Sir Winston Churchill and Queen Elizabeth, the Queen Mother. The Barons still hold a canopy over the Sovereign at the Coronation.

THE TUDORS

The coastal towns of Kent and Sussex had a different destiny from those inland such as Ashford and Maidstone. Their inhabitants were neither rich merchants nor the possessors of many acres with fine houses and impressive municipal buildings. In many cases, including Folkestone, they thrived economically but their wealth came from the sea - fishing, smuggling and the capture and ransoming of enemy ships and sailors. Their fortunes and dangers were affected by changes in British foreign policy and the varying relationships with France and Spain. The broad picture was that a watch had to be kept on the coast, invasions prevented, spies reported and boats and men provided when necessary.

During the reign of Henry VIII, in spite of the magnificence of his meeting with the French King, Francis I, at the Field of the Cloth of Gold, and the official declarations of friendship, England was in a state of simmering hostility with France. Henry entertained ambitions to win back the territories lost during the Hundred Years War. In 1522 it was reported that English fishermen were casting their nets in fear of the French. The Archbishop of Canterbury himself visited the sea defences at Folkestone, Sandwich, Deal, Dover and

HENRY VIII (NPG)

Hythe and wrote to Cardinal Wolsey to advise that beacons and watches should be organised and repaired. A chain of castles was built along the coast, at Sandown, Deal, Walmer, Sandgate and Camber. Sandgate was built in 1539, the year the Pope's Bull of Excommunication against Henry was reissued. It was designed on a clover leaf pattern like Walmer, with a keep, a gatehouse and three towers connected by galleries, all protected by a stout wall.

The building of the castle must have taken up all the available local labour with a daily average of 630 men working, rising at times to 900. The labourers came from as far afield as Somerset and Gloucestershire - stone masons, bricklayers, painters, metal workers and carpenters. They were housed in tents, a canvas pavilion or a lodge near the beach. The total cost was over £5,371

SANDGATE CASTLE

and 147,000 bricks were laid. Some of the stone was the Caen stone that had been used in the construction of the dismantled religious houses of Folkestone Priory, St. Radegunds and Monks Horton. In addition there were the resources of the Folkestone quarries which were covered by the sea at high tide. By the third month the labourers were *"breaking the rocks and carrying them from the sea, loading the carts and using boats to carry the stone."* Master Richard Keyes, the Paymaster, and Master Bryan Tuke put in their claims for horses, and time fetching money from London and Dover to pay for men and materials. (Master Keyes is also recorded for striking William Baker upon the eyebrow and drawing blood within the churchyard. He was fined 12 pence.)

Three years later these two were called upon again, when there was interest in building a harbour at Folkestone and a site was sought. The army was mustering on the coast awaiting an invasion and local harbours would be of great assistance. Master Tuke drew up a plan for which he was rewarded with a conger eel worth 20 pence. The King himself came down and stayed for five days at the beginning of May, 1542. Richard Cavendish, John Bartlett, John Borow and Anthony Aucher, who had already drawn up a plan for Dover, were called in as consultants. In the next two years John Thompson, Master of the Maison Dieu at Dover was also involved.

In 1574 there was a reference to *"money left over from the building of our harbour"*. It had become silted up and it was enacted that, upon the beat of a drum all inhabitants should assemble with a shovel and endeavour to clear it out or face a 6 pence fine.

The 1540s were a time of national emergency and ships were prohibited from passing over the sea. A watch was to be kept for Scottish ships as there was an alliance between Scotland and France. Orders were given to take French ships and boats and to seal up Frenchmen's goods. Finally war was declared on August 4th, 1543. Part of the army was mustered at Folkestone and 220 men, 10 bullocks and 40 horses were shipped from there. The local preparations were extensive - and expensive.

The town had to provide six armed men one year and eight the next. Their equipment was bought in Dover and needed an escort of *"Master Mayor and other company"* to fetch it, a journey which took three days. Six harnesses were bought, six upper garments and hosen, three doublets, six pairs of boots, six swords and daggers and two sword girdles, costing a grand total of six pounds fourteen shillings. As well as preparations for invasion, there were preparations for defence. William Baker, the Town Sergeant, rode to the Lord Warden at Cobham to fetch guns which were overhauled, taken to the old Priory site and tested by gunners from Dover. Bows, arrows and gunpowder were bought for them and trenches dug. Thomas Lambard made a quantity of targets with protective mounds or butts on the same site. These took seven loads of turf, rails and posts and cost 10 pence.

At this period there were 120 houses in the town and 25 boats in the harbour. The settled area did not vary much until the nineteenth century - The Stade, The Durlocks, the High Street, along the road to Dover and Cow Street (Sandgate Road). The names mentioned in medieval maps are familiar today: Bayle, Boucherisgate, Foard, Grace Hill, Terlyngham and Wiltighe. The inhabitants were mostly fishermen, shopkeepers and farmers, some living in tiny cottages and others in comfortable well furnished two-story houses, which had curtains and a store of household goods, brass pots, candlesticks and silver spoons. Some of the cottages had one room to each floor, similar to those still occupied in Hastings.

Alderman Henry Herdson, a merchant and member of the Skinner's Company, purchased the Folkestone estate from the Clintons. In 1578 in the days of Thomas Herdson, *"the ancient park of Folkestone seems to have been disparked as to the use of it for deer and the like and to have been used for feeding of oxen and sheep and for the purposes of agriculture."*

On the Bayle between 1550 and 1800 there was a building that served as a manor house. Thomas Clinton had abandoned the old large house and park and chosen a more central dwelling. It stood between the church and the sea, forming three sides of a square.

The re-issue of the Pope's Bull of Excommunication of Henry had served to increase France's hostility towards England. Whether it seriously troubled the consciences of the Folkestone faithful is doubtful. The oath of allegiance to the King as Supreme Head of the Church had only to be taken by those in office. There was no change in the pattern of church services, the Mass or offices for the dead, and Protestants were still burnt at the stake. In any case, the next heir after the short-lived Edward was to be the Catholic Mary. One innovation must have been a welcome one, the introduction of a chained Bible in churches, giving lay people a chance to read the Scriptures in their native tongue instead of Latin.

The suppression of the monasteries made the most impact locally. The larger houses, particularly in the North, offered valuable support for the poor and for travellers; their dissolution led to grave social problems and a dangerous revolt, the Pilgrimage of Grace. Some religious houses had lost their zeal and were declining in numbers, serving no obvious purpose. Commissioners had been appointed to make reports on their condition, which generally turned out to be unfavourable. The Folkestone Priory had been failing for years and Thomas Bassett, the Prior, submitted to closure in November 1535, when there was no more than one sick monk left in the community. Bassett was given a pension of £10 a year. Now only the parish church was left as a place of worship. There are still tantalising traces left of the old Priory, which had been built to the south of the church, in and around the Bayle, and the Priory House could have been the Prior's lodging. Leland in the 1530s saw *"in Castel Yard bones and great and long British brikes"* protruding from the storm-worn cliff. Hasted in 1800 saw only a foundation arch and a great sewer. He also says that the King's Commissioners had sold off any disposable parts of the building. Excavations may well bring more information to light.

The town's accounts show the provision of public entertainments. There were companies of players who moved from town to town. They had to be licensed or attached to a nobleman's household. Both the King's and Queen's Players appeared, giving performances at Master Baker's or Master Kennet's at the Cheker. The subjects were mostly religious and 8 pence was paid for a performance of 'Iope' (possibly Job). The Lord of Misrule, Master of Ceremonies at Christmas, was given seven shillings and sixpence when he carried out his duties at Folkestone and Sandgate. There were also performances by the King's Jester and William the Lutor (lute player), who played and sang. Bear keepers and their charges are mentioned seven times. One of the Queen's courtiers said: *"It was a sport very pleasant to see the bear trying to free himself from the dogs with clawing, with roaring, tossing and tumbling."*

Queen Elizabeth loved to travel round her kingdom. This necessitated extensive preparations, roads having to be mended and covered with gravel. In August 1573 she went to Mr. Tufton at Hothfield, then spent four days at Westenhanger, dined at Sandgate Castle and went on to Dover via Folkestone Down. She was greeted by Lord Cobham, Warden of the Cinque Ports, together with a great number of local gentry and Archbishop Parker, who was compelled to give Her Majesty his handsome horse which she had admired.

Traditionally Folkestone was a town of fools, who cast a net from the church tower to catch the smallpox and drown it in the harbour and buried beefsteaks to grow bullocks. Robert Holliday the Mayor, who was short of stature, climbed on a stool to greet Her Majesty, "Most gracious Queen, welcome to Folkesteen" he cried, *"Most gracious fool, get off that stool,"* she replied.

QUEEN ELIZABETH (NPG)

There was a great threat from Spain. Philip, having been married to Elizabeth's sister Mary, felt he had a right to the crown, having been misinformed by the English Catholics that he would be welcome. In 1570 her subjects were released from their allegiance to the Crown by the Pope, making Catholics automatically traitors. Spanish ships had been plundered of their rich treasures by Drake and others. Elizabeth, who was very averse to spending money, enjoyed the gold and jewels but did not want war. However, the provocation was such, she was powerless to prevent it, and in 1588 the great Armada was made ready for the invasion of England: 120 ships and 20,000 soldiers under the command of the Duke of Medina Sidonia, with more to come from the Duke of Parma. The fleet was sighted in June off the Cornish coast and might have been seen from Folkestone beach on July 28th when it was anchored off Calais. That week the Jurats of the Cinque Ports were quietly debating whether Sandwich owed a bill of £5 which had not been audited. The garrison of Sandgate Castle would have been in a state of the highest alert. The ships were *"built high like towers and castles"* drawn up in a crescent shape with horns seven miles apart, which were cumbersome and slow compared to the more nimble British. That night fireships were sent amongst the Spanish fleet and panic ensued. More ships were lost in storms off the Irish coast.

For coastal protection a harbour was to be made at Dover, financed not by the exchequer but by a levy on passing ships and a share of customs duties on wheat. The case for preferring Dover to Folkestone was put by Thomas Digges: *"Touchinge Foulstone Mole Sir Richard Greynvile is greatly abused for an hundred thousande powndes is not able to make any sutche mole there but every ebb eny of her Mayestyes great shippes should break out ther Rek on the rokkes. Wheras at Dover for £10,000 it may be done indeed serviceablye."*

There were interesting statistics on the Folkestone quarries supplied by the clerk of the works, William Hunt, in 1580. It seems 60 labourers broke out the stone and scapelled it and 40 hard hewers would shape and smooth and square it under the direction of John Trewe. The latter was paid 7 shillings per day but was later dismissed for wasting money. In 1580 there were 100 men at work, the hard hewers being paid 6 shillings a week, the labourers 4 shillings. The cost of sharpening tools was 5 shillings per day. The stone was taken to Dover by boat. At this time, after fishing, quarrying must have been Folkestone's main industry. Hasted remarked that *"Below the cliff on the shore, for some time towards the sea, is a long ridge of sunken rocks, occasioned by the fallen cliffs at different times."* He also says that rocks were taken for the piers of Dover and other places and that in the time of Cromwell's usurpation they were used for Dunkirk harbour.

Vigilance had to continue. In 1599 a watch was to be kept in several places in the town by the householders themselves, from seven at night when the bell was rung, till five or six in the morning *"uppon imminent danger of the enemy his landing within this land"* They were to gather at the place of rendezvous upon the ringing of the same bell. Thomas Godfrey, a common victualler, was to lodge only honest strangers who could be examined by the Mayor and Jurats. He should also charge reasonable prices. There was an emphasis on the purity of food, with an ale conner to ensure good and wholesome ale for sale and a flesh searcher to insist on good and wholesome flesh, suitable for man's body. Attorneys were to delay no man for lucre or malice, to do no falsehood and to be content with their fees. There was a constable, Ben Cloake, to keep the king's peace, to arrest felons and rioters, rogues, vagabonds and night walkers. These could be put in the small dirty cell underneath the Town Hall, put in the stocks to which was attached the name of the offence, or sent to Dover Gaol at the expense of the town.

Only freemen might trade in the town, a privilege granted on a payment of twenty shillings or a seven-year apprenticeship. Selling in the market was open to all but the goods were taxed. The other sources of the town's income remained the same: billet money, hookfare paid by fishermen who went to Yarmouth during the mackerel season, which was one of the privileges of membership of the Cinque Ports, crayerfare paid for North Sea voyages, taxes on market and shop sales, fines from unlicensed traders and even a tax of half its value on fish caught. This had to be lessened upon protests from the fishermen and settled at one penny per pound. In addition there could be additional cesses collected by the chamberlain on land and income, generally for the purposes of defence. Receipts amounted to some £65/100 spent on various expenses: £53 to the Mayor in 1607, to the Town Clerk £5, and the lavish freemen's dinner 36 shillings; rent of the Court Hall 2 pence and of the poorhouse 2 pence; given to a blackamoor 5 shillings and an Arabian 2 shillings; the expenses of those attending the Court of Brotherhood and Guestling; the upkeep of bastard children and pen and ink for the Clerk. The Town Chest contained various deeds from 1574 onwards, relating to sales of property and rent agreements for tenements on the Bayle. Documents were signed with personal hieroglyphics such as double or treble crossings. It was a narrow and in many ways a highly regulated world.

Deliberations were held in an ancient building, the Guildhall or Town Hall, for which a rent of one penny was paid in 1515. It was in a bad state of repair in the days of Henry VIII and sums for its repair - bricks, tiles and paint - appear frequently in the accounts. Of irregular shape, it stood at the junction of Mercery Lane (Church St.) and Butchers Row (Rendezvous St.). It would have resembled the Guildhalls in Rye and Hythe with a large room upstairs and an open space beneath for the market. It had to be shored up in 1730 and was eventually demolished in 1840.

The name of Folkestone was to enter medical history in 1578 when a son named William, who was to become the greatest scientific genius of the age, was born to Thomas Harvey and his second wife Joan, at a stone-built house near the junction of Church Street and Rendezvous Street. The Harveys were a well-to-do family who owned property in the district and were said to have owned a business carrying goods between Folkestone and Canterbury. Thomas was four times Mayor of Folkestone and another son John became MP for Hythe.

At the age of ten William attended Kings School, Canterbury, and went on to Caius College, Cambridge, where he would study various branches of science, including anatomy, physics and chemistry. Medical studies were then based on tradition. William's great achievement was to submit these theories to practical experimentation.

TITLE PAGE OF HARVEY'S BOOK

The circulation of the blood had been described in 1242 by an Arab physician, Ibn al-Nafis and several others, but the idea was completely unknown in the Western world. William's attention would have been drawn to this subject by his master at Padua, his next place of study. This was Hieronymus Fabricius who had described the valves of the veins in a way which William felt to be unsatisfactory. He did many experiments on animals and came to the conclusion that blood was pumped around the body by the heart and was continually recirculated. His great work 'An anatomical exercise on the motion of the heart and blood in animals', published in 1628, was followed up by other scientists. He also correctly observed the fertilisation of a human egg by sperm.

Given his scientific approach, it was no surprise that he was unimpressed by accusations of witchcraft and black magic. He headed an inquiry into some women who had been brought from Lancashire as suspected witches. The King pardoned four of the seven.

He had a successful career, being elected a Fellow of the College of Physicians and appointed one of James I's several doctors, attending the King on his deathbed.

Subsequently he was Court Physician to Charles I. The two men became friends and he was allowed to carry out experiments on deer in the Royal parks. After the battle of Edgehill he is recorded as attending to the wounded and following the King to his bolthole in Oxford, where he lived for four years and became Warden of Merton. His Whitehall apartment was sacked by the Parliamentarians and years of research were lost, particularly his work on insects, which he had intended to publish. His career had spanned a tumultuous period in English history, ending with the execution of his patron.

HARVEY ATTENDING KING CHARLES

After the death of his wife, William Harvey settled on living with his brother Eliab. His special importance in the history of Folkestone lay in one of his charitable bequests. He left money to found a library in Merton and

£200 for Folkestone's poor. This sum was used by his nephew, another Eliab, to buy a house for a school in Rendezvous Street for the sons of poor fishermen, to build a tanhouse (where nets could be treated to avoid rotting), and to purchase Combe farm, of which the rent should go to the upkeep of the school and the purchase of a fishing boat to give away to a poor fisherman. Thus did formal education in Folkestone begin.

THE UNVEILING OF HARVEY'S STATUE CLOSE TO THE LEAS, FOLKESTONE

He was commemorated by a statue erected in 1881 and by a window in the parish church. He appears on the town seal in company with St. Eanswythe. The large hospital at Ashford named after him has his statue in the car park.

THE STUARTS

The great national events which affected every family in the land in the seventeenth century were the Civil War, the execution of Charles I, the rule of the Commonwealth and the restoration of Charles II in 1660. The Kentish gentry had been affected by the imposition of ship money and some sympathised at the outset with the fervour for reform, as shown by various petitions to Parliament. But the killing of the King was seen by many as more than a crime, being a sacrilege committed against the Lord's Anointed. The King was condemned as a tyrant and a murderer and was led from the Banqueting Hall at Whitehall to the scaffold set up outside. When the axe fell, a bystander testified, *"there was such a grone by the thousands there present as I never heard before and never desire to hear again."* This happening was intimately connected to Folkestone, a shameful secret which was hidden for nearly four centuries and the perpetrator's name never appeared in the town's records.

It had to do with the history of the Manor. Basil Dixwell came to Kent from Warwickshire, inheriting the estate from the Herdsons, and becoming an MP, a sheriff and a Baronet. In 1625 he was living in *"my mansion and manor house of the Priory at Folkestone."* This was narrow and cramped so he built a new and more splendid house at Barham, Broome Park. The old mansion house gradually fell into decay and from then on till the nineteenth century the Lord of the Manor did not possess a Folkestone dwelling. His successor, his nephew Mark, was killed in the Civil War and the next inheritor was Mark's son Basil, who was three years old. Basil's guardian was his uncle,

KING CHARLES I

John Dixwell, an ardent Puritan and MP, who was a member of the Council of State, a Colonel in Cromwell's New Model Army and in charge of the defence of the South. When the decision to execute the King was taken, it had to be given a veneer of respectability by a trial in Westminster Hall and a death warrant. It was difficult to find signatories for this and pressure was put on the remaining members of the Long Parliament. Eventually fifty-eight men were found to take responsibility for the verdict, of whom John Dixwell was one. After the Restoration only twelve of the regicides escaped. He himself would have been imprisoned, possibly tortured and condemned to death, but he fled to America. In New Haven, Connecticut, he became a silversmith and died in 1689. The Dixwell assay mark is recognised to this day.

Support for the Commonwealth was considerably lessened by the rule of the Major Generals, laws against swearing (which caught out many Folkestone fishermen), the prohibition of any sort of plays, diversions or merry making on Sundays and Christmas Day. Church of England clergymen had been thrust out of their livings and replaced by Puritan preachers. The Folkestone clergyman was elderly and barely able to fulfil his duties, but in the parish records there was an entry reading IN THE TIME OF THE USURPER and two names, WILLIAM RUSSELL & JOHN BAKER. Weddings were performed by the Mayor or one of the Magistrates or Jurats. At the end of the Commonwealth era, Charles II was welcomed back with rejoicing and made a triumphal journey from Dover to London. Royalists were reinstated in Folkestone's Common Assembly.

THE STADE, FROM HASTED

The Quakers were constantly at odds with the authorities for refusing to pay tithes, take the oath of allegiance or attend the parish church. In 1655 there were travelling Quaker preachers in Kent, who were well received at Sandgate Castle and by Thomas Nichols of Folkestone, who was locked up in 1660 together with seven others. The meeting house was closed and, as no money was available for fines, goods were seized: silver spoons, candlesticks, wheat, sugar, stockings and a pair of linen drawers.

There now appeared a great danger to the town which did not lessen until the building of the 1807 harbour. The stone quarries had been valuable for employment and revenues but much of the greensand rock had now been removed. This left the lower part of the town at the mercy of wind and waves - the Stade, the fishermen's cottages and the cliff on which the parish church stood. The situation was summed up in a petition made to to Charles I in 1629:

"The town of Folkestone that hath flourished by shipping and trade and hath furnished very able pilots and hath contributed great sums of money towards the setting forth of ships, hath of late fallen into decay and the inhabitants become very poor; the sea hath fetched away their ancient stade where their vessels used to be laid up i safety. The sea hath encroached so much upon the land that it is approached within seventy paces of the church (as heretofore it hath fetched in two other churches there). They ask to be granted rights to build a pier and harbour with the same rights and benefits as other places of harbour have obtained."

Some sort of protection must have been made: in 1635 on the beat of a drum at the Mayor 's command every householder was ordered to repair to the harbour provided with shovels and other tools for expelling the beach. The communal nature of these efforts is interesting, though twenty years later the Corporation noted that people had been stealing stones from the jetties. These jetties, which needed to be protected by planks, cost some £600. As well as thieves there were storms, that of 1699 being particularly violent and again the inhabitants had to dig out the silt. In 1703, following the greatest storm, the fishermen proposed to pay 6 pence in the pound of their earnings for jetty repairs, though they could ill afford it, and the Corporation petitioned Jacob des Bouverie to let them take stones from the beach. By 1720 the stones had become dislodged. Jacob offered the fishermen a barrel of ale to replace them, but they pointed out the need for them to be cradled in large timbers, lest they be washed away again. The Mayor said the fishermen continued clamorous. Jacob was furious: *"This expression was not well used towards me. I desire you to acquaint Mr. Mayor that as I am Lord of the Mannor, I esteem it my right to proceed in the liberties of it as I think well. I will remove the stone or not and do what I please about the Stade, and if the Fisher Men don 't like it, let him and them represent to me by a petition what they would have done for the advantage of the Town and Corporation, and I shall resolve what may be best to do in it."*

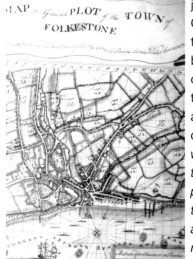

FOLKESTONE IN 1698 ABRAHAM WALTER

THE EIGHTEENTH CENTURY

In 1697 the last Sir Basil Dixwell sold the manor and lordship of Folkestone to Jacob des Bouverie. The family is still here after more than two centuries and, though stripped of much of its landholdings, is taking an active part in the modern development of the town. Jacob's father had a large fleet of ships which traded with the Far East via Aleppo and Constantinople and Jacob was a merchant agent. He returned to England and lived in London. He was probably anxious to invest his wealth and must have known the area, as he represented Hythe as one of the Barons of the Cinque Ports from 1695-1700 and was elected again in 1714. He also had connections with Lawrence des Bouverie, born 1542, of Flanders who married Barbara den Hove, niece of an opulent silk manufacturer in Frankfurt and emigrated to Canterbury at the age of 26. Jacob's notebook describing a trip around his new properties and his letter book from 1717 to 1722 give a good idea of his holdings and general policy.

As well as farms, his possessions included two tile lodges, a copperas house, the stone quarry on the shore, the Kings Arms at the Folkestone Cistern House and 300 acres of woodland, worth in all £1,204 per annum. He rode around Park Farm where

flowed St. Eanswythe's stream of clear water, Walton Farm and the Cheriton and Raidon [sic] Woods. He saw *"my Bayle land"* with its battery of eight guns and the remains of the old Priory. The stones would come in useful for building.

Jacob was a meticulous, indeed a grasping absentee landlord, intent on the last penny of his rights particularly if Henry Barton, his agent, had been dilatory in collecting the rents. He wrote to Margaret Boughton two days before Christmas,

THE CISTERN HOUSE MAP

"After heartily condoling with you on the death of your husband, wishing health and happiness to yourself and your little one, I think it proper to acquaint you that your husband stands my debtor in £200".

It was difficult to send money safely to London and guineas were advised as they attracted less attention than large amounts in small coin. Otherwise bills of exchange were used, a very complicated proceeding and Jacob had to acknowledge receipt and encashment of each one. However rents were sometimes two or three years in arrears. *"I am glad you go forthwith after tenant Dixon, he has broken his word with you a hundred times. His farm is undoubtedly a good pennyworth, (this was a favourite expression of Jacob's) and you can't fail of an able tenant for it."* He was particularly jealous also of his rights of wreck and salvage on the shore, making sure that the anchor and cable of the wrecked ship Neptune, cast ashore between the kiddle nets and the Shorne Cliff, fell to his share. This caused a dispute with Mr Brockman of Hythe and Jacob had recourse to Sir Basil to see if he had any remaining documents to support the Estate's claim.

He died without issue and the Estate passed to his nephew, Sir Edward, who also died without issue. The family seat was at Longford Castle in Wiltshire, which had been purchased from Lord Colerane in 1717. Sir Edward's brother, Jacob, who inherited the title and estates, was created Viscount Folkestone in 1747 and started the famous Longford picture collection. In 1761 he was succeeded by his son William, another noted picture collector, who was granted the Earldom of Radnor in 1765.

HASTED - THE FIRST PORTRAIT OF THE TOWN.

The problems of the fishermen were partially solved by the imposition of a new tax. In 1766 an Act of Parliament was obtained which placed a duty of one shilling on every chaldron (40 bushels) of coal coming into the town by sea or by land. The Mayor and Jurats undertook the task of administering the Act and keeping the accounts. In default of Lord Radnor, they also appointed the collector of coal dues with duties on the Stade, at Sandgate turnpike and Dover Hill. Yearly receipts could amount to £100. Oak planking was ordered and new jetties made.

Hasted's view of Folkestone published in 1790 shows a perfectly flat beach with rows of houses and cottages facing out to sea. In front were King's Bridge Street and Stade Buildings, behind lay Fisherman's Row, Old Sea-Gate, Froghole and New Island. The map made for the Radnor Estate in 1782 is more specific. There is one jetty and a clump of rocks near the outflow of the Pent Stream, a jetty beneath the cliff on which the parish church stood and three more at the Eastern end of the beach. This map also shows a dozen sites for capstans where boats could be pulled up, of interest to Lord Radnor because he could claim rent for them. In 1782 he formally demanded his rights saying that, having resided in a distant country, he had been *"very easy and indulgent"* with the inhabitants to date." The Corporation challenged him but, despite a thorough search, could not discover the necessary documents in the town chest. Eubulus Smith, the Radnor agent, wrote: *"I have observed that a very large part of the Stade is constantly taken up by large cutters to caulk, repair and rest there until they are again wanted for sea. This is of great importance to the merchandise of this town which is its chief support."*

Edward Hasted had also been granted access to the town chest to help him compile his History of Folkestone. This was not his only town history and there were eight others, including histories of Canterbury, Tenterden and Bexley. His major work was the History and Topographical Survey of the County of Kent. The expenses of publication brought him to penury. He fled to France but the war forced him to return and he spent seven years in a debtors prison. He was rescued by his friend William Bouverie, later the Earl of Radnor, who granted him the Mastership of Lady Margaret's Hospital in Corsham, which provided education for children and a home for six (later eight) paupers for five years till he died in 1812. Such posts were notorious sinecures.

KIDDLE NETS CAUGHT FISH ON THE INCOMING TIDE.

Vincent Pain, a boat builder, had three capstans bought for £27, which he used himself and let to other fishermen. The Corporation had threatened to withdraw his rights and he wrote to Lord Radnor, *"That your Petitioner, as soon as he became acquainted with the dispute regarding the Stade, being convinced of your Lordship's right to it, steadily adhered to the supporters of your Lordship's claim and having frequently repeated his opinion, he has given so much offence to the Corporation and they are become so much his enemies, that he cannot expect that any common request made to them will ever be attended to."* (Radnor Papers)

The centre of the town was still the Parish Church on the cliff and the Bayle, the pond, the Fair place and the Battery. The High Street with its shops climbed the steep slope from the harbour and the area of the Pent Stream, which had carved out the valley dividing the town, was now a peaceful rural setting with a mill and a tannery along its banks. William Gostling in his 'Walk around the City of Canterbury ' (1774) described it as *"a considerable fishing town, of such a hilly situation that it is hardly safe to ride in some of the streets of it."* There were a variety of small traders: blacksmith, hatter, basket maker, stationer, tailor, tanner, watchmaker, grocer, milliner, pastry cook, plumber, schoolmaster, chemist, cordwainer, cooper and shoemaker.

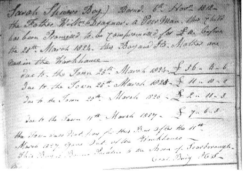

EXCERPT FROM BASTARDY BOOK

The Elizabethan settlement had decreed that the care of the poor, widows and orphans should now be the responsibility of the parish. Money for them and the upkeep of bastard children made regular appearances in the accounts until the latter were apprenticed, often as cabin boys on the boats. Girls went into domestic service but mistresses found them of little use as they had never lived in a proper home. Parishes were encouraged to build poorhouses where the elderly and sick could be cared for. In 1786 items bought for the Folkestone poorhouse start to appear in the accounts: two shillings' worth of beer, coals, seeds and plants for the garden, bedpans, pork, mackerel, mops and an apron for the mrs. There was relief for poor travellers and for other special cases; two shifts for widow Medgett, six shillings for a wedding, £1 for redemption of pawned clothes and two shillings for hire of a horse to carry a woman out of town, who had been whipped as a whore. There were occasional credits for the poor's employment in oakum picking or hemp dressing.

Parishes were anxious to avoid the expense of providing for a family where the father was unemployed. Every worker who came from another parish had to provide a settlement certificate that he could be returned there in case of necessity. Folkestone was a good place to find a job and there were certificates from many parishes. These cases, if involving enquiries, could be expensive. One such cost £21 and involved a night at Dover with tips to the boots and chambermaid, grog, beer and a bottle of porter for the officers involved. There were two poorhouses, one at the bottom of what was Sandgate Road, facing the Town Hall, and the other on the site of what was to become the Wesleyan Methodist Church. Then in 1785 a new poorhouse was erected at the bottom of Dover Hill. These local poorhouses were not centrally regulated and could be dirty and ill-run. Worse still the paupers could have the tight appearance of being overfed, as Sir Francis Head remarked when inspecting them. Beer and brandy were available to the Folkestone paupers in cases of illness, boots and shoes made to measure. There was actually a school for pauper children and a school master was appointed. But things had to change. Wages were being supplemented out of the rates on a sliding scale linked to the price of bread and the poor rates increased dramatically, from a million and a half pounds in 1776 to four million pounds in 1803.

In civic affairs the responsibility of inhabitants was emphasised, that those who enjoyed the privileges of the town should pay their cesses and take up their duties as freemen or Jurats or face fines. John Willis, who was from Dover and not a Folkestone

freeman, hired a house and sold baskets to the fishermen. He was fined six shillings and eight pence. Ham Tite, who owned the Gun brewery, attended the Common Assembly but refused to take the oath to support the charters, liberties and privileges of the Cinque Ports, but especially those of the town of Folkestone, on the grounds that he was a freethinker

THE BAPTIST CHAPEL, 1830

and an enemy to all corporations. Jesse Swaby, a Jewish pipemaker, refused to swear on the New Testament. A legal opinion was called for. The upshot was that Jesse Swaby could swear on the Old Testament but could not hold corporate office. Richard Hobday moved that Ham Tite's fine be rescinded and the motion was carried unanimously.

A Quaker meeting house was erected in Harbour Way in 1798 on land which had been a burial ground. Here Mrs. Lainley preached, though it was remarked that she needed to speak in a milder tone as she had talked herself hoarse.

Closely connected with the Quakers in their beliefs were the early Baptists. John Stace, the owner of Bradstone Mill, gave land for their burial ground and the meetings were held in his parlour. The first tombstone was that of Mary Stace in 1747 and the last that of William Pledge in 1856. No further burials were permitted after the municipal cemetery was opened in Cheriton Road. Some of the burial ground is still there, a forgotton corner of Folkestone. In 1730 a chapel was built in Mill Bay, then a peaceful rural spot, an orchard and a crescent-shaped meadow on the slope to the north, with the waters of the Pent Stream below. It had a gallery with room for forty singers, esteemed as one of the best choirs in the country.

JENNY POPE'S ALLEY

Discipline was strict. Mr. Anett was excluded for drunkenness and Ann Pledge for very awful immorality. The minister from 1784 was the Rev. Mr. Atwood until he married his housekeeper and had to resign.

The Methodists also tended to start with informal meetings and preaching in people's homes. The first Methodists in the area met at Sandgate in the parlour of Sgt. Gough, a Peninsular War veteran and the father of John Gough who became a famous American temperance orator. A chapel was later built and John remembered tweaking the wig off a fellow worshipper. The Folkestone Methodists met at the home of John Oliver Davies, above his chemist's shop. Then a centre was found in Elgar's Yard opening out of Jenny Pope's Alley which crossed Harbour Street. A sect which had links to the

THE PARISH CHURCH

Methodists was the Countess of Huntingdon's Connection which used the Zion Chapel, built in 1784. The registers are extant from 1799 to 1836. The early Congregationalists opened their own chapel at the end of Tontine Street.

There were many smelly herring hangs in the town, salted or smoked fish being a favourite item of diet. Quaker Jenkins, who came to live there in 1820, remarked on its reputation for ugliness but said that people in general had a wholesome and cleanly appearance. The boys he thought were worse than the lazzaroni of Naples. There were two tallow candle factories but darkness dropped like a thick cloud upon the town at night. Flickering oil lamps marked the street corners, but the many blind nooks, dark doorways and steps protruding into the streets aided the same small boys in their

THE TAN HOUSE

favourite occupation of teasing the grim-looking lamplighter, Jimmy Crummey. Pedestrians carried lanterns, as did the Town Sergeant when preceding the Mayor and Jurats in their journeys abroad after dark.

Many houses had their own wells but the drains discharged into the harbour where, it was said, the smell was enough to knock a horse down. There were occasional plague and typhoid epidemics and in 1765 there were 158 victims of smallpox. In 1796 a private Act of Parliament was passed for 'Paving, repairing and cleansing the town of Folkestone'. A special body of Paving Commissioners, a Chairman and 6/8 members were set up to enforce the duties laid down therein. They had powers to name the streets, to pave them with stones from the quarry, clear drains, lay extra pipes and to remove bow windows and intrusive steps, all paid for by a special rate. This was collected by the same official who collected the coal dues and the proceeds of the turnpike gates on Sandgate Hill and near the Valiant Sailor on Dover Hill. They could award the contract for clearing rubbish or scavenging amounting

THE PENT STREAM

to a payment of some 2 guineas, which at one time went to Parson Pearce. Ashes and rubbish were valuable for roadmaking, as proved by Noddy Boffin, the Golden Dustman of *"Our Mutual Friend."* In the first year of operation 117 complaints were investigated.

Along the South East coast smuggling was combined with the trade of fishing ever since duties had been imposed on imports and exports in the reign of King John. The export was fine English wool much, prized by Continental weavers, which was exchanged for luxury goods such as wines and spirits, tobacco, silk and tea. The Customs service was established with ships to patrol the coast. In 1724 Daniel Defoe noted: *"As I rode along this coast I noticed several dragoons, riding officers and others. armed and on horseback, riding always about as if they were huntsmen beating up their game; upon enquiry I found their diligence was employed in quest of the owlers, as they call them and sometimes they*

SMUGGLERS ON THE BAYLE CLIFF, (TURNER)

catch some of them, but I found too that often times these are attacked in the night with such numbers that they dare not resist or, if they do, they are wounded and beaten and sometimes killed". Defoe's account is borne out by the fate of Lt. Peat, an officer residing in Folkestone who was shot fourteen times in an ambush – and still survived. In spite of the violence, there was no particular moral disapproval, as so many were implicated, including on one occasion, the Mayor of Hythe. Lord Liverpool, when Prime Minister, in 1820, called Folkestone, *"a nest of damned smugglers"*. There were many hiding places in the cottages built along the Pent stream, inside hidden cupboards and cavity walls. Women also were participants, hiding contraband in laundry baskets or mattresses. The stream survives still under Tontine Street, ending as a feeble trickle into the inner harbour.

Turner came to the area many times, sometimes to visit his mistress in Margate and to Folkestone to paint. In 1845 he executed sheets of studies in colour and light, 'Ideas of Folkestone', anchored to the landscape by the faint silhouette of the viaduct. He also did watercolours of the smugglers whom he must have known well. They are shown, first sinking the kegs tied together with rope to escape detection, then pulling them up again and hauling their booty up the Bayle cliff where they buried it and lastly, having been caught by the revenue officers, being compelled to dig it up from the beach. These were turned into popular prints. Punishments could be transportation for landsmen or service in the Navy for fishermen.

There were countless stories about smuggling exploits: an exciseman was on Sandgate beach when a boat was hauled ashore. He called out *"I smell tea"* when a young sailor came ashore with some packets concealed in his tall boots. A dozen knives flashed and the officer fell dead. The culprits were never even accused. Juries displayed a great reluctance to convict and the flimsiest excuse was sufficient for an acquittal. A lugger the 'Four Brothers' was carrying a hundred tons of leaf tobacco and fifty casks of brandy destined for Ireland and had a crew of 26. It came across a revenue cutter, the 'Badger', and a fight ensued in which four smugglers were killed and six wounded and some of the opposing crew were also killed. They were captured and served eleven weeks in the King's Bench prison. They had an able defence team and were warned not to speak any English as they claimed to be Dutchmen, who had been flying the Dutch flag. Pregnant English women would go to Holland to be delivered and it was a difficult claim to disprove. They were aquitted and were conveyed back to Folkestone in triumph, all the town turning out to meet them.

In 1830 a whole crew consisting of Folkestone and Sandgate men was taken by Lt. Lilburn, known as Billy Hellfire, and lodged in Dover Gaol. A rescue attempt was swiftly decided upon and a large force of men, boys and women made their way there, resolved to knock a hole in the wall. The Governor was in a terrible state of alarm and sent for the Mayor, who sent for the soldiers from the Castle. The mob was now augmented by reinforcements from Dover. The Mayor attempted to read the Riot Act but the women, acting like Furies, snatched the paper from his hands and tore it up. Lt. Lilburn, who was zealous but foolhardy, asked McCullock who was in charge of the troops, to fire upon the excited mob. He refused and told Lilburn to give the order himself. The Mayor fled, pursued by the insults of the crowd and the shop keepers barricaded their shops. Meanwhile the activists had succeeded in freeing the prisoners who were taken to Folkestone where their manacles were removed and they went into hiding. This exploit gave rise to a ballad:

> *"Oh then a hole in all the wall*
> *Was everybody's cry*
> *And Lilburn's and McCulloch's men*
> *Were soon obliged to fly."*

The coastguard service provided lodgings for its officers. One house was destroyed in a landslip and was replaced in 1832 by an unusual dwelling, the 'Pelter' brig, left over from the Napoleonic wars and beached in East Wear Bay. It was cosy but inconvenient as shopping had to be carried from the town along the beach and bread was delivered by a boy on a horse. It was superceded by cottages, which were again destroyed in a landslip; finally the row of Coastguard Cottages with a station were built at the end of Sandgate High Street, still standing but now sold off and in private ownership.

There was another side to smuggling. During the Peninsular War Wellington was in need of money to pay his soldiers and allies. The bags of golden guineas, supplied by the great banking house of Rothschild, were sent via Folkestone in fast-rowing galleys painted black to escape detection and sent to Spain through a network of spies. Napoleon actually knew of the traffic but allowed it to continue as he thought it would drain Britain's gold reserves. The story went that this same spy network informed Nathan Rothschild of the allied victory at Waterloo. He was a familiar figure on the Stock Exchange and sold his Government bonds with maximum publicity. Others took the hint of a defeat and Consols slumped alarmingly. His agents then repurchased them and he made another fortune. Throughout the century Folkestone handled bullion exports, a lesser tonnage than Dover, but of high value.

Voyages were not always successful and there were four shipwrecks in two years, 32 women becoming widows and 146 children fatherless, all dependent on charity. The

fishing community were helpful and Parson Pearce never allowed any family to go hungry. For this he was rewarded by the occasional gift of smuggled goods left at his door. Indeed smuggling involved a great deal of social cohesion and clan loyalty. But it was a closed, secretive and somewhat sinister world, suspicious of strangers. There could be no holiday traffic or smart visitors till the trade had vanished, conquered by the impact of modern times, new roads and railways.

Foreign rivalries now menaced the small town. The Kent coast was twice in danger of invasion. Napoleon, master of Europe, made immense preparations to destroy England, his one unconquered enemy. The first time was in 1798 when the country was ill prepared. There was only a small force of regular soldiers and a large force of untrained but enthusiastic

NAPOLEON

volunteers. The uneasy peace of Amiens in 1802 was but an interval in the struggle which continued for eleven long years. Between 1802-5, the peril was extreme. *"The English don't know what awaits them,"* he declared: *"If we have the power to cross for only nine hours, England is no more."* The ports of Boulogne, Etaples and Wimereux were widened and deepened. A force which was eventually to build up to 100,000 men was being trained and provisioned and over 1,000 boats built for transports and landing craft. The troops took rowing and swimming lessons. Encampments of huts appeared on the slopes round Boulogne. Napoleon himself paid several visits.

In 1794 the War Department bought 229 acres of land at Shorne Cliff which was to become one of the foremost military establishments in the Kingdom. Here Sir John Moore, a humane and intelligent man, commanded the Light Infantry Brigade, training the men in tactics of mobility and speed which were to be so useful in Spain. These tactics he had learnt in the campaign in America. Stout officers were made to run up the hill to the Camp. Nervous inhabitants were immensely reassured by the fact that he brought down his mother and sister to live in York Cottage in Sandgate.

Meanwhile the Royal Navy was constantly on the watch in the Channel. In the popular prints, a miserable Boney was opposed by a stalwart John Bull, fuelled by beef and beer. Every town, even as far as Edinburgh, was becoming a garrison and the volunteers, who eventually numbered 380,000, trained diligently with whatever weapons came to hand. The cavalry might produce swords and pistols, the infantry volunteers firelocks and the pioneers or labourers, pickaxes, shovels, spades, saws and billhooks, a motley collection. All boats, their masters and their tonnage were listed, with those serving as privateers or the sailors as sea fencibles. The press gangs were busy, out to capture young men for the navy. Such a raid was reported as taking place at the New Inn, Sandgate. Folkestone itself was protected by its steep cliffs, the battery and the Camp but there were many landing opportunities on the flat sands of Romney Marsh. Between 1796 and 1803 there are numerous documents in the town records empowering the constables, churchwardens and overseers of the poor to make lists of supplies which might be useful in case of a general evacuation: oxen, cows, sheep, pigs and horses. Cattle should be branded with a parish mark to prevent confusion. There were 14 bakers who could supply 100 loaves daily with an extra supply of flour. There were lists of all the male inhabitants aged between 15 and 60 with their available arms. Quakers were exempt. There was considerable difficulty locally about finding lodgings for the militia and a Billetting Officer was appointed with a salary of £5 per annum.

Folkestone ships, while playing their part in the defence of the coast, also brought prosperity to the town. The merchants and mariners armed their vessels and were granted Letters of Marque as privateers, which gave them powers to take and then ransom enemy ships and their cargoes and crews. Several valuable prizes are recorded. Some of the boats were built by the Sandgate ship-builders who had already provided frigates and sloops for the Navy in the American War of Independence. These ships were from 40 to 400 tons and some carried large crews which included a surgeon and carpenter. The 'Ant' a Folkestone cutter, captain John Cornish, was captured by a

French brig from Dunkirk, with 140 crew, in 1793, but in a storm two Frenchmen were shut in the hold, another jumped overboard and the ship was recaptured. The sailors were rewarded with 30 guineas by the Society for the Encouragement of Recaptures. The 'Fame' under Captain Tapley took a French ship of about 400 tons laden with indigo with an estimated value of £60,000. Unfortunately the following year the ship was sunk, the crew had to swim ashore and were taken prisoners. There was great rejoicing in Calais when the 'Flying Fish' of Folkestone was taken, this having been a terror to the French for a long time. She had previously taken a valuable cargo of silk from Martinique and had landed it at Deal. There are many stories of valiant deeds, narrow escapes and deaths from drowning. It was recorded that in times of war, pots full of golden guineas stood upon the table.

In the event of an invasion, the alarm could be given by telegraph and hence conveyed to thousands of volunteers across the country by fire beacons, bundles of faggots or barrels of tar kept always ready, as had been prepared for the Armada. In September 1803, a signal was fired. General Moore was at Dungeness and came galloping back at top speed to find the alarm false but the volunteers, sea fencibles and all were in high spirits at the prospect of meeting the enemy.

Informed opinion in England, including that of Nelson, was sceptical about the French chances of success. The Navy was on a perpetual alert and French boats could only be launched over several tides. A limited rehearsal in 1804 with Napoleon present, resulted in a scene of confusion. Nevertheless the Légion d'Honneur was presented to the soldiers in a special ceremony near Boulogne and a medal inscribed with his head bearing the legend 'Descente en Angleterre, frappe à Londres 1804' was struck. In the winter of 1804 preparations seemed to be in abeyance and relations between France and Austria were worsening. The Emperor was now turning his attentions towards Europe and the battle for England was to be abandoned.

When the danger was nearly over, it was ironical that the most extensive Government preparations against the French were begun. These were the digging of the Royal Military Canal through Romney Marsh to Rye, which Napoleon, who had crossed the Rhine and the Danube, would have found no obstacle. Another new defensive idea was the building of a line of 74 round forts at danger points along the coast, of which three were in Folkestone and four in Sandgate. These were 33 feet high with immensely thick walls and housed a powder magazine and small garrison. They were called Martellos, after one that had been very successful at Mortella Point in Corsica. Sandgate Castle was remodelled. William Cobbett fulminated later against the expense, the work of Pitt and Dundas, *"Here has been the squandering! Here has been the pauper-making work!... the causes which are now driving some farmers to the workhouse."*

THE MAKING OF THE MODERN TOWN
THE COUNCIL, THE ESTATE AND THE MPS

By 1800 Folkestone's population amounted to some 3,500 - 770 families living in 762 houses, with 70 men employed in agriculture, 212 in trade and (in 1811) 659 seamen. After the Napoleonic wars economic conditions were bad and there was much unemployment. The overseers reported on the conditions in the fishing trade, especially in stormy weather. There was no work to give them,

THE ELHAM WORKHOUSE
BUILT 1836, NOW DEMOLISHED

save a little fishing-net braiding for those in the workhouse. *"Casual relief is one shilling a head, sometimes only sixpence. It would grieve anyone to take this relief wholly off when there are gales of wind and no fish."*

The concept of workhouses was changing. For economy the reforming Whig Government introduced the Poor Law Reform Act in 1834. Parishes were to form unions and build new large workhouses. These were to adopt a prescribed dietary, no more than the poorest labourer could obtain by his own efforts. There was to be no more monetary relief and a pauper family had to give up all their goods on entry. Husbands were separated from wives, parents from children (who were generally looked after by the feeble minded amongst the inmates). There was such a dread of these institutions that they were known as the 'New Bastilles'. Folkestone joined the Elham Union of fifteen parishes. The poorhouse was built at Each End Hill, costing £6,500 with room for 300 people, though at first it housed only 65 men, 28 women, 38 children and 7 lunatics. The old poorhouse was bought by Stewart Marjoribanks M.P. and became the first British school. Goods were bought for it: knives, teaspoons, porringers, boots (which were passed on, ill-fitting, from one pauper to another), flock beds, (shared except in the infirmary), 200 yards of dark fustian and 20 yards of unbleached calico for clothing. Folkestone, though it provided 1/3 of the revenue had only one representative on the Board of Guardians. The paupers took up residence in 1836.

The health of the poor generally was also the responsibility of the Guardians of the Poor. In 1851 there was cholera in Sandgate and medical attendants were allowed an extra two guineas daily. Some fifty letters were written to landlords who were responsible for filthy privies and blocked drains. These duties were eventually taken over by the Inspector of Nuisances.

But there were occasions for rejoicing such as the annual Mayor's dinner at the Apollo rooms or the Guildhall. There was a splendid procession at the proclamation of a new monarch - George IV, William IV and Victoria - of all the town's officials in their robes and uniforms. At the young Queen's accession in 1837 a new national spirit was perceptible, one of idealism and respect for innocence compared with the cynicism of the eighteenth century. This was especially strong in the field of religious belief and gave a new impetus to Evangelicalism.

Matters settled back into their original peaceful state. The Harbour Company was being formed and the Corporation contributed towards its costs. Its members were also those who were shareholders and later mortgage holders of the Company – men like Henry Butcher, a blacksmith and five times Mayor who sat on a Committee to check the Chamberlain's accounts and James Tolputt, a painter, who attended the court of Guestling and helped to decide the fate of the old Guildhall, which was leaking badly; several times meetings, obviously at great inconvenience, had to be adjourned to the neighbouring Kings Arms.

The Guildhall was also used as a Court Hall. In 1829, during a murder case, the Recorder complained of overcrowding and inadequate ventilation and that prisoners could not be separated from the jury or bystanders. Lord Radnor received the market dues – why should not he contribute to a new building? Lord Radnor equivocated whether *"in the excitement*

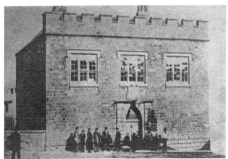
THE CISTERN HOUSE

occasioned by a temporary inconvenience they were not about to land themselves with a very serious and permanent burden." The correspondence with the Committee continued and three plans were put forward which would all require Radnor assistance. *"Even in the days of your excellent and much lamented father, the building was too small when crime was of comparatively limited extent, but now trials are of all too frequent occurrence."* The cheapest alternative was chosen, the alteration and use of the existing Radnor Cistern House with the Radnor arms over the door. The upper floor was to be a court with rooms for the jury and magistrates, the ground floor a flat for the gaoler and the market place was to have a light roof. A 21 year lease was granted for £70 per annum and the Corporation was to keep it in repair. This arrangement lasted for 36 years.

There were several legal changes which made improvements easier to put in place. In 1835 the Municipal Corporations Act tidied up the status of all old boroughs which had been governed under a variety of ancient charters. It gave all the ratepayers of three years' standing the vote, instead of only the freemen, and councillors took the place of the jurats. This was an age of municipal reform and large towns, such as Leeds, Manchester and Birmingham with an influx of population that had overwhelmed the old order, were similarly opening up their systems of government.

The Folkestone Improvement Act of 1855, was the most important piece of legislation to affect the town in the nineteenth century. It was an act to extend its limits, to enable the Corporation to construct a market house, to make new streets and other improvements and to pave, light, drain and otherwise improve the borough. There was a considerable amount of disquiet about the cost of obtaining this act, but its consequences were far-reaching. From then till 1898 the Council held special monthly meetings to implement it. The Councillors could make compulsory purchase orders on property owners in order to widen streets or make new ones. They could sell off the building sites thus created and could borrow money to execute the works. In future new roads were to be no less than 40 ft.

THE KING'S ARMS HAD BEEN DEMOLISHED TO WIDEN THE CORNER OF SANDGATE ROAD AND GUILDHALL STREET

wide and widening of existing roads could be carried out where practicable, for example Upper Sandgate Road, Rendezvous Street. Grace Hill, Radnor Street and Tontine Street. There had been constant complaints that it was impossible to drive a carriage to the harbour through the jumble of buildings at the end of Tontine Street, so Harbour Street was created. There was to be a new carriage road from Mill Lane to Foord Lane, affecting 242 properties; a notice was issued to the owner or leaseholder of the dwelling house, yard or pasture land indicated on a numbered plan. A separate claim form was enclosed. Along these new frontages, freeholds could be sold off. This was setting the shape of the modern town and marked the change from narrow crowded alleyways to wide streets and large shops.

The evidence given before the passing of the Bill to the House of Lords Select Committee is also interesting. There was much mention of the coking ovens, 40 in all on the East Cliff, which inhibited building there. Sidney Smirke, the Radnor Estate architect, gave evidence that the construction of Radnor Bridge had been intended to facilitate building in that area but that the presence of the ovens made it impossible. Richard Hart the Bill's solicitor was also examined. He stressed the importance of making a new carriage road to the harbour. Hart was an example of the new men of official Folkestone. He started his career as Disraeli's agent in Maidstone but returned to his native town scenting the possibilities given by the arrival of the railway. Holbein's Visitors' List said that he designed and developed the future of the town and it was hardly possible to name a single agency which promoted its progress in which he was not concerned.

The Earls of Radnor, Lords of the Manor of Folkestone and owners of most of the land to be developed, together with their agents and advisors (collectively the Folkestone Estate) must surely be ranked as the most powerful unofficial influence on the development of the town. The foundations of the Estate date from before the Norman Conquest. In 1863 its rights on the foreshore and the taking of wrecks were challenged by the Lord Warden, who exercised such rights at Dover and the rest of the Cinque Ports. The matter went to a Committee of the House of Lords. Their judgement traced the history of the Manor through the centuries and concluded the Lord Warden's claim to be *"a thing of yesterday"* compared with the seven centuries such rights had been exercised by the Lord of the Manor.

The Estate documents are now in the Kent Archives collection. They form a fascinating, largely untapped source for the town's early history, including court rolls, hundreds of leases, the wills of John Herdson and Basil Dixwell. There is a notebook with observations made by Jacob des Bouverie on his purchase of the Estate in 1697, the family account book, and many exchanges with the Corporation regarding Estate rights and duties, down to the railway correspondence of the 1880s about the proposed loop line. One document of 1391 concerns two hens from a fee farm in a tenement by the churchyard. Others relate to the 1449 rental of John, Lord de Clynton, arranged by streets; the 1559 lease of a shop in Le Bochery; an 1810 survey of Folkestone, again by streets, with lists of occupiers. The Estate still holds the originals of the maps of 1698 by Abraham Walter and of 1782 by John Powell.

The Estate Office did not preserve these documents so carefully out of mere antiquarian interest. In The Folkestone Chronicle, October 22nd 1859, appeared the following announcement by Ralph Brockman, Deputy Steward, that the Courts Baron were to be held at the King's Arms:

"All Folkestone freeholders and copy and service holders who owe suit and service to William, Earl of Radnor, lord of several manors of Folkestone, are required to make their personal appearance, to pay up arrears of quit rents, copy rents and reliefs, and to enter their estates with proper descriptions on the Court Rolls."

Similar courts were held for the outlying manors at the Maypole, Hawkinge. Such independent registration of tenancies, boundaries and transfers, with the fees thereon, was of obvious importance in any dispute, such as that of 1782 over the Stade. The Estate being organised, motivated and in possession of the documentation, was able to pursue a more coherent and long-term policy than ordinary owners who held scattered parcels of land. This accounts for its importance in the eyes of Estate tenants during the railway negotiations. The leases it granted trace the history of the town's development. Between 1780 and 1800 43 leases are extant, whilst there are 12 between 1800 and 1829. The former period involved the use of the ground at Sandgate. Fabian Clayton Wilson built himself a spacious residence and 30 tenements for his men working in the Sandgate shipyards. The industry thrived and other shipwrights followed. Between 1775 and 1787 seven 28-gun frigates, four 16-gun sloops and two fire ships were built for the

Royal Navy, as well as sturdy privateers. This activity, together with the purchase by the War Department of land for the new military camp at Shorncliffe, was the beginning of the village of Sandgate.

On the land below the cliffs, formerly the property of Plain Farm, Cuma House was erected by Captain Gill, R.N. Rent for the land was a peppercorn the first year and £15 per annum subsequently. The building, which was to be to the satisfaction of the Earl and his surveyors, was subsequently to be used by the sixth Earl. There is the lease of the Cistern House (for use as the Guildhall), to the Mayor and Jurats of Folkestone in 1830, for 21 years at £70 per annum payable half-yearly, to include the stable yard, garden and pasture; two rooms were to be kept for Lord Radnor's steward. There are the leases of Walton Farm to Hunt Jeffrey in 1843, of Terlingham Farm and Broadmead Manor. There are pub leases: 'The Valiant Sailor' with 37 acres in 1861 at £45 per annum, 'The Black Bull' leased to Messrs. Rigden and Elmar in 1858 for £18 per annum and 'The Ship Inn' in Sandgate to George Ward in 1865 at £50 per annum. The large-scale development of the town from the 1850s involved a flood of leases of plots of land, generally for 99 years. They incorporated restrictive covenants prohibiting trade signs (in fashionable areas) or drying washing in the garden. Proposed designs had first to have the approval of the Estate architect, Sidney Smirke. No freeholds were granted before 1910, a prohibition which was sometimes criticised and contrasted with the more liberal policy adopted by the Duke of Devonshire in relation to Eastbourne.

Having surrendered its control over the Stade to the Harbour Company (and its successor, the South Eastern Railway Company), the Estate still kept a firm hold on its other foreshore rights, the rights of wreck and of quarrying building stone. The former may not have yielded much profit as, on all shores, the local inhabitants had always been the first to reap the harvest which the wrath of the sea had given them. In 1859 a Dutch galliot, the 'Frederick' went aground off Radnor Cliff with a cargo of coal and the Sandgate villagers laid in a store of cheap firing. The 'Princess', a West Indian brigantine was wrecked off Sandgate Castle; a crowd scrabbled for coconuts and barrels of rum and sugar, while Thomas Baker and George Kennett climbed aboard and were later arrested for stealing the Captain's gold watch.

Building stone was valuable, but quarrying had to be carried out with caution in case it caused cliff falls. In 1790 Richard Hodgmen had a lease to take stone from Eastwear Bay to Sandgate Castle, but the Earl still kept the copperas stones (used to produce a green dye), thunder stones (fossils), and enough stone to repair the streets and houses in Folkestone. There was an interesting case in 1860 in which the 1783 lease of the Stade to the Corporation was cited. The Railway Company was taking Stade rock to build a new north wall and to extend the pier. The local men on the job said they had decided to take the rock and that they had the power to do so. Messrs. Bailey and Norman, the Radnor surveyors, denied such a right. The railway officials in London were more conciliatory and a negotiated settlement was reached. Earlier Lord Radnor had received £8,296 cash for land used for the line. The Estate was indeed well served by its agents, from Henry Barton to the cautious and pragmatic Mr Norman.

William, the third Earl, succeeded to the title at the age of 49 and lived till he was three weeks short of 90. He was educated in France where he was introduced to Louis XVI and Marie Antoinette. After being in the Commons for 27 years, he subsequently became that rare species, a Liberal peer, supporting the abolition of the slave trade, Catholic Emancipation, and the 1832 Reform Bill. His lifetime saw the coming of the railway. Under his guidance the Estate adopted an expansionist and forward-looking policy which was also intended to be financially remunerative. At no previous time had Folkestone been considered other than an investment property. It had lacked the dignity and benefit of a resident Lord of the Manor.

The Earl was not often seen in the town, though he held various honorary offices, being patron of the Working Men's Educational Union, the Dispensary and the Harveian Literary Institute. He always gave generous subscriptions, such as £70 annually to the Dispensary in the 1860s. Land was also granted for good causes: religious, educational or recreational. He presented the ground for the Sandgate National Schools, built Christ Church and endowed it with £30 per annum, and his son built Holy Trinity. Both churches were regarded as refuges for those of an Evangelical persuasion from the High Church practices at St. Eanswythe's. The Leas was kept in good order as a promenade and completely re-turfed in 1866. Shrubs and trees were planted along the Lower Sandgate Road, which had been made up in 1828 as 'The Earl's New Road'. Later the Estate gave ground for the Marine Gardens, Radnor Park and the Leas Shelter. The Earl was the largest shareholder in the Waterworks Company and represented its interests in Parliament. In his later years he was known as 'The Old Earl' and Lord Folkestone transacted Estate business on his behalf.

Helen, the Earl's grandson's wife, wrote of him in her memoirs, 'From a Great-

Grandmother's Armchair'; he was a kindly old gentleman, delighted with her first baby Jacob, the new Radnor heir. She did not, however, get on so well with her in-laws. Lady Radnor, wife of the fourth Earl (who had borne 15 children in 18 years) disapproved of her eldest son's wife, who was neither rich nor titled; she made Helen feel extremely uncomfortable on her visits to Longford. The young Folkestones lived at the other family home, Coleshill, under considerable restrictions, unable to invite their uncle and aunt to the house, as Lord Radnor had quarrelled with them both. In 1877 their adored daughter died of typhoid fever and was buried at Coleshill. The Radnors took such offence that Nellie was not in the family vault at Britford

HELEN, DOWAGER COUNTESS OF RADNOR, 1928

that they forbade her parents to use Coleshill any more. Helen Radnor's unfavourable impression is reinforced by the facts of a case heard by the Salisbury magistrates. While Lord Radnor was Chairman, the Bench tried George Stay, aged eight, who was one of three children who had stolen greens and was sentenced to 20 shillings plus costs or a month in prison.

Though the fourth Earl was not widely loved by his tenants, visiting Folkestone rarely and staying in hotels, family public relations in the next generation were excellent, thanks to Lord and Lady Folkestone. Lady Folkestone was a talented musician and singer who could have turned professional, had she been born into a different class. She appeared many times at charity concerts and sang duets with Tosti. Lord Folkestone learnt to play the cello and joined in with the family. She organised concerts for the poor with the People's Entertainment Society and sang for the Primrose League at the Albert Hall and Covent Garden. There was a memorable concert at St. James', Piccadilly, when she persuaded all the leading musicians and conductors of the day to play in the Toy Symphony. She also

JACOB FOURTH EARL OF RADNOR 1869-1889

organised the 'Ladies' String Band' with sell out performances - 82 instrumentalists and 120 in the chorus, naturally all ladies of good family. She sang for the Queen and was a great friend of the Princess of Wales who asked her to be a Lady-in-Waiting, but she had to refuse for health reasons.

Folkestone was not forgotten by Lady Folkestone. She gave a London concert in aid of St. Andrew's Convalescent Home and the whole family performed at a free entertainment for fishermen at the Congregational Schools. She sang often and brought the String Band to the Exhibition Building, notorious for its cold draughts. On these visits, the Folkestones stayed at a hotel - the Westcliff or the Leas - or at 39 Augusta Gardens. After his accession to the title in 1889, the new Earl decided to build himself a home in Folkestone, thus satisfying a persistent desire

MANOR HOUSE

on the part of the inhabitants for the Lord of the Manor to have a marine residence and attract good society around him. The Manor House, for which George Gordon, son of the Dean of Salisbury was the architect and Daniel Baker the builder, is still standing on the Leas. It was not to be long in Radnor occupation, however, as their son found it too small for his family of ten children and used Cliff House, Radnor Cliff. Lord Folkestone, or 'F' as he was known, and Helen were constantly in the town in the 1890s, and their daughter was much in demand for amateur theatricals. Radnor influence at this period was strong in local politics by way of the Primrose League and they attended many Town Hall meetings.

The year 1900 was a sad time for the family. Jacob joined the Army during the Boer War and was sent to South Africa, but became very ill with enteric fever at Bloemfontein. His wife and Julian went out to nurse him, with his Uncle Bert, Canon

Bouverie. The death of Jacob's father in June was due partly to anxiety over his son's health. The fifth Earl had been popular in the town, attending meetings in person rather than sending a subscription. His father had been a rich man, leaving £288,548, with landed property of 20,000 acres in Wiltshire and Berkshire and 3,003 acres in Kent. However, much of this went in legacies to the rest of the family and the Folkestone property had to be mortgaged. William felt the need to be a prudent landlord and to ask a proper price for building land, though he was faced with a considerable demand that the Estate should be responsible

THE FIFTH EARL for providing cheap working-class housing as well as expensive mansions. Land was set aside for allotments; Radnor Park was laid out by the Borough Surveyor and presented to the public. At the opening of the Leas Shelter, which had been built by the Estate but transferred to the Corporation at a percentage of the cost, the Earl remarked that he read newspaper comments and had no desire to be a grasping landlord.

His son now drew the ties uniting Estate and town even closer. He was suggested as Mayor by a Radical, Cllr. Payer of the East Ward, and accepted the office in 1901. In his official capacity he insisted on being addressed as 'Mr Mayor' and gained a favourable verdict from the local press:

> "He has sacrificed leisure and many personal enjoyments,
> he has done much to raise the tone of municipal government
> and make a seat on the Town Council an object worthy the
> ambition of cultured and leisured citizens. Trained in the
> Imperial Parliament, he has been a firm but courteous advocate
> of order and has insisted firmly upon Council rules in their deliberations."
>
> (Folkestone Herald, October 1902).

On July 11th 1902, Lord Radnor was presented with a silver cradle bearing the Radnor arms and the Mayoral seal, a traditional gift to a Mayor to whom a baby was born during his year of office. (It was a boy, Bartholomew.) Ironically, only a few months later there was considerable public controversy when Gordon Hotels, the owners of the Metropole, erected barriers either side of the hotel barring access to the part of the road facing the Leas. The Estate retaliated by putting up a large fence in front of the hotel itself. The matter went to law and the case was found in favour of Lord Radnor. Both fence and barriers were removed.

Contemporary views on the Radnor Estate were mixed:

An Act for the support and preservation of the lower part of the town and the parish church, 1760:

"We are sensible of your Lordship's favour in contributing so largely to the expenses of preparing and passing the said Act. It will be our study to put the same into execution for the power thereby intended in such manner as we hope will merit your Lordship's esteem and favour."
> (The Corporation, Rev. Dr William Langhorne, the minister and all the principal inhabitants of the town).

"His (Lord Radnor's) interest in the town of Folkestone except what comes into his purse is exceedingly small and would doubtless require a candle and lantern to find it."
> (A liberal, protesting against Lord Radnor's refusal to allow Sandgate to be supplied with Hythe gas, Folkestone Chronicle July 10th 1858).

"Before 25 years ago, his Lordship's name was not mentioned with the respect it is now. It was not his fault, but that of his advisors and now a better feeling prevails."
> (The Mayor, speaking at the Tradesmen's Dinner, Folkestone Chronicle. February 22nd 1868).

"The Earl relies solely on the agent's report and accounts. He really ought to have a marine residence here and could understand the needs of the area better."
> (Folkestone Chronicle October 21st 1871).

"His strict rules (with regard to the size of houses and the preservation of the Lower Road) may seem harsh at present, but posterity will appreciate their value. That firmness will insist that this magnificent inheritance is worthy of its situation and its frame."
> (Folkestone Chronicle January 2nd 1886).

"Every bit of local enterprise and activity has to pay tribute to the Lord of Longford Castle and it is principally due to this fact that Folkestone is kept from her proper position as the leading summer health resort of the South Coast."
> (Cllr. Jones, a Radical, Folkestone Herald, March 15th 1895).

"Everyone knows that to get popularity in certain quarters, the thing is to 'have a go' at the Earl. We like to know that his sympathies have not been alienated in spite of all the attacks made in recent years."
> (Editorial, Fokestone Herald, May 4th 1895).

The Earl is seldom seen now in person and the Leasehold Reform Act has meant the break-up of large estates. The Estate still owns part of the town centre and exercises a watching brief over new developments, the Sports Centre and the Warren. There is co-operation with developers over the new plans for the town.

Compared with the local presence of the Estate and its agents, the members of Parliament were remote figures whose activities seemed to affect the town little. But

AN ELECTION 1844 (PUNCH)

Parliamentary representation in the nineteenth century must be seen against the background of the gradual extension of the franchise, the introduction of secret ballots and the prohibition of bribery. Interest in politics was growing by the last quarter of the century, expectations of M.P.'s duties were higher and there was a greater polarisation of opinion between Conservatives and Radicals. Until 1895 Folkestone was nominally Liberal, as perhaps befitted a town with strong trading and mercantile ties. While agricultural constituencies mostly returned members linked to landed interests, Folkestone and Hythe were fortunate, in having as members four men of wealth and initiative, with experience of a wider world than county society. The Reform Bill of 1832 caused a few broken windows on the Bayle, the sort of incident that occurred nationwide. After the Bill, Folkestone was joined to Hythe, which returned one member instead of two. There were 469 inhabitants qualified to vote.

By the end of the century the electoral roll had risen almost tenfold to over 4,000. Stewart Marjoribanks, the member from 1832 to 1837, was a Whig and a ship owner, living at Cuma House, who presented a picture of Charles James Fox to Hythe Town Hall. He accepted the Chiltern Hundreds in 1837 and was succeeded by Viscount Melgund who held the seat until 1841 when Stewart Marjoribanks was again returned. In 1847 Edward Drake Brockman succeeded in gaining the seat against the opposition of Baron Mayer de Rothschild, a fellow Liberal. A barrister and Recorder of Hythe he was the son of James Drake Brockman of Beachborough. The election was fought with great bitterness and, never, according to local tradition, had the right of a vote in Hythe been so valuable. In 1857 he retired because of indisposition and Sir John Ramsden, a Yorkshireman, was elected in his place. He had been opposed by Colonel (later General) Hankey, a local figure of some note, especially in Sandgate. Sir John returned to his native Yorkshire in 1859 and this time Baron Mayer de Rothschild was returned unopposed, four rival candidates having withdrawn. He was to keep the seat till shortly before his death in 1874.

The Rothschild connection had begun in the days of the Napoleonic Wars. Mayer Amschel Rothschild was a coin dealer in Frankfurt who expanded into international finance. He had five sons, one of whom, Nathan Mayer, handled the export of gold to the Continent via the port of Folkestone. Nathan's oldest son, Lionel, raised various large sums for the Government: to compensate expropriated slave owners; to relieve the Irish famine; for the Crimean War and the Suez Canal purchase. He also wanted to become an M.P., an ambition as yet impossible for Jews, who had to take an oath *"on the true faith of a Christian"*. For

BARON MAYER ROTHSCHILD (CENTRE)

eleven years he persevered - ten times a bill was introduced to revise the oath and ten times the Lords threw it out. At last in 1858 he was successful and the way was open for his brother Mayer to take his seat peacefully at Folkestone. Had Baron Mayer won on his first attempt in 1847, he would have faced the same struggle as his brother.

All the Rothschilds were very rich and Mayer was no exception. His only child, Hannah, married Lord Rosebery, a future Prime Minister, after her father's death. She was described as the richest heiress in England, being the possessor of a fortune of seven million pounds. Mayer engaged Joseph Paxton, the architect of the Crystal

HANNAH ROTHSCHILD

Palace, to build Mentmore Towers on his 700 acre estate in the Vale of Aylesbury. It is a vast and impressive 'Jacobethan' pile. He filled it with one of the most outstanding and varied collections of art treasures in private hands in Europe: quantities of French furniture; Marie Antoinette's milking pails; Gobelin tapestries; crystal, silver and enamels; pictures by Rubens, Boucher, van Loo and Moroni. The washing facilities for

guests were Louis XV commodes, fitted with basins and taps. The sale of the treasures and the house by the Rosebery family in 1977 excited much interest. A bust of the Baron was standing forlornly on a pile of horsehair mattresses in the stables. Lot 2461 in the sale, subsequently withdrawn, was 'Luggers awaiting the departure of the Steamer from Folkestone Harbour' by John James Wilson, a Folkestone artist, presented to the Baron by his grateful constituents in 1873. It

MENTMORE

had been hung at his residence, 107 Piccadilly, where the Prime Minister, Foreign Secretary and Chancellor of the Exchequer were invited to lunch to admire it.

No one could expect that such a man, described as *"the huntingest, merriest, ridingist baron in England"* would be at the beck and call of his electors. In 1868 he voted in nine divisions out of 168 and apologised that the pressure of duties kept him away from his constituency. He was known as a moderate Liberal and supporter of Gladstone, approving of education for the working classes and the extension of the franchise. He was generous to local charities, subscribing £30 for the poor at Christmas, and giving a clock to the new Town Hall. At the 1865 election he was returned unopposed, though there was a complaint that he had not been seen in the town for six years. After that, he made a point of turning up for the Mayor's dinner. In the 1868 election he had two rivals, Captain Merryweather, a fellow Liberal, who subsequently retired, and Albert Nugent, Conservative, a simple honest soul who did his best and promised to be more attentive to the wishes of the electors. The Baron was called *"an absent member of the House and a silent and neglectful one out of it"*, who had refused to intervene when Captain Boxer was oppressing the fishermen by refusing to let them enter the harbour till their fish were stale.

The only recorded anti-Semitic remark came from Thomas Denne, *"Why do you vote for a Jew and an unbeliever against a Protestant and a Christian?"* Election fever lasted for weeks and there were noisy scenes at the Town Hall and the Artillery Rooms in Sandgate. However, the Baron's return was a foregone conclusion, the results being Nugent 521, Rothschild 1,268. Fighting an election did not come cheaply, election expenses being £2,130 for the Baron and

THE BARON'S MARE, HANNAH

£1,284 for Albert Nugent. The Baron exerted his influence in circles where it mattered and promoted Folkestone's commanding position in the bullion export trade. He was also remembered with affection by those interested in racing - *"Follow the Baron"* they advised. He had a magnificent stable and in 1871 his mare Hannah won the Thousand Guineas, the Oaks and the St. Leger, while Favonius won the Derby. Rev. Woodward disapproved but the church bells were rung.

He was succeeded as MP in 1874 by Edward Watkin who held the seat until 1894. Watkin was an obvious choice for the town since he already influenced its fortunes to such an extent as chairman of the South Eastern Railway Company. It was also convenient for him to find a secure seat. In 1857 he had been returned for Great Yarmouth but was unseated on a petition. He was M.P. for Stockport 1864-8 and then unsuccessful in Cheshire and Exeter. Unlike the Baron he was indefatigable in the performance of his duties, always ready to attend civic meetings and presenting the prizes at the Science and Art classes sixteen times. Nominally a Liberal, he appealed to members of both parties, occupying a middle of the road position. He sometimes voted with the Tories - taking the patriotic side in the Zulu and Afghan wars - and was given a baronetcy in 1880 by Disraeli's government. His lukewarm attitude over the favourite Liberal cause of Church disestablishment earned him the scorn of the Nonconformist ministers, Rev. Sampson and Rev. Foster Jeffery, who formed the backbone of the extreme Radicals. He did not support school boards.

In his first election Watkin had been opposed only by the resurgent Capt. Montague Merryweather, a good-looking and gentlemanly man, as the Folkestone Chronicle commented, his only fault being a deficiency of brains. Although the Captain did not have a chance, the Watkin party set about their task as though they were fighting a tough contest. Volunteers were sent out, back streets and alleys canvassed while the candidate was busy shaking hands and generally making himself known. The figures were: Watkin 1,347, Merryweather 300. His standing with the electorate increased in 1878 with his activities over the new harbour at Boulogne, when he went with a fellow director to see M. Gambetta. The discussions lasted till cockcrow and he was supposed to have returned with the Boulogne Harbour Bill in his briefcase. He equally earned some unpopularity with the Railway Company's tactics over the Sandgate Branch line. At the 1880 election he was returned unopposed, Folkestone being only one of about a dozen boroughs to experience an uncontested election.

Opposition was not dead, however, and as the middle ground was already occupied, this tended to extremism. In 1881 a new party appeared, its mouthpiece 'The Folkestone Advanced Liberal Association', organised by the Rev. Sampson. Premises were found, radical literature together with tea and coffee distributed and regular meetings held. One was addressed by Thomas Pilcher, an organiser of the Agricultural Labourers' Union, which had organised strikes in Kent and Sussex. There were demands for manhood suffrage, the abolition of the House of Lords and Church disestablishment. Any mention of Sir Edward was greeted with hostile laughter. A radical candidate, Mr Morton, stood against him in the 1885 election, advocating free education, the abolition of grants to Royalty and leasehold enfranchisement, but Sir Edward was again triumphant with a majority of 1,450.

The Conservatives were also wooing the working man, with the foundation of the Conservative Working Men's Association in 1883. Lord Radnor was chairman and remarked that, in his youth, he was called a Radical and had been in jeopardy of being injured or even killed for his beliefs – by whom, he did not make clear. But the great success story of the 1880s in politics was the formation of the Primrose League in memory of Disraeli. This was patriotic and universal in its appeal, aiming to defend the Monarchy, the Empire and the Church. A habitation (branch) was started in Folkestone in 1886 at a crowded meeting in the Town Hall. Lady Folkestone sang 'Auld Lang Syne' and 700 members, knights, dames and associates were recruited, which total later rose to over a thousand. The sharp divisions of politics were starting to be felt. In March 1889 £30 worth of damage was done to the Town Hall, at a meeting summoned to discuss Irish Home Rule, always a contentious subject. There was an inebriated old lady waving her shawl; cries of *"Chuck him out"* and *"He's a Dover rough"* were heard.

Rev. Russell Wakefield spoke on this occasion and also at a Women's Suffrage Meeting. Although Church of England clergymen were almost overwhelmingly Tory, the Dissenters Liberal and in favour of Church disendowment, Rev. Russell Wakefield was an exception. Educated in Germany, Vicar of Sandgate and eventually to become Bishop of Birmingham, his Liberal sympathies were strong enough to disconcert his brother clerics. He was also a close friend of Sir Edward, who was godfather to his son, and officiated at Sir Edward's second marriage to Mrs Blanche Ingram, widow of the founder of the Illustrated London News. This marriage was the subject of unkind rumours that Sir Edward was marrying her for her money, which he was at pains to deny.

> *"From Snowdon's breezy summit to Dover's chalky strand*
> *He carries us the slowest of any in the land.*
> *He bores the Channel Tunnel, he builds the Watkin Tower,*
> *But neither helps his income like Mrs. Ingram's dower.*
> *He'd blacken Kent with coal pits and cave St. John's Wood in*
> *But these are merely trifles in his career of sin,*
> *For he doth run the Underground in whose mephitic air,*
> *The gasping, choking Londoner doth think of him – and swear."*

In 1887 Sir Edward paid yet another visit to North America; he was one of the great advocates of a railway line across the continent. The following year he went to India, planning a railway through to Burma. On his return he was given a dinner at the Winter Garden in the Royal Pavilion, an event said to be the largest gathering ever held in Folkestone. Here he was described as a captain of industry and brilliant manager on whom thousands of working men depended for their jobs, but one often made the subject of bitter attacks. At the Science and Art prize-giving in 1889 he told the students of plans to erect a 'Watkin Tower' at Wembley, to be modelled on the Eiffel Tower, of octagonal shape and 1,200 feet high. In 1892 there was another election and Sir Edward, with united Conservative support, was again returned unanimously. When he opened the Marine Garden, everyone was agog to see the new Lady Watkin. In his election speech at the Town Hall he promised an extension to the harbour. He mentioned that he had done his best to have Folkestone made a torpedo station, but competition from Dover was too strong. By 1894 his health was declining and he gave notice of his resignation from Parliament.

After a period of peace, politics were once more to be thrown into a state of turmoil. On the extreme Radical side were Cllr. Jones and the Municipal Reform League, demanding the public

ownership of gas, electricity, railways and water, together with all landed property. The Primrose League, still strong with regular meetings and Radnor support, was attacked for its *"inflated income, derived from farm labourers and servant girls, its fanciful and childish parchments, bogus Brummagem badges and enamels."* The Conservative and Liberal candidates had now finished with their truce and fielded separate candidates. Sir James Bevan Edwardes for the Conservatives was a former military man, whose longwinded speeches were guaranteed to empty any hall.

SIR PHILIP SASSOON (RIGHT)

His Liberal opponent, Sir Israel Hart, should have appealed strongly to Folkestonians. He had lived in Tontine Street till the age of 29, moving then to Leicester, where he had opened a successful clothing factory and was three times Lord Mayor. He spoke to an audience of working men, advocating Home Rule and an eight-hour day for workers. It was a fierce battle and the result - Edwardes 2,189, Hart 1,776, - surprised many. However, there were national factors at work, while the recent massacre of the Christians in Armenia had helped Gladstone. Furthermore, the Liberal espousal of a temperance bill was not popular in a town owing its prosperity to the holiday trade.

Sir Bevan Edwardes resigned for health reasons in 1899 and was succeeded as Conservative candidate by Sir Edward Sassoon, head of another famous Jewish family. But while the Rothschilds had been a banking family of German origin, the Sassoons were merchants and manufacturers who came originally from Baghdad and settled finally in Bombay. Here they gained great wealth, though not on the Rothschild scale. Abdullah (later Albert) Sassoon, the first Baronet, brought his cotton spinning machinery to England and set up in business. His heir was Edward, born in Bombay, who married Aline Rothschild, daughter of Baron Gustave of Paris. Aline was a 'Soul', member of an exclusive and intellectual society coterie. The couple had many houses in Trent Park, Hertfordshire; Park Lane; Bombay, Poona and Paris. They wished also to have a residence in the constituency and from the Countess of Chichester bought Shorncliffe Lodge on the hills above Sandgate.

Although Sir Edward was head of the house of David Sassoon and Co., he was more interested in politics. In Folkestone he became the first President of the Chamber of Commerce, President of the Victoria Hospital; he spoke at the Cheriton Oddfellows dinner. On a national scale he was interested in wireless telegraphy and, as Chairman of the Commons Committee, he tried to bring down the cost of cable messages and introduced an unsuccessful bill to make telegraphy compulsory on passenger ships. He also took up the cause of English fishermen and French poaching in English waters.

Sir Philip, his only son, became M.P. for Folkestone and Hythe on his father's death in 1912, the youngest member at Westminster. He was a millionaire at 23, and although one of the most eligible young men in London, he never married. An aesthete and a dandy, he was disliked and admired in society in about equal quantities for his ostentatious display of wealth, and best known in Kent for building Port Lympne, one of the few great country houses of the twentieth century. During World War I he served in the army and became Haig's secretary, smoothing the path of that irascible man. After the war he was Lloyd George's Parliamentary Private Secretary. The Prime Minister found the facilities and hospitality of Port Lympne useful for semi-political gatherings, such as that attended by the French President, M. Millerand, who came to discuss the reparations question. Sir Philip entertained a wide spectrum of guests from Charlie Chaplin to the Duke of Windsor, his sister or his cousin, Hannah Gubbay, acting as hostess. Like his father, he did not play much part in the family firm but was very keen on flying, becoming Under Secretary to the Air Minister, Sir Samuel Hoare. He died in 1938, aged fifty. Folkestone had cause to remember his generosity – he opened and maintained for 15 years a free dental clinic and built a model working-class housing estate of 16 cottages and 8 flats.

THE HARBOUR

Recent discoveries have brought to light some evidence of early attempts to make a harbour. A twelfth century masonry wall and an expanse of cobbles on the site of the car park in Tram Road were discovered in 1988. A wooden piled-and-planked retaining wall of the seventeenth century was found on the western side of the Pent, possibly a long timbered quayside.

The interests of the town and the Estate were to coincide with the idea of providing a commercial profit-making harbour which could take up to five hundred boats. In 1803 Mr Hodgson's survey was laid before the Trustees and William Stace was asked to communicate with Henry Cull of Ramsgate, the deputy engineer who had advised on the construction of Ramsgate harbour. Their correspondence shows the original scheme for a harbour from Copt Point using blocks of hewn stone which would cost £184,000. It would be cheaper to use 'Ruff rocks', of which there was a quantity available. The plans and estimate were sent to Lord Radnor and Lord Folkestone approached the Government for aid, which was not forthcoming. The plan was then temporarily dropped and further jetties constructed. Henry Cull settled at the sum of three guineas for his expenses.

The idea of a harbour persisted and it was agreed in 1807 that the proceeds of the coal dues could pass to a new company. Mackie's guide of 1856 attributed the harbour to Thomas Telford, one of the greatest canal and harbour engineers of the day. However, the Kentish Companion of 1810 mentions only William Jessop, who worked with Telford, and the existing plans of 1806 are in his name. These show, firstly, the harbour enclosing 16 acres of water, then the same with a small extra pier at the entrance and lastly a larger and more ambitious scheme, utilising the semi-circle of rocks which extend into the sea from Copt Point as the basis for a long breakwater. The smaller scheme was chosen and the Harbour Company formed, raising £22,000 in 440 shares of fifty pounds each, Lord Radnor being the chief shareholder. In 1807 the Act was passed to construct a pier or harbour in or near the town of Folkestone. It stated, *"Jacob, Earl of Radnor, as Lord of the Hundred or Barony of the town, waives his rights for the benefit of the undertaking"*.

The new Company had the right to make byelaws and receive dues at six pence a ton on cargo unloaded for foreigners, two pence for English boats. Fishing boats had to pay one shilling every time they left the harbour. The foundation stone was laid in 1808 by Thomas Baker, the Mayor, with the words, *"May Heaven reward the endeavours of spirited men and prosper the Folkestone Harbour"*. The band played 'Rule Britannia' and guns fired from the Bayle battery, while the population were regaled with a butt of real British stout. There is a watercolour in the library of a horse-and-crane being used to lift the great stones quarried from the sea bed, laid slantwise to minimise the force of the waves. They are still in their place today. The contractors were Messrs. Spedding & Crawford. By 1810 the first dues were being paid. Much profit was envisaged from the

THE OLD JETTY

vessels that would use the new harbour - Channel packets; fishing boats; cargo boats; the regular service of hoys from the Gun and Shot Wharf, London (Masters J and K Spicer). The jettee [sic] vouchers show expenditure on men and horses, winches and rope. Ships such as the 'Annabella', the 'Betsy', the sloop 'William', the 'Scarborough', the 'Sarah' of Sunderland and many others were frequent visitors. However, all was not well financially.

William Wilberforce had already resided at Sandgate for two successive summers and was to return again. He wrote to Joseph Marryat at the House of Commons in December 1814, asking him to use his influence with the Lords of the Treasury to obtain a Government grant of £12,000 to finish the work, following a suggestion made by Mr Stace. This would enable a measure to save both lives and property. He shrewdly observed that Folkestone, already noted for smuggling, was treated by Government with a stepmother's behaviour whereas Dover gained the parental fondness. (Dover was always seen as being of national strategic importance.) The Corporation did their best to help the harbour's cause by petitioning

THE OUTER HARBOUR

the Lords of the Admiralty to have it made a harbour of refuge and a headquarters for pilots, who could spot a ship in trouble as soon as it rounded Dungeness Point. *"It would provide employment for a hardy race of men accustomed to the sea from their childhood who have proved themselves ready to risk their own lives in saving ships but are now nearly destitute from want of employment"* (Common Assembly minutes, 1833). Silt was the trouble. It made entrance difficult save for small fishing smacks and herring luggers at high tide. Fishermen's wives dried their sheets on the banks of sand and shingle, while the pier formed a good promenade on warm evenings.

A further wall was suggested and a memorial signed by 209 merchants, owners and masters of ships of the Port of London in 1828. They emphasised the usefulness of the harbour to shipping in northerly and easterly gales. Telford certainly drew up the plan of 1829, proposing to build a wall with sluice gates which would divide the harbour into a permanent wet dock and tidal basin. The gates were intended to channel the force of the Pent waters which would clear out the silt when released, but this would keep clear only a small area. Local mortgages were raised from men such as Thomas Elgar, cabinet maker, James Tolputt, painter and glazier, Thomas Cook, mariner, and Henry Butcher the Mayor, most of whom were already prominent in the town's affairs. Regular interest was paid on the loans. However, all this was not enough and the whole enterprise ran out of money. It was mortgaged to the Exchequer Loan Committee for £10,000 and the Company went bankrupt in 1842.

Although the Government was not interested in running a small harbour, its availability was noticed by the surveyors and directors of the South Eastern Railway Company as the line to Dover advanced. Presumably it had not entered into their calculations at first, as the main line was made to the north of the town some way from the sea. This was to present great difficulties of access later, when the advantages of a port to the powerful and wealthy Company became obvious. If it owned its own harbour, it could run a cross-Channel service without the necessity of paying harbour dues.

The actual purchase of the harbour was made by Joseph Baxendale, the Chairman, for the bargain price of £18,000. He bought it on his own responsibility after being given a take-it-or-leave-it decision on a Saturday afternoon in March 1843, with no time to consult his fellow Directors – at least that was his version as told to the shareholders:

"If you sanction the purchase, it is well. If not, I will take the harbour myself. I do not know if I have had in my whole life anything which gave me greater pleasure. I hope

THE HARBOUR

within ten days to find steamers to take passengers at a cost of between ten and twenty-five shillings from London to Boulogne. Dover had a monopoly of the Channel traffic and a monopoly is a bad thing. We were subjected to a toll at Folkestone but now we have the toll in our own hands. We had to run to Dover, otherwise we would never have got our Bill, for there was no idea then of the value of Folkestone Harbour."

The step was approved and the cheque drawn on April 15th. This sum is comparable with the £15,000 spent in October on locomotive purchases. Herapath's Railway Journal applauded the move as the wisest step the Company had yet taken. This was also a turning-point in the history of the town. Till then, it had been an insignificant stop on what was popularly known as the 'Dover line'. Now, with the establishment of the cross-Channel service, the furtherance of the town's prosperity and amenities, along with the speed and comfort of the whole journey from London to Paris, were to become of great concern to the powerful Company.

Disposing of the mud and shingle which had presented such problems previously was an easy task for the railway contractors, who used it as ballast for vessels which had come into the harbour loaded with materials and machinery for the railway. *"We have cleared out the accumulation of the past forty years"*, remarked William Cubitt, the chief engineer. No other building operations were found necessary before the boats started. On June 24th 1843, a well-publicised excursion opened the railway line and inaugurated a new era in the history of travel – London to Boulogne and back in a day. Eighty-four travellers, including William Cubitt and Benjamin Cubitt, the locomotives superintendent, left London Bridge at 6.00am, reaching the temporary station at Folkestone at 8.40am. They walked three-quarters of a mile down to the harbour and embarked on the steamer 'Water Witch' amidst the firing of guns and waving of flags by the townspeople. Copies of the London morning newspapers were presented to the astonished Boulogne authorities on arrival and the party was generously, perhaps even over-generously, entertained with toasts to Louis Philippe and the directors of the Company. They left at 2.00pm in small boats to rejoin the steamer, now lying in low water half a mile offshore. The wind had got up and, in spite of the use of steadying sails, the boat rolled and pitched. The merry conversations flagged, the participants scattered to the boat's side or to lie quietly below. Notwithstanding the seasickness, they reached London in safety by 10.05pm, a highly successful trip.

At first the Company did not have Parliamentary permission to run its own steamships, nor did it wish to do so. The boats were managed by the New Commercial Steam Packet Company. Lewis Cubitt was in charge of arrangements and an agreement was concluded in July 1843, that the Company should be guaranteed £30 per sailing for two steamers daily and should receive a lump sum of £1,000 from Boulogne. For its part, the railway company received the fares for passengers, carriages and merchandise. The steamers used had been built originally for other services: the 'City of Boulogne' for the London-Margate run, the 'Emerald' for London-Gravesend and 'Sir William Wallace' for London-Perth. By October there were difficulties. The 'Sir William Wallace' had been taken out of service and replaced by an inferior boat, the 'Ramsgate Packet'. There were frequent delays and occasions when no boat appeared at all. The Railway Company refused to advertise the steamship services or to issue its timetables. Herapath's Journal referred to railway expeditions being destroyed by the slovenly and irregular conduct of the marine department and its old lumbering tubs. Matters reached such a pitch that Mr Baxendale refused to meet Mr Bleaden, chairman of the Steam Packet Company and negotiations were left in the hands of solicitors. Mr Bleaden appealed to him:

"Why not you and me sit down and discuss our differences?
I put the boats on to Folkestone contrary to the wishes of my
colleagues. I relied on you – you wished the port to be tried.
I have not withdrawn the vessels, I will do nothing unhandsome
notwithstanding the contumely you have mistakenly heaped on
me. A fortnight has been suffered by you to elapse. Is this handsome?
Remember, I have to account for my conduct to a large body
of shareholders not always disposed to view directors' acts
with liberality. To be candid, who can arrange the port of
Folkestone but yourself? Why not do it? I do assure you,
I do not desire to treat the matter but as a Merchant and Gentleman."
(South Eastern Railway Company minutes, October 24th 1843).

In the end the matter was happily settled, as the Steam Packet Company was bought out for £150,000. The Railway Company formed its own subsidiary company to run the boats but did not take them over directly till 1853. Parliament did not like railway companies also running boat services.

At the beginning there were eight small ships on the run, averaging 251 tons per vessel. Between 1861-5 a new generation of paddle steamers was ordered: the 'Victoria',

the 'Albert Edward', the 'Alexandra' and the 'Napoleon III', named for the new entente cordiale between Britain and France. The 'Victoria' was 200 feet in length and did the run in the record time of 1 hour, 34 minutes. It had an eighty-foot-long main cabin with leather settees and birdseye maple panelling. Single fares were 8 shillings first class, 6 shillings second class and all boats had direct train connections. In the early 1880s there were new ships: the 'Louise

A STEAM PACKET CROSSING THE SAND
BAR AT THE HARBOUR ENTRANCE

Dagmar', the 'Albert Victor', the 'Mary Beatrice' and the 'Duchess of Edinburgh'. The latter was found to be unsatisfactory and taken out of service. The older steamers were sometimes brought out for special occasions, not always with success. In 1882 the Duke of Edinburgh took a party to France in the 'Albert Edward'. They started at 12.15 on Tuesday afternoon and did not return till 2.37 on Wednesday morning. The engines stopped due to a small fault in the piston rod and the vessel drifted helplessly toward Cap Gris Nez. No warnings had been sent as the submarine telegraph was out of order. In 1902 the first turbine vessel, the 'Queen' was introduced and the old boats were gradually replaced, though one, the 'Brace', stayed in service till 1909.

Even the improved larger boats tossed about dreadfully. Several papers referred to the favourite pastime of disengaged Folkestonians in rough weather, which was to walk to the harbour and mock the pallid faces and forlorn aspect of the returning passengers as they tottered to the shore. The public cabins became crowded and unpleasant and many people preferred to travel on deck. Dickens described one passenger:

"One lady as I looked, one resigned and far-seeing woman, took her basin from a store of crockery as she might have taken a refreshment ticket, laid herself down on deck with that utensil at her ear, solemnly covered her countenance and, on the strength of these preparations, appeared by the strength of her volition to become insensible."
(Out of the Season, Household Words).

NEPTUNE'S VICTIMS

Letters and diaries in the Maidstone archives emphasise the sense of apprehension before a Channel crossing, especially felt among women, and the agony of those two hours. In 1868 Captain Tyler informed the Board of Trade in a report on the Channel Tunnel that the majority suffered extreme discomfort from seasickness and lack of shelter. Queen Victoria said that the Tunnel promoters would earn her gratitude and that of every lady in England. There were several experiments to produce a steadier boat, that of M. Bessemer being the most ingenious. This had a suspended saloon for first class passengers fixed in the middle of the boat and prevented from rolling by a hydraulic apparatus. However, it was unmanageable at sea and made only one voyage.

In the early days the station was up a steep hill and passengers had to be conveyed from train to boat by omnibus. Also the Company wished to unload coal to be turned into coke at the ovens on the East Cliff since coke was easier to burn for the trains and produced less smoke and smuts. In 1843 a branch line was planned down the incline to the harbour.

"A natural channel formed by a gap between the hills carries it at an inclination of 1 in 43 down through the town of Folkestone, and it is carried on arches of no great expense to a pier running out into the harbour, alongside which colliers and other vessels can unload their cargo and arrangements may hereafter be made for conveying passengers and their luggage to the steamers". (Directors' Minutes, November 8th 1843).

This was the Tram Road, at first used only for the unloading of coal, but opened to passengers in 1849. In the same year a wooden swing bridge, 138 feet long, was opened over the stretch of water between the South Quay and the jetty. The gradual build-up of shingle on the sea side of the quay meant that train sheds and a station could be erected and passengers could board the train immediately upon disembarkation.

THE SWING BRIDGE, INNER HARBOUR AND NEW CUSTOMS OFFICES

There was a need for hotel accommodation at the harbour. This was first provided by the conversion of a boat builder's workshop called the Pavilion, with a canvas marquee erected in front as a dining and reception room. It was described by Dickens as:

"A strange building which had just left off being a barn without having quite begun to be a house. Nobody expected your coming or knew what to do with you when you were come, and you were usually blown about until you happened to be blown against the cold beef and finally into bed." (Out of the Season, Household Words, September 29th 1855).

The first instalment of a permanent hotel was put up by Messrs. Grissell and Peto. Designed by Lewis Cubitt, it was somewhat bare and barrack-like with brick walls and small square windows. This being before the establishment of the Water Company, a pipe had to be laid to the Foord brook to ensure clean fresh water with a similar supply for the boats. The Pavilion was for many years Folkestone's largest and most fashionable hotel, rented by the Company to a succession of managers, the first being M. Vantini. In March 1844, the total cost of the harbour, hotel and improvements was over £87,000, but by 1861 it amounted to some £300,000. A customs house was built in 1845 and there was a breakwater at the harbour entrance to deter the old enemy, sand and shingle. Mr Barlow, the engineer, donned diving gear to inspect the rocks at the harbour entrance and recommended their removal.

Folkestone and Dover were now in a great race to capture the lucrative cross-Channel passenger and cargo traffic. Dover had always been the port for both Boulogne and Calais. By 1843 the Admiralty ran a daily mail service to Calais and 30,000 passengers were taken annually by the steamers. There were troubles, as at Folkestone, with blockage by sand and shingle and in 1837 fifty men had to be employed to keep it clear. Until the opening of the Admiralty Pier in the 1850s passengers had to be conveyed to the boats by small craft at low tide. This exposed them to the waves and the rapacious demands of the local boatmen, who would ask two shillings for the journey. In 1843 the opening of the Folkestone-Boulogne service was greeted with fury by the Dover Telegraph: *"Folkestone may be a useful little harbour for fishing smacks and colliers, but we cannot allow the ridiculous puffs of the place to mislead the public into supposing it will engross the traffic to Boulogne"*. It claimed that in every instance the Dover packet had beaten the boat from Folkestone and often carried up to five times the number of passengers. Ladders had snapped asunder with the swell in Folkestone harbour, endangering the lives of passengers. Ridiculous or not, in the 1840s and 1850s Folkestone drew ahead. The sea passage was longer but the direct rail link to Paris via Amiens was faster. The South Eastern itself invested money in the French line and built a hotel in Boulogne on a par with its own Pavilion in Folkestone. The expansion of both services and Folkestone's later decline relative to Dover can be seen in the table:

Number of Passengers		
Year	Folkestone-Boulogne	Dover - Calais
1845	70,809	18,642
1850	82,016	54,036
1865	118,553	133,352
1895	103,910	251,324
1900	174,676	316,156

(Southern Railway's Study of the Channel Tunnel Project, 1928.)

However, Dover Harbour was of a different order to Folkestone. It was controlled by the Harbour Board and owed its great size to the Government's decision to make it a national harbour. The original small commercial venture was completely engulfed by the new Eastern arm and Admiralty pier. It was served by two railway companies, the South Eastern and the London, Chatham and Dover. The South Eastern also ran boats from there in the 1850s and 1860s. Folkestone, on the other hand, had to try harder in the way of superior passenger facilities. The local press in its turn lost no opportunity of making unfavourable remarks about its neighbour *"Dover has lost caste during the past few years – it is melancholy to walk the streets of this benighted town. Its visitors decrease yearly, it has seen its day and we regret its backward progress"*. (Folkestone Chronicle, May 6th 1861).

Of course at a hint of trouble from Folkestone, the Company was always free to transfer the boats to Dover. In 1872 during the loop-line controversy it was suspected that the harbour would be sold and the Company apply for running powers out of Dover. This rumour may have been spread deliberately to force the Council to contribute £100,000 towards the new works which were being planned. The idea of losing Company patronage drove commercial interests in Folkestone frantic. Hotels would close and unemployment rocket. The threat was mentioned at the Mayor's dinner in 1873 and a Council resolution passed to let the Company have the extra land it needed. In 1886 it was proposed to empower the Council to raise one quarter of the £400,000 needed for the new harbour works and to take shares in the Company for security. This envisaged a close financial link between the Council and the Company and aroused a great deal of opposition.

There was also the danger that some other means could be found of conveying traffic across the Channel, perhaps a bridge or the tunnel that had been the subject of local speculation since 1855. In the able hands of Edward Watkin the prospect of a tunnel became more of a reality and was one of his most favoured projects. A private company was formed and an excavation - 2,200 feet long by 1885 - was dug under the Channel by compressed air engines, the debris being removed on trams drawn by Welsh ponies.

EXCAVATION WORK ON THE FIRST
ATTEMPT TO BUILD A CHANNEL TUNNEL

"Large parties of visitors, dressed up in white canvas coats and felt hats were taken into that long, round, clean, dry, white and beautifully lighted perforation which took everyone completely by surprise. It was brightly illuminated by incandescent electric lights from M. Siemens and for the whole way there was not a drop of water to be seen or heard falling anywhere and not even an approach to 'weeping' in any of the numerous close-fitting joints by which the beds of chalk are naturally divided."
(Folkestone Chronicle, February 25th 1882).

Works were also underway at Sangatte on the French side and Watkin prophesied that the whole enterprise could be completed for under three million pounds. It was stopped by the Government, not for any consideration of the havoc it would wreak to the fortunes of the steamers and harbours, but for strategic reasons. The Government considered that an army would have to be kept at Dover to deal with possible armies of French invaders as they filed out of the tunnel. During these excavations seams of coal were found which led to the establishment of the Kent coal mines.

Folkestone and Dover both did well in the nineteenth century with their Channel traffic except during the Franco-Prussian war of 1870-71. The war caused an interruption in the Folkestone-Boulogne service, though the London, Chatham and Dover Railway continued to carry mail via Dover. All the boats save two were laid up and the officers put on half pay. British sympathies were firmly on the side of their old enemies, the French, and Folkestone was a good place to gather first-hand information of the crops destroyed and houses looted by the advancing Prussians.

An influx had begun of middle-class holiday makers seeking instruction and pleasure on the Continent. Many people stayed in Boulogne which was known as a good refuge for those in financial difficulties, since food and lodging were cheap. French guest houses and hotels advertised in English papers. The traffic was not all in one direction. A party of French workmen arriving in Folkestone for a music festival amazed inhabitants by the noisy volubility of their conversation, though their uniformly polite demeanour was noted with approval. Eugenie, Empress of France, stayed overnight at the Pavilion in December 1860, and charmed everyone with her beauty and elegance. Prince Arthur, the fourth son of Queen Victoria, saw his delicate brother, Prince Leopold, off to Cannes and returned to the shore in tears. In 1875 the Sultan of Zanzibar came with his exotic entourage who caused some amusement with their curious dresses and household utensils. He had visited Queen Victoria to discuss the abolition of the slave trade. The Mayor read an address of welcome, translated by Dr. Badger, the Sultan's physician, and in return he was presented with the Sultan's portrait and a sword, richly ornamented with gold. In January 1860, were seen the tattered remnants of Garibaldi's army, still wearing their famous red blouses, some of whom were penniless and had been forced to beg their way through France. A collection was taken up to assist them. Queen Victoria herself passed through the harbour in March 1899, on a private visit to the Riviera. She was carried in a wheelchair and attended by three princesses. The town was decorated in her honour. There were also some strange cargoes, such as the two elephants from Astleys and the entire hunt of the Duke of Beaufort - fifty hounds, huntsmen, and servants. They were off to the Continent to chase wolves and were recorded as having had good sport, even if the hounds seemed bemused by their unfamiliar quarry. When visitors took their own carriages, there would be a groom on board to look after the horses.

The passage of the Indian mails through Folkestone was described by the Illustrated London News in 1844. It consisted of letters, and later included news of the Indian Mutiny and commodity prices, of vital interest to the City. Thirty or forty heavy boxes were made up at Bombay, shipped to Suez, sent in carts to Cairo and on to Marseilles by the Oriental Steam Navigation Company. An abstract of the most important items was telegraphed to Paris and conveyed to Boulogne. There it was put on the fastest vessel available to Folkestone. The South Eastern now offerred the superior facilities of a crossing in 1 hour, 45 minutes. If the steamer could not enter the harbour because of gales or low water, the harbour was signalled and an eight-oared galley sent out, the captain himself carrying the precious packet to the shore. There is a picture of a crowd assembled at night to watch its arrival. This was before the days of the Harbour station and the swing bridge so the mail had to be taken to the Upper station where a special train was waiting to take it to London. The South Eastern ceded the right to carry mail by boat to the London, Chatham and Dover in 1862, as it was considered an unremunerative service.

THE ARRIVAL OF THE INDIAN MAIL

At this time, the service of boats was not paying its way for either company once depreciation was taken into account. The boats were expensive to keep in order and to run, costing £20 a trip. In 1899 the South Eastern workshops in Folkestone employed eighteen men and cost a total of £103 per week. Steamer fares were low because there was competition from the cheaper Newhaven-Dieppe route which had third class facilities. The South Eastern limited its liabilities by running only one daily boat from Folkestone until 1897, whereas the London, Chatham and Dover ran three from Dover, two of which carried mail. The services were looked upon as being feeders for the profitable expresses of the South Eastern which had a monopoly at Folkestone and a good share of those from Dover.

Increasing commercial activity meant new buildings. The harbour administration had offices, the Harbour House, with a clock tower near the Pavilion Hotel. There were platforms on the South Quay to suit all stages of the tide. In 1855/6 new Customs Offices were erected, along with ticket offices, refreshment and ladies' rooms, a bullion room, loose boxes for sixty horses and a goods shed. Baggage could be examined and taken to the passenger's hotel or booked straight through from London to Paris, which saved a great deal of waiting at the customs. Goods for export were put directly on board. Imports were examined and loaded into trains so swiftly that frequently less than twenty-four hours elapsed between their despatch from Paris and arrival in a London warehouse. From 1850 a daily Company cargo vessel ran to Boulogne. The quantity of goods passing through Folkestone in the 1860s totalled 35-38,000 tons a year. These were not large bulk cargoes but small amounts of comparatively high value goods, such as bullion, which was charged at the highest rates because of the extra security involved. Much of this trade was still done by Messrs. Rothschilds, remembered by the inhabitants as a link with the smuggled bullion of the Napoleonic War period. There were also laces, silks, gloves, dresses, wine, fruit and vegetables from France, wool and fish from England with salmon from Scotland for the Paris gourmet. By 1900 the Folkestone-Boulogne route handled fifteen million pounds worth of cargo yearly.

The steamers, while they still arrived and departed from the South Quay inside the harbour, had to time their arrivals and departures according to the tide. This was good for the hotels, especially the Pavilion, as many passengers preferred to spend the night on shore, but it was inconvenient and could lead to unfavourable comparisons with the journey through Dover. The grand aim of the improvements made to the harbour during the latter half of the nineteenth century was to make berthing possible for the larger boats at all stages of the tide, at the same time keeping direct access to the trains for passengers and goods. The same process was taking place at Boulogne, but needed much encouragement from the English Company. In 1870 there was a scheme put forward by Mr Fowler to build a completely new harbour at Audresselles, half way between Cap Gris Nez and Boulogne, with accommodation for much larger boats which could hold twenty-four railway carriages, running from Dover. Folkestone opinion was that, in collaboration with Boulogne, the same facilities could be provided for one tenth of the vast sums necessary for the new scheme. Baron Mayer Rothschild, the local M.P., and the South Eastern promised to oppose the scheme in Parliament. It was eventually adjourned, due to the outbreak of the Franco-Prussian war. Looking at the harbour now, the eventual solution of running a single pier out into deep water at Folkestone seems obvious enough, but there were several other plans drawn up by Sir John Hawkshaw in 1870 and 1875. Sir Edward Watkin visualised enclosing 200 acres of water.

The actual improvements at Folkestone were more modest but effectual. At first the Company's duties were to keep the harbour free of silt. It cost £500 a year for men to shovel it out at low water. The Pent stream, held up for twelve hours by sluice gates, was a valuable ally. In 1863 a new jetty called the Promenade Pier was made of

Allington stone, projecting into deeper water from the end of the South Quay. It was this pier that halted the shingle and made possible a build-up of land where the harbour station could be sited, and which the new and larger steamers could use at all times. The lines were altered in 1876 to allow trains to run through the end of the harbour station and on to the pier itself. This made it easier for passengers with their luggage to get off the boat and step on the train, though at first they were much exposed to the weather. In 1881 after bad storms, further improvements were effected: the structure was strengthened and extended, and a new station and sheltering parapet made. After this the steamers practically ceased to use the old South Quay, which was given over to cargo ships. Tidal passenger boats ceased in 1886. Between 1897 and 1905 the

harbour took the basic shape that we know today. The old pier was widened to 75 feet, encased in piling, with a new 600-foot arm added. There was a new lighthouse at the end of the pier. Low-tide landing stages were constructed with slipways for the embarkation of horses. There was also a repair yard near the East Head (which generally had plenty of work), a boiler factory and other workshops, and a gridiron pier which ran at right angles to the tram road jetty.

IMPROVEMENTS TO THE HARBOUR WHICH LED TO ITS SHAPE TODAY.

Boulogne had a new Customs house in 1868 and a floating dock was installed. The Chamber of Commerce did not want the train sheds on the quays and had to be reminded that it owed its prosperity to the Channel traffic, without which Boulogne would be no more than a landing place for fish. Passengers had to take omnibuses to get to the trains and the North of France Railway Company was considered to be dragging its feet. Watkin and Eborall were financially involved in promoting improvements. By 1875 passengers could step directly into the trains and a new refreshment room was built, considered to be markedly superior to the dismal establishment at Folkestone. A Harbour Committee had been formed to promote improvements and a Company set up with English involvement, though the French Ministry of Works announced in 1875 that it did not wish too much power to go to foreign concessionaires. By 1897 a deep water port had been made.

The Folkestone harbour was not the exclusive preserve of the cross Channel packets. The fishing and cargo boats had to accommodate themselves to the new regime, under which the Harbour Master was appointed by the Railway Company. His powers were exercised under the original Act of 1807. He was to direct the order of sailing of every ship and its going out. If anyone neglected to obey his instructions, they could be fined 40 shillings. Ships' captains did not appreciate being kept waiting, sometimes for days, before they received the signal to enter. The captain of the 'Jason' was fined for entering without permission when there seemed plenty of time to do so, at

THE LIGHTHOUSE

which the Mayor said that the Harbour Master, Captain Boxer, seemed to consider only the interest of the Company. He would keep a boat waiting outside till dark and, when it had no lights as the oil had run out, its captain was prosecuted for an infringement of regulations. Captain Boxer seized another seaman, the captain of the brig 'Isabella' and shook him like a dog. Even the swing bridge was shut up at his pleasure. We must suppose that his anxiety was for the safety of all, as photographs show the harbour crowded with boats. Great skill was needed in manoeuvring when the steamers tied up at the South Quay. Their captains would sometimes give the fishing boats a tow out to sea.

Captain Boxer's own recollections as narrated in his diary indicate his concerns:

"The difficulty I had to contend with was extraordinary due to the dogged obstinacy and ignorance of the masters. They looked upon the Company and their officers as foreigners and held it to be their right to berth ships as they pleased and in some instances defied me to interfere. A few sentences before the magistrates and a little kindly reasoning at length led to a general obedience to the laws".

Captain Boxer was Harbour Master and General Superintendent of steam ships from 1856 to 1873. His predecessor, Captain (later Vice Admiral) Hathorn, was a jolly and popular old sea dog more conversant with the days of sail than those of steam. In his time discipline was lax all round and it was common for ships' stores to be purloined by the officers. Upon Captain Boxer's arrival, any attempt by him to attend to his duties was met by, *"Now, Boxer, I will tell you a good yarn"*, accompanied by clouds of smoke from an old pipe. Hathorn considered the people of Folkestone as being but little above the old regime of smugglers: *"If you attempt to curb these people they will simply smash your windows and some day do you a bodily injury. Take my advice and if the masters of colliers quarrel, let them fight it out on the wharf"*.

Boxer prided himself on the increase in passenger and cargo traffic due to improvements he had been the first to suggest – enlargement of the pier, building of groynes which were barriers to lateral movement of sea water, to prevent erosion, a repair jetty and more powerful ships. He was also responsible for the running of the Company's boats from Dover to Ostend and Calais and for reaching agreement with the agents in Brussels and Paris regarding goods traffic. He retired in 1873 when his health broke down due to overwork.

In Folkestone, coal was unloaded either outside the Pavilion Hotel in the inner harbour or on the tram road jetty, where it could go straight into the railway trucks. It was generally bagged on the boat, loaded on to the labourer's back and run up a plank. Some was intended for the coking ovens of the railway, some for the gas company, whose works were originally situated by the harbour, and some for the coal merchants of the town. The old coal dues imposed in 1766 brought in £2,000 a year to the council, the equivalent of a four-pence rate. They were not abolished till 1920. Coal was also brought in by train or landed on the beach at Sandgate. Timber came from the Baltic, ice from Norway for packing fish, bricks from Belgium and slates from North Wales. In 1875 Samuel Plimsoll (who retired to Folkestone and is buried in the churchyard of St. Martin's, Cheriton), was fighting hard to ensure that ships should not be dangerously overloaded. How many from Folkestone harbour were unfit to leave? There is a collection of fishermen's stories in the library. One man remembered the last voyage of the 'Cambois' in 1891 visiting Blyth, Lapland, Archangel and Amsterdam, carrying a variety of cargoes. The seamen reported that there was hardly a sound bit of timber in her, food was short and the galley fire lit only every second day. When they remonstrated with the owner on their return, he took them to the pub, stood them a drink and said, *"I am a very poor man"*. They agreed he must be to own such a rotten old tub and left it at that.

Life afloat for the fishermen cannot have changed very much over the centuries, hard exacting work at the mercy of winds and tides. Fishermen are like farmers, gluts and shortages being almost equally unfortunate. In 1875 the catch of herring was so great that it reached half way up the pillars of the market and the load of a coster (who sold from a barrow) fetched only two shillings and sixpence. It was the same all the way round the coast and, as one fisherman observed, *"If we had one quarter of this we would have done well, but all that number be a'most a dead loss"*. Charles Golder, the Harbour Master in 1836, gave evidence before the Parliamentary committee enquiring into the feasibility of the proposed railway line, as to the statistics of the fishing and cargo trade. Two hoy boats of 50-60 tons took an average of thirty tons of cargo to London, leaving every twelve or fourteen days for Griffins Wharf, Tooley Street. There were twenty fishing vessels in the mackerel and herring season of 20-30 tons and forty smaller boats of 4-8 tons. The season was from May onwards, mackerel lasting till the end of June and herring till October, along with crabs, lobsters, prawns, dace, sole, turbot and brill. Carriage to London was expensive at over £8 a ton, sometimes amounting to as much as the value of the fish. Mr Golder felt that more could be sent and sold at better prices by means of the new railway. Folkestone fish could be sent to Boulogne and Paris by the same means.

THE FISH MARKET

Fish was still sold on the Stade, an ancient right which was specifically protected in the Folkestone Improvement Act of 1855. A packing and washing place was provided in 1862 with a supply of water, and in 1883 a new open market, 200 feet by 50 feet, with a roof and pillars.

The best description of harbour activities, as so often with Folkestone affairs, comes from the pages of Dickens:

> *"We are a tidal affair at Pavilionstone. At low water, we are a heap of mud with an empty channel in it where a couple of men in big boots always shovel and scoop with what object I am unable to say. At that time, all the stranded fishing boats turn over on their sides as if they were dead marine monsters; the colliers and other shipping stick disconsolate in the mud; the steamers look as if their white chimneys would never smoke more and their red paddles never turn again…*

> *"But the moment the tide begins to make, the Pavilionstone harbour begins to revive. It feels the breezes of the rising water before the water comes in and begins to flutter and stir. When the little shallow waves creep in, barely overlapping one another, the vanes at the mastheads wake and become agitated. As the tide rises, the fishing boats get into good spirits and dance, the flag-staff hoists a bright red flag, the steamboat smokes, cranes creak, horses and carriages dangle in the air, stray passengers and luggage appear. Now the carts that have come down for coals load away as hard as they can load. Now everything in the harbour splashes, dashes and bobs. Now the down tidal train is telegraphed and you know (without knowing how you know) that two-hundred-and-eighty people are coming. Now the fishing boats*

THE ARRIVAL OF THE TIDAL BOAT

> *that have been in, sail out at the turn of the tide. Now the bell goes, and the locomotive hisses and shrieks, and the train comes gliding in, and the two-hundred-and-eighty seven come scuffling out. Now there is not only a tide of water, but a tide of people, and a tide of luggage, all tumbling and flowing and bouncing about – together."*

(Household Words, September 29th 1855)

8

THE ARRIVAL OF THE NAVVIES

O f all the achievements of the nineteenth century the use of steam to power locomotives running on rails - and the gradual development of the railway system that spread like a spider's web across Britain - is surely the most far reaching in its effects. Thackeray compared the experience of those who remembered the days of the stage coaches as akin to living in the Stone Age, so much had life changed with the increased speed of travel. Folkestone mackerel could now travel to London more quickly and cheaply and new markets were opening up everywhere.

A ROMANTIC VIEW OF THE RAILWAY

John Gough, the American temperance reformer who was born in Sandgate, remembered in his autobiography the great days of the stage coaches and a trip from Sandgate to Maidstone in 1825. He recalled the coachman and guard in scarlet livery, four shining spirited horses, the crack of the whip with dogs barking, the bugle of the guard playing a merry tune, people throwing up their windows and running to the doors to see the gaudily painted mail coach. For a small boy it was the very perfection of travel. Coaches from and through Folkestone had run daily to London, Ashford, Maidstone, Brighton, Hastings and Dover. The Rose Inn, the George and the Folkestone Arms had been busy centres for passengers and goods. Now their day was over.

Railways made possible the mass production and distribution of goods and encouraged a variety of new employments. They changed the way people thought about the possibilities of their own lives; they could visit relations, go abroad, take a trip to London or get to market in comparative comfort and at low cost. To travel by train was at first a unique and thrilling experience. The famous actress,

MAY 3, 1830. THE OPENING OF THE FIRST PUBLIC RAILWAY, CANTERBURY TO WHITSTABLE.

Fanny Kemble, wrote in 1830 of a journey with George Stephenson on the Liverpool to

Manchester Railway: *"You can't imagine how strange it was to be journeying on like this, without any visible cause of progress other than the magical machine."* Such a journey was soon to be taken for granted as part of everyday life. Every town and village through which a line passed was changed in some way. Folkestone was changed more powerfully than most, because the Company's purchase of its harbour made it an important link in the golden chain binding two capital cities, London and Paris. The town would certainly have developed facilities as a resort in the course of the century, but the increased flow of passengers to the Continent meant an assured traffic for the hotels and boarding-houses – visitors who, in the leisurely habits of the middle and upper classes, would break their journeys on the way.

The powers necessary to buy land were granted by Parliament in a series of private bills, the procedure being much the same as for the building of the canal network. The

promoters of a company would see the possibilities of a particular line and have it surveyed and costed. It was usually presented to a Parliamentary Committee. The cost was at first generally underestimated until experience was gained in this field. Expert witnesses were called and could be disrespectfully handled, as was George Stephenson by William Cubitt over the London to Birmingham line. The promoters would produce evidence favourable to their cause; objectors could put their case - those who felt sparks would set fire to their houses or frighten the horses; farmers whose fields would be split up forever; the representatives of competing lines who wished to make the case that the district was already well served. The members of the various Committees gained much knowledge of railway matters, though Herapath's Journal felt that

FOLKESTONE TRAIN EMERGING FROM BLETCHINGLY TUNNEL

hundreds of thousands of pounds' worth of investment was at the mercy of absentee and ignorant members. There could be jobbing and bribery involved; large landowners could hold companies to ransom by threatening a prolonged and expensive battle in Parliament.

The year 1836 was a great one for railway expansion, when fifty-seven Bills came before Parliament, involving a projected outlay of £28,000,000. Before permission was granted, many considerations were discussed - other means of transport; possible competing lines; the number of passengers and weight of freight to be expected; the railway's course and costs and the number of roads that would be blocked. The Committee heard the evidence for the South Eastern line between April and June.

There seems to have been little local financial support, the shareholders being mainly from London, Liverpool and Manchester. Some potential investors were turned down as they were not considered to have enough means to pay for their shares. From London to Dover, there were twenty turnpike roads and seventy-three parish roads to be crossed. There were two coaches plying between London and Dover making twelve journeys a week. Fears were expressed as to the stability of the chalk cliffs, but H.R. Palmer, the engineer, said that the danger was remote. The labourers would earn three shillings a day for ten hours' work and the total cost was estimated at £1,334,649. Some of the Committee expressed doubt at these figures and in fact the total cost was to be over three million pounds.

At this time the Folkestone population was put at 4,296. The local witness was Charles Golder, Harbour Master for five years and part owner of ten ships. His views, which provided valuable evidence about the Folkestone fishery, are described in the Harbour chapter. Although the fish carts which left at 7pm and arrived in London at 5am provided a reasonable service, the charges were enormous; cheaper carriage, such as the railway could provide, meant that more fish could be sent and larger profits made by the fishermen.

LONDON/BIRMINGHAM RAILWAY - NAVVIES AIDED BY HORSES AT TRING

There were twenty-four petitions against the Bill from landowners whose property would be adversely affected and from those towns left out of the plan, such as Sheerness, Sittingbourne and Canterbury. The Act for making a railway line from the London and Croydon Railway to Dover (to be called the South Eastern Line) was passed on June 21st 1836. In November an item appeared in the accounts for £11,898, the amount which had been spent on advertisements, maps, engraving and the calling of expert witnesses. As was usual, the whole amount did not have to be paid at once by shareholders, who were called upon only as expenses were actually incurred. Railways could be backed by those with no ready cash who were gambling on success. This led to the great boom of the 1840s, when the whole country seemed gripped by railway fever and hundreds of miles were planned with no chance of being built.

The bubble burst in 1845 and many were ruined. A contemporary account describes sons being recalled from academies, daughters going out to seek their daily bread and the Queen's Bench prison filled to overflowing with debtors. Confidence could also be lost while the line was under construction, when investors would refuse to pay their dues and their shares would become forfeit to the Company. This

GEORGE HUDSON
THE RAILWAY PROMOTER
AND FRAUDSTER

65

happened with the South Eastern in 1837 when Cubitt had to be called in to reassure investors of eventual success and again in 1839 when calls on shares in arrears totalled £66,525. Disillusioned shareholders were writing to Herepath's Journal advising the trustees of widows and orphans not to touch the shares. They intimated that five thousand pounds' worth of traffic weekly would be needed to cover expenses, an impossible goal, and that the new steam boats going from Herne Bay to London would do the journey for half the railway fare. Local opinion, particularly in those districts through which the line would pass, was generally favourable to the South Eastern. A railway deputation which went to the Dover Town Hall met with unanimous approval. There was a good deal of correspondence with the poor law authorities on the question of the employment which could be provided by the railway for Folkestone fishermen. Steps needed to be taken, it was said, since out of eight hundred houses in the town only two hundred were occupied by ratepayers and the rest were on poor relief. The Folkestone Corresponding Committee for promoting the fisheries on the South Coast of the Kingdom issued a pamphlet in 1835 - 'The Utility of Railroads as a means of increasing the British Fisheries'. It was recognised that, if cheaper distribution were available, gluts of fish which now went stale could be bought by poor people in the capital. John Dunk's great grandfather represented the town opinion otherwise: *"A Railway to Folkestone? Why, there is a daily coach and very often no one in it"*.

To aggravate the problems, the advocates of a Kentish railway disagreed over the

1844 SIGNAL "ALL RIGHT"

actual route of the new line. An article in the Dover Telegraph of 1837 suggested it should go through the towns of the densely populated north of Kent -Dartford, Gravesend, Rochester, and Chatham - with 120,000 population and two million visitors annually. As planned, it would pass from Croydon to the quiet town of Tonbridge, then on to Ashford with its population of three thousand chiefly supported by selling brown sugar, butter, and treacle to the farmers on market day. *"From Ashford to Dover the passengers will see nothing human, save the little dirty children with aprons full of cockle shells at Folkestone."* The surveyors had spent three years discussing the most suitable route, the decision being finally made on the grounds of ease of construction. The North Kent line meant hills and the crossing of the Medway; the planned line was easy and straight till it came to the Pent valley at Folkestone, necessitating the building of a viaduct and tunnels through the chalk cliffs at Dover. A good level it may be, said one objector, but so is the Arabian desert!

The missing connections were to be provided and the Kentish monopoly preserved by numerous branch lines: the North Kent loop via Dartford, Strood and Maidstone; a line from Ashford to Rye and Hastings to take in the sheep and cattle area of Romney Marsh; another from Ashford to Canterbury, Margate and Ramsgate, which would give prospects for the development of Ramsgate Harbour as the port for Ostend, Belgium and the Rhine. Additionally it was proposed to go onwards to Sandwich and Deal from Dover, a route the Directors walked for ten miles in 1837. Whilst the branch line was actually built via Ramsgate and Minster, there was no Dover/Deal route until 1881.

It is noticeable that in all the preliminary discussions there was never an encouraging word as to the advantages of making a stop at Folkestone. *"The town itself is but a poor affair"* said the Railway Journal in 1843. The project was always known as the Dover Line and William Cubitt drew his plans for the railway to cross the Pent Valley and over the hills to the North of the town, disregarding the harbour approach completely. However, all this was to change with the Company's purchase of Folkestone Harbour in 1843.

LAND BOUGHT FOR THE VIADUCT COMPENSATION AWARD

Baxendale must be counted as one of the makers of the town's prosperity in the nineteenth century. He was an enterprising and imaginative businessman with experience as Manager of Pickfords and General Superintendent on the London to Birmingham Railway. In an age when the great Brunel advised a minimum of rules, leaving each line to make its own decisions as to safe running and timetables, Baxendale was cautious, an advocate of a Government Regulatory Board. He felt - and the 1840s boom and slump were to prove him right - that a mad competitive scramble for lines with sixty or seventy Bills under way at once would lead to disaster. He stated, *"Holding a large stake in railways I certainly felt so alarmed in seeing what was passing that no power on earth could induce me to hold that property unless there were some security very different to what we have at present"*. Railways were eventually put under the regulatory powers of the Board of Trade in 1844. Unlike some railway chairmen he invited shareholders to fully investigate the financial matters of the Company, whether by personal interview or by inspection of the books.

One of the first steps in the making of a new line was the appointment of a chief engineer. The South Eastern's choice was William Cubitt who had been born in humble circumstances, the son of a miller. He designed agricultural machinery for Ransomes of Ipswich, inventing a patent treadmill for animals which was later adapted for prison use. A successful canal and bridge designer, he was consultant to the Great Northern Railway, a director of the Berlin Waterworks, and an advisor on French Railways for the

WILLIAM CUBITT

Boulogne/Amiens and Paris/Lyons stretches. In 1851 he was knighted for his work on the Great Exhibition buildings. After the Chairman, who was responsible to the shareholders for overall policy and finance, Cubitt had the most important voice. It was he who planned the route, specified the work to be done and superintended its construction.

The local surveyor was Thomas Thurston, an Ashford civil engineer who produced many tithe maps. He made his way through the Weald of Kent and on to Folkestone, for which he found he had to charge as much as two guineas per mile in consequence of the standing crops and number of hop gardens. An old inhabitant remembered Mr Thurston and his assistant:

> *"A mysterious stranger appeared in and around Folkestone in the late 1830s – he had been perched on the highest point of land near the 'Valiant Sailor' on Dover Hill and the brow overlooking the rope walk where Stace's windmill stood, minus two of its sweeps lost in a storm, and where the Eastern end of the viaduct is now built. He came into the town and haunted the Durlocks, the Harbour, Haigh's yard and Jinkin's Lane and even the High Street. He had an attendant who, at his bidding, stuck little flags of different colours in every conceivable and inconceivable position to the great mystification of the juvenile mind. This was the incubation period of the South Eastern Railway and the immediate results were soon to be seen in the neighbouring meadows where the turf was removed in a narrow line marking the direction and width of the coming iron road."*
>
> (Holbein's Visitor's List, December 31, 1890)

The land purchase was always a contentious and complicated matter. Lord Radnor

RADNOR BRIDGE

received £5,550 for fifty-four acres. Prices were between £100 and £120 per acre for freeholders but very different for tenants, compensation being reckoned according to the value of the crop and the length of the lease. Thus the Rev. Thomas Pearce asked for £300 for an acre of land and received £250, but his tenant, Henry Ashtell, got £5. Mark Tapley, a Folkestone grocer (whose name Dickens borrowed in Martin Chuzzlewit), mentioned damage by persons trampling over his property and asked the Company to give *"what they thought fit."* William Stace, who owned the Bradstone water mill, hoped for £3,685 for his land on which a small windmill was situated and where the viaduct was to be built. He was to get £1,000, his relative William Harvey Stace £85, and William Bennett owner of the rope walk £150. The windmill - pictured in a Constable watercolour - was to be pulled down two years later.

The main line in the Folkestone area went mainly through fields, whereas the branch line and the Pavilion Hotel involved tenements and lands held in a variety of different ways, such as Mary Baker's copyhold (a tenure less than freehold), Mrs. Pope's ground rent and John Stredwick's freehold. The branch cut the town in two and must have entailed a great deal of inconvenience. Lord Radnor received £2,746 for lost rent on fourteen copyholds, quit rents, the building stone which had come from two parcels of land excavated to a considerable depth and land covered up by a slip from an embankment. The Company also agreed to make a bridge in the parish (to be Radnor Bridge). His Lordship earned the thanks of the Company meeting in 1836 for his zealous assistance in Parliament and for his kindness in taking charge of the Bill in the House of Lords.

Cubitt divided the line into four districts: Godstone, Tonbridge, Ashford and Dover. He appointed a resident engineer for each section and instructed each man to take a house near his work. Mr. Wright was the engineer for Dover (which included Folkestone). He had to keep a daily journal to measure the work done by contractors and to keep in constant touch with Cubitt himself. The relative complexities of the different stretches were shown by the eventual cost: £32,615 for Dover as against only £12,012 for Ashford. When the main contractors were appointed, those tendering in 1837 for the double tunnel through Shakespeare Cliff were asked to bring in two persons as sureties for £1,000 each for the performance of the contract. Cubitt liked to put exact prices to the work to be let out. He had a great aversion to what he called lumping sum contracts. A large contractor employed thousands of men. They could amass great wealth, though their fortunes rose and fell with the number of lines to be built.

The line began to make its way slowly through the Kentish countryside, taking eight years to complete, and opened to Tunbridge Wells on May 28, 1842. The receipts for that first day were only £60 but the Railway Magazine advised investors not to be apprehensive, since partial opening of long lines was very often not successful. By June there were 70 passengers on a Saturday and by August the Company was taking £900 a week. In September twelve horse boxes, twelve carriage trucks, and twenty sheep trucks were ordered. Staff were being taken on – porters; switch-men; head and under-guards; railway constables and engine drivers.

Entry to the metropolis and establishment of a terminus was a complicated and expensive business for any line. At first the South Eastern was content to share the lines of other railways. It passed over the lines of the London to Croydon railway and onwards to the terminus at London Bridge, using three miles of the Greenwich railway, which was built on a viaduct. The Greenwich

LONDON BRIDGE TERMINUS

railway exacted a toll of 4 pence per passenger, the maximum permitted by Parliament. In an attempt to avoid this payment, the Croydon and South Eastern built a terminus at the Bricklayers Arms, but it was never popular with passengers and was eventually used for freight only. The same lines were also to be shared by the London and Brighton railway.

At last came the turn of the Folkestone district as the line continued from Saltwood tunnel. Railways might bring prosperity in their wake but the arrival of a vast army of navvies was greeted with dread according to contemporary accounts:

"They were rude, rugged, uncultivated and drunkenness and dissolution prevailed. They lived in huts of damp turf too low to stand upright in. Depredations among the farms and fields were common and they often

committed the most outrageous acts in their drunken madness. On Sundays the most beautiful spots in England were desecrated by their presence."

(J.A. Francis, 1851)

They certainly changed the face of England with no other tools than their picks and shovels. One man could shift twenty tons of earth a day. They were well paid by labouring standards, eating and drinking enormously.

NAVVIES ON THE CRYSTAL PALACE LINE, 1853

"Soon another apparition settled on the spot whose presence was unmistakably felt in every sphere of local life. This was the navvy, pioneer to all Folkestone's greatness, hard, stout, muscular thick-set navvies, trousers strapped at knee with narrow leather thongs and for full dress, blue plush velvet vest with two rows of white pearl buttons. Swarms of the tribe literally squatted in the Warren where payment of rent, rates and taxes was avoided by building mud huts against every bank. Beer, beef and bread were consumed in prodigious quantities and those Folkestonians who saw the opportunity made the most of it and their fortunes at the same time."

(Holbein's Visitors List, Dec. 31, 1890).

Contemporary records hardly bear out the belief in universal depravity. Local labour was often employed and the register shows forty-nine men had children attending the local Sunday school. They lived in the poorer areas: North Street, Fancy Street, Prospect Place and one family in the High Street. There is a sketch of one of the navvy huts near Saltwood with a neat roof and a barrel to catch the rainwater. The Rev. Thomas Pearce made a temporary chapel in the old wooden theatre on the Bayle.

There was certainly an illegal tommy shop (where men had to accept goods in lieu of wages). Mr. Morris, the subcontractor for the viaduct, was reported to the Company Secretary by the Mayor, David Major, and Mr. Wright was instructed to repress the practice. Mr. Morris was also reported for failing to complete his share of the work on the due date.

The main contractors for the viaduct, the early harbour works, the Pavilion Hotel and the coke ovens were Messrs. Grissell and Peto. They had a very different reputation, paying their workers weekly in cash, encouraging clergymen and Scripture readers to visit their men and ensuring that no one who could read was without a Bible. Samuel Morton Peto, knighted in 1855, was the greatest railway contractor after Thomas Brassey. He contributed to the funds of the first Folkestone Baptist chapel and said about a typical navvy, *"I know that if you pay him well and show you care for him, he is the most faithful creature in existence."*

There was, however, one unfortunate incident in Folkestone, long remembered by the inhabitants. A drunken, blaspheming mob held possession of Radnor street for five hours, finally retreating to the Radnor Inn. The Mayor had to summon the aid of forty excise men and two horsemen with their cutlasses and muskets, under the command of Captain Shillingford R.N.. The street was in an uproar with children screaming and women huddled together with aprons over their heads. The Mayor read the Riot Act, the excise men charged forwards and the cowed navvies dispersed peacefully.

THE VIADUCT

The steep sides of the Pent valley were filled with a huge network of scaffolding for the viaduct with its nineteen arches. It is 780 feet long and 100 feet high, made according to Cubitt's designs and still the most impressive architecture in Folkestone. In May, 1842, according to the Kentish Gazette,

"The town presents a scene of bustle and confusion to be compared to Lower Thames St., London. This is occasioned by the preparations for the railroad. It is calculated that fifty vessels have been in the harbour within the last two weeks with implements for this purpose. The streets leading to the harbour are frequently impassable, the number of carriages employed being so great. Several acres of ground have been broken up and hundreds of persons employed in making bricks. Stables and cottages are also building near the line and it is expected a great deal more work will be done this summer; there is scarcely a stable, house or lodging or store of any kind unhired."

There was plenty of work for the local brickmakers. The viaduct is variously described as taking seven or eleven million bricks. Some of the clay was dug from what is now Kingsnorth Gardens and the works were near the site. Between July and October 1843 John Kingsnorth was paid £5,090 for bricks, Charles Golder £1,973, and

Messrs. Tite & Jeffrey of the Cheriton Brick Kilns, £1,857. In September, 1843, the carpenters went on strike in consequence of an inequality of wages.

BRICKMAKERS AT PARK FARM 1880s

At the same time a sad decline was apparent amongst other forms of transport. The traffic of the Herne Bay to London steamers served by the Red Rover coaches from Deal, Dover and Canterbury was nearly all gone. *"We never Sir,"* said a coachman, *"thought the railway would cut the fares as low as this. We must soon shut up, we shan't stand this long"*. The turnpike trustees of the Dover, Deal and Sandwich roads begged the Houses of Parliament to consider the interests vested in the roads, the panic and subsequent road decay which could be caused.

On June 28, 1843 the first train open to the public stopped at the small temporary station in the fields near Darlington Arch before the viaduct was finished. On that same day the London coach vanished from the roads for ever. It was not, however, the end for horse transport and employment, which was on the increase. Carriages, hansom cabs and short haul carriers were in great demand, due to a greater movement of people and goods to the station.

TEMPORARY STATION AT DARLINGTON ARCH

The railway authorities organised two celebrations in connection with the line opening. The first on July 24, 1843, to celebrate the first trip from London to Boulogne and back in a day is described in the chapter on the harbour. The second occasion on August 1st was the turn of a French party to visit England. Visitors flocked in, flags were flown from the church tower and 'Dillum' Golder kept up a fusillade from a small cannon. The French, together with two hundred distinguished ladies and gentlemen, were taken to Ashford and back and at 4.30pm were entertained in a canvas marquee, from which the Pavilion Hotel was to take its name. Toasts were drunk and songs sung. M. Adam expressed his hope of a Boulogne to Paris rail link. It was nearly midnight when the steamer started on its homeward journey. The sounds of the band and singers on board could be heard fading slowly over the water.

DINNER AT THE PAVILIION HOTEL 1843

All was not yet perfect for travellers. Shareholders were told:

> "The arrangements at the temporary station require the utmost
> exertion on the part of the Company's servants and those at
> the boatbuilder's shed converted into the South Eastern Pavilion,
> the unfinished state of the harbour and the unavoidable
> inconveniences attending the first establishment of the
> Customs Department have been submitted to with much
> good humour by those who have been travelling on the line."
>
> (Directors' Minutes, Nov. 8, 1843.)

The line was by no means finished at this point. Work in the Warren had started in November, 1837, and went on until the opening of the line to Dover in February, 1844. There were considerable doubts all along as to the safety of the proposed route. The quantity of springs, beds of slippery chalk and the exposure of fragile chalk cliffs to the action of the waves make stability a matter of concern to this day. There were tunnels to be made: Martello, Abbots Cliff, Shakespeare and Archcliff. For some two-thirds of their length the tunnels were lined with bricks wedged solidly against the chalk to leave no chance of slippage. They were masterpieces of engineering; galleries were dug from the front of the cliff and vertical shafts sunk from the surface. The Kentish Gazette of April 25, 1843 gave an account of a visit made by a party of Directors who had arrived from London to view progress:

> "Passing through the tunnel entailed gropings in unfathomable
> darkness, goings down of innumerable ladders, wadings through
> filth and traversing planks over cold, wet, slimy pools. The clay
> is as slippery as an Irish bog. Imagine twelve directors toiling up
> this Jacob's ladder, each with his enshrined candle in hand. You
> come across a group of excavators who grin at the sufferings you
> endure, another moment and you are nose with a blind horse that
> drags a wagon load. The perfected part is brilliantly lit with blue
> lights and innumerable candles."

Public imagination was powerfully caught by the use of gunpowder, particularly for blowing up Round Down Cliff. Cubitt and Wright were advised by Major General Pasley and Lieut. Hutchinson of the Royal Engineers in blasting a portion of cliff 300 foot long and 375 foot high, thus saving the Company £4,000 in labour costs. Three shafts and galleries were made and some ten tons of gunpowder used, ignited by the use of electric batteries. There was a faint low subterranean grumble and the whole cliff

BLOWING UP OF ROUND DOWN CLIFF

subsided gently into the sea, the debris forming the platform for the sea wall. Ten thousand visitors had crowded the town to see the event, kept at a respectful distance by railway police, while others watched from steamers. There were similar but smaller explosions in March and April. As each section was finished and open, the Railway Gazette complimented the Company on its neatness. There was no litter lying about, no surplus or broken rails, sleepers or tools and no untrimmed embankments or cuttings displayed in disorderly haste. The line might have been open for years.

In a speech to a special meeting of shareholders held at the London Bridge terminus on February 10th, 1844, Mr. Baxendale hailed the opening of the line to Dover as a week of considerable excitement in the railway world. Shares were up in price and dividends secure. There was still much to do and application was being made to Parliament for the branches to Canterbury, Margate and Ramsgate. The Dover line was to be the highway, not only to the Continent, but also to the East. *"We have got the first stage on the road to Pekin"*, he declared.

9

RAILWAY PROGRESS AND CONSOLIDATION

A great tide of visitors was now about to sweep down to the South coast – travellers to France; holidaymakers; business men; invalids in search of health; unemployed in search of work; relatives visiting their families. The early steam engines with their tall smoke stacks had a driver and fireman standing on the foot plate. Then came the coal tender followed by the passenger coaches, on top of the first of which sat the guard and train attendants, in their uncomfortable and chilly posts. The third class passengers were not much better off as they travelled in open coaches. *"We give them seats, we give*

FOLKESTONE TRAIN, 1846.

them sides above 4 foot high", said Mr Baxendale, in his evidence before a Parliamentary committee in 1844, *"In fact, we give such accommodation that the number of what we term the broadcloth (or middle class) is greater than that of the lower class, the accommodation is so good. I must say that I, going as Chairman, often by choice take my seat in a third class carriage – if the weather is at all tolerable"*. It was on this account that a parish officer testified that paupers had to be provided with second, rather than third class tickets because of the thinness of their clothing.

Train travel was still a great improvement on the coaches for speed and cheapness. These had been cold on the outside, dank and cheerless inside, compared by Dickens to the interior of a mouldy dog kennel, and always bumpy. The third class train fare to London was six shillings and passengers disembarked at New Cross instead of London Bridge; 4/7 of the fare was railway profit and 3/7 expenses. For eleven shillings the second class passengers had plain box-like compartments, often very crowded, with roofs but no lighting or corridor. The first class passengers paid seventeen shillings to secure space, arm rests and padded seats. By 1873 the new rolling stock being constructed at Ashford had first class smoking compartments lined with dark blue morocco leather, brass spittoons with drainage holes and brass plates

THIRD CLASS CARRIAGE

75

with chequered surfaces for striking vesuvians (matches). There were no cheap day tickets to Folkestone, as it was considered unnecessary to encourage the lower class of tripper who would feel more at home in Margate or Ramsgate, but a frequent, speedy and punctual service was important. A traveller wanting a day in London could leave by the 8.25am, arriving 10.50am and returning by the 9.25pm would be home by midnight. By 1874 there were ten trains daily, the expresses taking a time of 2 hours, 12 minutes. Standards seem to have been higher in the 1840s and 50s than later.

One event connected with Folkestone which aroused a great deal of public interest was the Great Train Robbery which took place on May 19th 1855: three large boxes in transit from London to Paris were robbed of their contents, Australian gold bars worth £14,000, and the weight replaced by lead shot. The loss was only discovered when the boxes were opened in Paris. Folkestone was a port through which large amounts of bullion often passed, £15 million a year in the 1850s. With the elaborate precautions taken, it seemed impossible that the chests had been tampered with in transit, but they had lain all night in the Folkestone office - where the door was open - and not in the strong room appointed for the purpose. The Company's law clerk Mr Rees, and his father who was a well known solicitor, played detective; they interrogated the unfortunate station master who, they thought, quailed at their glance. Even so, no clues were found until Fanny Kay, (an associate of Agar, who was an experienced thief), called upon Mr Rees and revealed the plot. There had been a conspiracy between Agar and several others: Pearse, a company ticket printer; Burgess, a guard; Tester, who was employed in the passenger manager's office and had actually been given a certificate of character enabling him to take up a post as General Manager of the Royal Swedish Railway. They managed to make copies of the keys of the bullion boxes, one having been stolen from the Folkestone office while the clerks were busy. After proving the keys and waiting two weeks, their opportunity came. Tester informed them that a large consignment of gold was on the train and Burgess was the guard on duty. Pearse and Agar got on the train with the lead shot in carpet bags. Burgess opened the van and the men were able to undo the boxes, take out the gold and reseal them. They alighted at Folkestone Junction with their booty and went to Dover, returning to London by the mail train. The mystery would have remained unsolved but that Pearse and his wife refused to support Fanny Kay and she sought revenge. The conspirators were tried in January 1857; Pearse got two years hard labour, Burgess and Tester fourteen years transportation and Agar was sent back to Portland prison where he was already doing penal servitude for another robbery.

There had been considerable co-operation in this criminal case, between the South Eastern and the North of France Railway Company, no more than one example of the many times when their interests were identical. Even before the harbour was purchased, the English Company was clearly convinced of the need to encourage the formation of a line from Boulogne to Paris and was often seen to be taking the initiative. In April 1842 Robert Stevenson was commissioned to make a report for presentation to the

French Government. It was hoped that London and Paris would be within a 12 hour link in 1844, the projected Boulogne to Amiens line having been laid down according to the advice and estimates of Mr Cubitt and supported to a great degree by the shareholders. At the time it was quicker to drive from Calais to Boulogne and catch the Paris train there. It was also vital that improvements should be made to Boulogne harbour facilities to match those provided at Folkestone. When the station was made on the Quai Bonaparte in 1875 the English Company had put up half the capital of 160,000 francs. Closer links still were forged when it was decided to appoint a French director to sit on the English board. Monsieur Alphonse Rothschild, the President of the French Company, was too busy. The veteran Alexandre Adam too old, but he was given a gold pass and his nephew Achille Adam (a deputy for the Pas de Calais) appointed in his place. The Company was to acquire offices in Paris in 1876, a portion of the old Opera House near the Boulevard des Italiens.

Trains had been running down the steep incline on to a jetty in the Folkestone harbour to pick up coal for the coking ovens on the East Cliff even before Parliamentary approval had been gained. With the opening of the branch line to passengers in 1849, Folkestone now had two railway stations: Folkestone Junction known as the upper station, and the Harbour, which proved to be more popular and accessible for local traffic. The working of the line was nevertheless highly inconvenient. As the Dover Chronicle put it, *"Passengers are to be shot down a terrific tram road and swung slap into the harbour."* There were through carriages to the Harbour on most main line trains, but a delay ensued while they were taken into a siding where the special engines used for the branch line were attached.

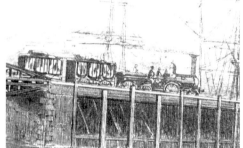

TRAIN GOING TO THE HARBOUR

After the siding the train travelled over a thousand yards down a steep gradient, over the wooden swing bridge and into the station. At first the station was situated on the South Quay where the shingle had conveniently built up against the harbour walls which arrested it in its eastward drift. Four engines had to be used for the heaviest trains and each coach had double brakes. As soon as the new pier was more used than the South Quay for steamers, the trains were run on to it by means of turntables. In 1876 the station itself was transferred to the pier, at twice its present length. At its opening working men from the Friendly Societies in full regalia presented an address of congratulation to Sir Edward. A contingent from Boulogne was present at a dinner in the evening, when Monsieur Achille Adam made a speech prophesying two deep sea harbours and large comfortable boats. A

A HARBOUR ENGINE. IN USE UNTIL 1888

toast was drunk to free trade and the manufacturing and commercial union of Great Britain and France. In 1881 the station was further improved, with a replacement swing

bridge opened in 1893. Final developments took place between 1897 and 1905, when a lengthened pier was rebuilt and improvements made in passenger and goods handling.

Harbour facilities had certainly been improved by the end of the century. Even so, the company

BOULOGNE HARBOUR 1852

had never been happy about the operation of the harbour line (an unplanned expedient in the first place), and the delay incurred by the cross Channel traffic compared badly with the approach to Dover. Attempts to provide an alternative route were to be a bone of contention for nearly 30 years between the Company, the shopkeepers and commercial interests. On the one hand the railway meant increased prosperity, but Lord Radnor and the property owners along the shore feared a line would deter bathers and holiday makers. In 1860 there were two proposed routes for

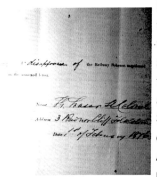

the Board to consider. One was a line from Cheriton, which would pass to the north of the main line, under the viaduct and so to the harbour. The alternative and cheaper way was from the main line via Risborough Lane to Sandgate and along the coast. Between the harbour and the village of Sandgate (along the base of the Leas Cliff), the Estate had constructed a pleasant carriage drive in 1828 with a toll gate. At the Sandgate end, there had been a development of villa residences, all on Radnor land on 99-year leases with direct beach access called Radnor Cliff. The largest of these dwellings was built by Captain Gill, a naval man. Formerly the

LORD RADNOR'S QUESTIONNAIRE FOR HIS TENANTS

residence of Folkestone's M.P., Stewart Marjoribanks, it was now the home of General Hankey and his wife, Lady Emily, well known figures in local affairs. This was a substantial house with ten servants, extensive gardens down to the beach, stables and kitchen gardens on the other side of the road. The second line would have run along the bottom of all these plots cutting them off from the sea. General Hankey felt that his daughters would certainly not be able to bathe if exposed to public scrutiny.

Some property owners objected to a line. One such was James Morris (Governor of the Bank of England) of Encombe, at the other end of Sandgate. Sir John Bligh of Enbrook was another, a retired diplomat and younger son of Lord Darnley of Cobham Hall. Yet a third way was suggested, along the coast as before, but joining the main line via Hythe and Saltwood. This was the line the Company chose to promote, since, although it was longer, it reached more people. Opinion in Folkestone was generally hostile. A petition, backed by Radnor, Bligh and Hankey, was left at the Pavilion Hotel for signatures with the aim of presenting it to Parliament. The only drawback to the Council's opposition was the expense, which would have meant raising a special rate to meet it. Matters progressed slowly. In 1862 a town hall meeting was held and Richard Hart, town clerk and local solicitor, suggested the line should be put in a tunnel. The minutes of the meeting were sent to Lord Radnor who, together with his son Lord Folkestone, felt that his interests were very much involved. The latter commented, *"Such an intolerable nuisance would be a high price for Folkestone to pay for improved communication with Paris."* However, the tunnel plan appeared less destructive. Sir John Bligh seemed prepared to compromise, providing he could have adequate compensation and a bridge over the carriage road, though he later changed his mind. In February 1863, the new electric telegraph brought the announcement that the Commons by a majority of 11 had thrown out the Bill, a message so unexpected that the townspeople at first refused to believe it. It has been suggested that James Morris may have been exerting influence behind the scenes. For the next twelve years the matter of the branch line lay dormant but not forgotten. In 1863 also the new station called Shorncliffe and Sandgate was opened, chiefly to provide for the needs of Shorncliffe Camp, which had been utilised for the British German Legion during the Crimean War and was now a sizeable military establishment.

Edward Watkin - a man who did not easily give up - was the moving spirit in the second attempt to make the Hythe to Sandgate line. Already a well known figure, he secured a place on the South Eastern board in 1865. A year later he became chairman and in 1873 also managing director on the death of C. W. Eborall - a move he announced as being for reasons of economy. Watkin was M.P. for Folkestone and Hythe between 1874 and 1895. With Baxendale he was the second railwayman powerfully to influence the affairs of the town but, unlike his predecessor, he was a great believer in enterprise, competition and, above all, freedom from Government control. He spoke in 1872 of the French railways, protected and partly controlled by the Government: *"Having had to do with French railways since 1855 in connection with the English traffic, I am bound to say that neither in speed, nor price, nor comfort, nor in anything that involves good travelling has there been the slightest improvement in them."* He was the archetypal Victorian businessman, forceful, energetic and conscientious in the

SIR EDWARD WATKIN

performance of his many duties - M.P.; Chairman of the Manchester, Sheffield and Lincolnshire Railway; Chairman of the Grand Trunk Railway of Canada; Chairman of the South Eastern Railway and the Metropolitan Railway, (which gave London its first underground trains). He spent a lot of his life in railway carriages and was reputed to keep a portmanteau with a change of linen in all the principal hotels of the kingdom.

A visionary, he advocated rail tunnels, to link Scotland with England and England with

SIR EDWARD'S RAILWAY CARRIAGE
WHICH COST £1000

France. The Company under the control of such a man carried almost too much weight to be entirely welcome to all the citizens of Folkestone. They recognised the importance to its economy of keeping on good terms, but expressed their unease in metaphors, *"To oppose the Company is like a poor son quarrelling with a rich father in law"*. (Dr. Gill, 1876 enquiry.) *"Folkestone has been much neglected – they have eaten the oyster, we have had but the shell; they have dug gold from our earth and we are only the mud hole from which the treasure has been taken."* (Folkestone Chronicle, January 10th 1874).

A positive step was taken towards the formation of a branch line when in 1872 amidst much rejoicing Prince Arthur dug the first sod of the new Hythe station. Nearly every house was decorated and the streets were impassable for the crowds. Sir Edward was present, together with Baron Mayer Rothschild M.P and the Lord Mayor of London. In 1874 the 'Sandgate' station was opened, situated actually outside the village at Seabrook. The Company plan was now to push on to the harbour; the small line so far barely paying the porter's wages. The Bill, which went to be considered by the Commons in March 1875, passed the committee stages by May. There were several circumstances which made the second attempt more acceptable to the Council (though it still wished to add extra clauses to the bill to safeguard drains and footpaths), notably the support of Sir Edward. Moreover, there was a threat that, if the Company's wishes were not met, the Continental steamer services would be removed from the harbour and centred in Dover, with consequent loss of trade to the town.

In April 1875 a deputation of directors waited upon the Mayor. Sir Edward himself explained the plan in the Council chamber, giving the assurance that the line would be built piece-by-piece rather than having navigators, bricklayers and masons spread over the site for years. Lord Radnor was not in favour but perhaps he, so seldom present in the town (which was a calculated insult) did not appreciate its commercial importance. The Company had opposed Mr Fowler's plan to enlarge Dover harbour at a cost of a million pounds, but could not promise to support Folkestone indefinitely if its wishes were not

THE HEROES FROM LADYSMITH ALIGHT AT
SANDGATE FOR BEACH ROCKS
CONVALESCENT HOME, 1900.

met. The Council was by now fully supportive of Sir Edward; the Mayor, John Sherwood, said bluntly, *"I hope you will succeed and Lord Radnor will be floored"*.

The plan was then explained to a wider public at a Town Hall meeting packed with railway supporters held on February 2nd 1876. From the Chair, the Mayor, Richard Hart, explained the line's course. Following Sir John Hawkshaw's survey in October the previous year, the Company was prepared to put the line in a tunnel for three-quarters of its length under the Leas, so as not to interfere with the Lower Road, and the rest could be screened from sight. The bathing beaches would be almost uninterrupted and the line would only reappear in front of General Hankey's garden. Moreover, the protective groynes necessary would mean a build-up of shingle, making the beaches more extensive than before. There would be no objectionable smoke, as the Company would agree that no coal should be thrown into the furnace while passing between Folkestone and Sandgate. The Mayor was supported by Alderman Banks, a jovial local house agent, who suggested that the Company were not going to spend £300,000 for the purpose of ruining the town. Folkestone needed to improve its commerce as well as being purely a seasonal watering place. This was reaffirmed by Dr. Gill who said many invalids were not sent to Folkestone by their medical advisors because it was too cold. The town needed resident business men, able to reach their London offices speedily. As for the Lower Road being spoilt, the visitors would positively enjoy the pleasant sight of trains passing as they did in the Warren. The Bill's opponents were attacked by Edward Knatchbull Hugesson - Lord Radnor for his lack of interest in the town and General Hankey, whose property would actually increase in value and who would feel a monstrous fool for his former opposition. A ratepayer interrupted with a derogatory comment about the General's cesspool and the three stinking drains which ran on the beach. Sir Edward summed up the debate, referring to General Hankey's campaign of slander against him personally and the posters now appearing on the walls. He reassured the audience about the Company's aim of promoting the prosperity of the town,

PRINCE ARTHUR DIGS FIRST TURF OF SANDGATE STATION.

which showed that the interests of Town and Company were identical. It would be a calamity if Folkestone ceased to be a great continental port with the many visitors the service brought.

It is interesting that the tenants of the Lord of the Manor looked to him to protect their interests in the environment at this period of crisis. The Estate office received many anxious letters, *"The line in question will render our properties useless by cutting us off from the sea. I would entreat your Lordship to use your influence to protect us from a ruinous scheme in the course of being carried through by the grossest falsehood and deception."* (Radnor papers.) Lord Radnor was to a certain extent dependent upon his advisor (his agent Mr Norman), whose first impressions of the Bill were cautiously favourable. Lord Radnor's reply to the letter was forthright, *"It looks all rubbish so far as I am concerned and I do not think it will do a pennyworth of good to the Estate"*.

The whole plan was eventually abandoned as extra expenses became apparent. If Sandgate Castle had to be demolished, the War Department requested that a similar defensive building should be put up. Furthermore, the plan for the new line would necessitate a tunnel being built under the cliff.

By now there was a main line in that populous portion of Kent which the South Eastern had passed over when it planned its route in 1836. In 1859 the new line was named the London, Chatham and Dover Railway, L.C.D., and a year later had trains running from Canterbury to Victoria Station. As had happened with the South Eastern, entry to London was gained by running over the lines of other companies, which entailed paying tolls and reduced profits. In 1862 it won the Government contract to carry mails, short-sightedly relinquished by the South Eastern, and started its own channel ferry service from Dover. At this the South Eastern withdrew its boats from the port and concentrated on Folkestone.

The new South Eastern termini at Charing Cross (1864) and Cannon Street (1866) attracted a more numerous and better class of passenger than Victoria, but many journeys to London - such as those from Maidstone, Canterbury, Ramsgate and Margate - were shorter by the L.C.D. For the shareholders there was no comparison. In the 1870s the South Eastern was paying its accustomed steady 4-5%, while for the L.C.D. ordinary shareholders there was, as yet, no chance of a dividend. *"Happy is the man who has a basket of South Eastern stock"*, said Sir Edward at the Company meeting in 1876. Why could they not amalgamate and make one profitable Company? The fact that they did not is often put down to the autocratic and obstinate Sir Edward. He was determined to wage war upon his opposite number at the L.C.D., James Staats Forbes, an astute, plausible and cultured business man. Sir Edward was at pains to refute this at the July 1875 shareholders' meeting. He had recommended amalgamation in 1861, but the proposal foundered over the division of fares and profits. *"Peace and Union are worth buying at a price, but we cannot recommend you to buy it at a price which would not appeal to our best judgement."* In 1876 again shareholders and city interests appealed to both sides. The L.C.D. was particularly short of money, as it had just taken over the Crystal Palace line, but Forbes refused to go to arbitration.

The nearest the two companies came to fusion was the Continental Agreement of 1865 (made retrospective to 1863). By this agreement fares were pooled for continental passengers to coastal stations only, receipts being taken in proportion to the size of the expected traffic - 68% to the South Eastern, 32% to the L.C.D. By 1864 the L.C.D. had received £558,000 which enabled it to continue running. This made it all the more bitter for the South Eastern when the L.C.D., continuing its ambitious policy of expansion into all areas, proposing in 1884 to build a branch from its Canterbury-Dover line to run via

Kearsney and the Alkham Valley into Folkestone. With a terminus in Earls Avenue, the branch would give Folkestonians a choice of two lines to London Victoria. The whole town was in a high state of excitement, split between the two rival parties. Not only was the L.C.D. offering cheaper rates for passengers and fish, there were doubts about the safety of the South Eastern line to Dover through the Warren following a serious accident in January 1877; after a very wet spell, a landslide had killed three men and opened up crevasses 6 feet wide. The line had been blocked until the beginning of March and the Martello tunnel converted into an open cutting. Navvies had to set to work again, a thousand men with their braziers for cooking, and shanties and tents to live in, reminding inhabitants of the railway's first beginnings. The tunnel was shored up with planks to prevent further falls and gas jets threw their light on the enormous works. Forbes hastened to offer aid in conveying passengers and mail to Dover via the L.C.D.

The weight of opinion in the town was on the side of the South Eastern, including Lord Radnor and the Council, even to the point of spending rates on the expenses of Parliamentary opposition to the L.C.D.'s proposed Bill. The line would chop up the West End, cheap fares and day trippers would spoil Folkestone's exclusive atmosphere and there was the ever-present threat of the South Eastern's withdrawal of the Channel steamers. A pamphlet compared Forbes to Napoleon who diverted attention from domestic difficulties by schemes of foreign adventure; Forbes did the same with the ruined L.C.D. investors. The evidence called by both sides for the Select Committee in 1884 is of great interest, as these were the views of tradesmen and builders, investors and hotel keepers, men judged to be the very backbone of the town's financial prosperity, all of whom were given first class rail passes to attend. First for the L.C.D. came William Jeffreason, Chairman of the Folkestone Committee in favour of the line and Chairman of the School Board; he had interests in house property and the cement works on the East cliff. Jeffreason mentioned the landslip, the petition in favour of the line signed by 1,200 people and the advantages of access to the Alkham Valley for lodging-house keepers on holiday. Thomas Vaughan, who owned 2 grocer's shops and 16 houses, felt the line would not injure property values. Mr Hilder of Tonbridge, who had built 40 houses and owned 27, preferred cement from Faversham to that from Folkestone. His evidence was somewhat devalued as, on cross-examination, the houses were admitted to be cheap cottages, unlike the West End mansions built by James Petts in Earls Avenue, worth up to £2,000 each. Donald McKay, a lodging-house keeper, always travelled between Folkestone and Dover in fear and trembling. *"He makes a fresh will each time"*, said Counsel.

Against the line were two men whose employment would be directly affected and who were not to be tempted by generous offers of compensation; one was Arthur Hussey of the Grange, Shorncliffe Road, whose spacious school took 60 boys and had cost £10,000 with its classrooms, dormitories, chapel and cricket field. The other was Mr Salter, a laundry man of 5 Melbourne Gardens, who employed 20 hands regularly and 40 in the season. He visualised an embankment 60 feet high cutting across his spring of fresh water and ruining his two-acre meadow and drying ground. Henry Worsfold Poole, the Mayor, said that in 1842 there had been 850 houses, the number now being 3,450. Development in the West End would cease if a new station was built

there. Alderman Sherwood was a grocer and house agent, a director of the Gas and Coke Company and of the Water Company. He was Chairman of the Bathing Establishment and a member of the Burial Board. A former Mayor, he remembered Folkestone as a small fishing village, and did not wish the town to become like Ramsgate. Alderman John Banks, another former Mayor, said that he must

WORKMAN ON THE SLIP, 1877

have sold half the property in the town and thought that the South Eastern had made its prosperity. Important evidence was also given by Francis Brady, an engineer with the South Eastern for 36 years. There had been substantial drainage works in the Warren to prevent any recurrence of the landslip, though he complained of the difficulty of getting permission from Lord Radnor for access to the land. He was supported by two other engineers with experience of coastal railways, Peter Margary and Peter Barlow. Due to the greater weight of local opinion on the side of the South Eastern, the Bill did not pass.

The South Eastern also had two cards to play which helped to defeat the Bill. In 1884 it opened the long awaited station in the West End with easier access than that of

the Harbour or the Junction. It was a small wooden station called Cheriton Arch, where the road traffic went under the railway. The arch, narrow and inconvenient, was widened in 1890, when the station became known as Radnor Park. Finally in 1895 it was renamed Folkestone Central to avoid confusion. Local trains were gradually withdrawn from the Harbour, leaving it only for boat trains. It could now plausibly be argued that the new station and Shorncliffe

CHERITON ARCH STATION

Station did not serve continental passengers, so the Company did not include them in its fare-pooling arrangements with the L.C.D. This enabled it to offer cut-price tickets from Shorncliffe which increased its traffic from 6,000 passengers in 1866 to 29,000 by 1883. The L.C.D. sued the South Eastern for its lost revenue, said to amount to

£70,000. It won the case but lost on appeal. The L.C.D. then took the matter to the House of Lords where judgement was given in its favour for £85,000 and costs, reckoned to amount to £250,000.

Another project was of interest to the town, for which Parliamentary approval had been gained in 1881 and which was now to be pushed forward in haste. This was a line from Cheriton to Canterbury by way of the Elham valley, Lyminge, Elham, Bishopsbourne and Bridge, though it promised meagre financial returns. The first turf was cut on August 28th 1884 at Peene, by Sir George Russell, and the line was finished in June 1889. The advantages promised by the L.C.D., a West End station and a direct line to Canterbury were now achieved by the South Eastern and Folkestone felt it had made a wise choice in supporting Sir Edward.

FOLKESTONE CENTRAL

Fares to Folkestone in 1887 were: 18 shillings and sixpence, 1st class; thirteen shillings and sixpence, 2nd class; six shillings, 3rd. The boat train fares were twenty shillings 1st class and fifteen shillings 2nd class, there being no third class. Comfortable Pullman type carriages were used for the boat trains in the 1890s which increased the popularity of the route. However, they entailed inconvenience to other traffic and were a part cause of public disillusionment with the South Eastern. *"The South Eastern manages to secure more ill-will from the public than any other line. It is audaciously unpunctual and makes a ruthless sacrifice of local convenience whenever Continental trains are in question."* (Foxwell & Farrer, Express Trains English and Foreign, 1899).

When Sir Edward retired in 1894, the way was at last open for a peaceful agreement with the L.C.D. In 1899 the two companies formed a Working Union to be known as the South Eastern and Chatham Railway, administered by a Managing Committee under the chairmanship of Cosmo Bonsor. At last uneconomic services could be eliminated, carriages and engines modernised and made to a uniform design. The new Company was also able to rationalise the boats, the combined fleet of passenger and cargo boats being reduced to 18, including two new boats, which could be interchanged between the Dover and Folkestone Services.

TRADES AND SERVICES

In old Folkestone, the shopkeepers and merchants who could at least read, write and count and enjoyed some measure of prosperity provided many of the candidates for public offices, such as mayors, Jurats, chamberlains and overseers of the poor. In the later years of the nineteenth century there were more residents who could be styled gentry, being of established families possessing independent incomes. But the shopkeepers, builders and professional men, seen as their social inferiors because they worked for their living, were still prominent in public affairs. It was their sons, not the sons of poor fishermen, who were given the educational opportunities offered by the Harvey Grammar School and later, the numerous private schools for young gentlemen.

The number, size and sophistication of shops increased greatly during the century. The working life of shop assistants then has been described elsewhere, but the majority of shops were run by the owners and their wives. In his Autobiography, H.G. Wells gives a moving account of his parents, trapped in their dismal, unsuccessful shop in Southsea, which must have been typical of many in Folkestone.

The exchange and purchase of goods is an activity as old as civilisation itself, but fashions in shopping have changed across the centuries. Larger and more varied arrangements of goods were made possible by the introduction of gas lighting and plate glass. Shop windows were crammed, with every inch of space filled with goods and no efforts made at artistic display. Price tickets were being used, though not in the expensive shops. Much service was provided as long as wages were low. Goods were delivered, often arriving home before the customer. A new customer, entering a fashionable draper's, would be greeted by the floorwalker who would beckon an assistant to take charge. The photographs of Messrs. Plummer Roddis' saleroom show elegant surroundings, ferns, potted plants and a thick, patterned carpet. Goods were either in glass cases or contained in tiers of drawers, each neatly labelled with its contents.

The large number of tailors and dressmakers indicated that clothing was often made to measure. They generally worked at home on materials purchased by the customer from the draper. A display of ready-made wear, especially gentlemen's clothing, generally indicated a lower class of goods, since a discriminating clientele preferred clothes made to measure. There were shops, however, such as that of Miss Owen in Alexandra Gardens or Mr Brett in Rendezvous Street which offered both ready-made and bespoke clothing.

There was no self service; the assistant would pile the counter until the customer made a choice, after which all items had to be returned, neatly folded into their boxes before anyone else could be served. Money was placed in a small metal canister sent whizzing along an elevated wire to the cash desk, the change being returned in the same fashion. Messrs. Plummer Roddis kept this system until closure in 1971. Demanding customers had to be humoured and flattered if a job was to be kept, as described in Kipps (H.G. Wells)]:

SHOE SHOP - PUNCH

"Sometimes people would stay long after the shop was closed. 'They don't mind a bit at Shalfords', these ladies used to say and while they loitered it was forbidden to touch a wrapper or take any measures to conclude the day until the doors closed behind them. Mr Kipps would watch these later customers from the shadow of a stack of goods and death and disfigurement was the least he wished for them."

The commercial centre of the town was the area around the Town Hall from where the shops spread out in a web pattern. According to Russell's Guide in 1885 there were 68 shops in the narrow crowded High Street, 20 in more spacious premises in Sandgate Road, 20 in Guildhall Street, 53 in Tontine Street, 35 in Dover Street and 42 along the Dover Road.

LEWIS & HYLAND

The two largest and most important shops in Folkestone both described themselves as 'drapers'. They sold high class ladies' and children's wear, millinery, gents' clothing, as well as china, glass and furniture. In 1837 George Alexander Lewis lived above his old-fashioned shop in Rendezvous Street. It prospered, and was to be replaced in 1887 by a new large four-storied block, built with plate glass windows, incorporating every modern improvement in shop fitting. By 1886 it was a partnership of Messrs. Lewis, Hyland and Linom, with branches in Ashford, Ramsgate, Hastings and Pluckley. The firm was described as being in touch with the leading fashion centres in London, Paris and Berlin. There were large well-stocked departments, dresses and suits being made on the premises.

Messrs. Plummer Roddis & Tyrell (formerly Beecroft) were another partnership. They occupied the commanding block at the corner of Rendezvous Street and the High Street. This shop, the great rival of Lewis & Hyland, had also sprung from small beginnings, three premises which were altered and adapted to make a large and magnificent emporium, which made a feature of soft furnishings, china and glass; there were branches in Hastings, Eastbourne and elsewhere. Both chains of shops were essentially similar to the modern department store and depended for their trade on visitors as well as residents. They employed large staffs, not only shop assistants but also tailors and dressmakers. Although they survived until recently, they were in the wrong part of town as trade shifted into the Sandgate Road. Herbert Bobby, who had taken over the business of C. J. Saunders in Rendezvous Street in 1906, moved to Sandgate Road premises in 1931, becoming the best known and successful store, and eventually selling out to Debenhams.

There were also many small drapers and outfitters of a standard and price proportionate to the neighbourhood in which they were established. Tontine Street specialised in gents' outfitting. The largest of these shops was the Monster Clothing Store, belonging to Philip Hart, which was taken over in 1875 by Simeon Hart, who was also a pawnbroker. Selling working men's ready-made clothing and thick jerseys for fishermen, he advertised 'Every Article marked in Plain Figures at Lowest Possible Price for Cash'. Another was T. Logan, a tailor, hatter, general outfitter and proprietor

LOGANS / R.J. WOODS

of a bath saloon, whose shop survives largely intact at the corner of Rendezvous and Tontine Streets. He introduced prizes of £100 for customers and on one occasion gave away a pony, but eventually he went bankrupt; the shop was taken over by R. G. Woods, who kept Logan as manager. In his time, Logan was a fighting Radical, who represented the East Ward in the Council and began the newspaper Folkestone-up-to-Date in 1894, a livewire paper to champion the cause of "the working men, the struggling tradesmen, oppressed cabmen and brave fishermen". More detail is given in Chapter 14.

Adolphus Davis, mentioned in Kipps, described himself as 'House Furnisher and Draper'. He had a shop in the High Street and bought four properties in the Sandgate Road, occupying the two largest himself. He specialised in furniture which was displayed in fantastic profusion. No provincial shopkeeper had yet learnt the impact of an

ADOLPHUS DAVIS

elegant display of a few choice pieces. Yet it was remarked how much the art revival had affected home interiors – less clutter, bright colours and lighter furniture, the modern drawing room in the 1890s being furnished at less than half the cost of forty years before.

There was a great number of boot and shoe makers producing their own designs. The best shop, Messrs. Clements & Sons, was founded in 1840 in Rendezvous Street, where three spacious windows displayed every style from ladies slippers (some imported from France) to heavy working boots. C. Bull & Son, of 4 Cheriton Road, sold cheaper and less fashionable shoes, all made on the premises. Daniel Walter, who opened his first shop in Hythe in 1849, moved to Folkestone in 1919 and eventually took premises at 108 Sandgate Road, the firm has recently ceased to trade.

Hall & King from Wigmore Street traded as the West Cliff Pharmacy in Bouverie Road West. At the Folkestone Drug Stores in Tontine Street qualified chemists mixed medicines of their own brand. You could also buy perfumery and toilet requisites, medicines for horses, cattle and dogs and Oporto Coca Wine, a specific against fatigue, popular with cyclists. Much in demand were patent medicines, widely advertised in newspapers, which claimed to alleviate every disease afflicting mankind. Holloways Pills cured 33 diseases, including consumption, fits, gout, worms, ulcers, dropsy, ague, indigestion, leprosy, local debility (the especial annoyance of the female sex) and *"that retributive disease which seems to be the penalty of sensual grossness"*.

Branded goods were rare in grocers' shops. Shopkeepers made up their own packets of tea, currants, flour, sugar and dried cereals. Adulteration was not unknown - sand in the brown sugar, powdered chalk in the flour and dried tea leaves sold by servants were mixed with fresh. Credit had to be given if customers were to be kept, a practice which led to the ruin of some small shopkeepers. The arrival of the small account books lettered in gold in which the butcher's or grocer's accounts were rendered monthly was frequently a cause of heated family debate. Bills for dresses and millinery could equally be a source of contention, in an age when these were often expensive to denote social status. Poor people could not afford good clothes and second-hand dealers offered a source of supply.

Food shops, grocers, greengrocers and licensed victuallers formed the majority of trading establishments. These were scattered throughout the town and varied greatly in size and turnover. J. W. Pittaway advertised in verse:

> *"In Rendezvous Street, very near the hill top*
> *Stands a general warehouse or well arranged shop*
> *Where good things in abundance are nicely displayed*
> *At prices as low as you'll find in the trade.*
> *And if houses or lodgings you're anxious to see,*
> *There's a register kept by J.W.P."*

John Sherwood, four times Mayor, kept the largest grocer's shop in Folkestone at 3-5 Rendezvous Street. Every month he also issued a register of furnished and unfurnished dwellings for sale or to let. He owned a great deal of property in the town himself and died with a fortune of £230,000. W. F. Gosling at 6 High Street was another good class grocer and wine merchant, said to date from the days of the railway navvies and the tommy shops.

SHERWOODS

Bakers advanced rapidly with the coming of bread baking in primitive ovens used also to cook the Sunday dinners of the poor. George Strood was an example of a tradesman who moved to better himself, starting in the High Street in 1876, moving to the Dover Road and finally to Guildhall Street. His gas-fired ovens turned out bread and rolls untouched by hand. The longest-running baker's business was that of W. K. Marks, started in 1840.

Butchers were highly important and generally prosperous tradesmen. Large quantities of meat were eaten in all households except the very poorest. A father of eleven related how he bought a tin of Australian meat for two shillings and sixpence. The tin, opened amidst the breathless interest of all, provided a good meal on Sunday, another on Monday and he finished it up on Tuesday. *"This,"* he concluded, *"will urge*

DURBAN BROS. CHRISTMAS DISPLAY

the butcher to lower his price." The most famous Folkestone butcher was Stephen Major. He started in Beach Street in 1850, then bought the old Wesleyan chapel, later the Queens Hotel site, and finally moved next to the Town Hall. At a time when butchers killed their own animals, his slaughterhouses were on the Bayle. All slaughterhouses were seen regularly by the Sanitary Inspector, but the disposal of blood and offal presented difficulties and polluted the Pent Stream before it was covered over. (Eventually a public abattoir was opened.) Animals were driven through the crowded streets and accidents could occur, as when a bull entered Mr Jenner's china shop in Sandgate and caused much damage. All butchers made a tremendous display of meat at Christmas - with joints and turkeys hanging in rows - and made a great selling point of which farmers they patronised.

The washing of clothes being a heavy ill-paid occupation for women, laundresses were too insignificant to be noted in early directories. An advertisement for Fosters Laundry in 1886 recalled the bad old days when the laundry was done in unwholesome back kitchens and hung out between walls on which the dirt of ages had accumulated. The growing hotel trade demanded new methods. There were several laundries in Cheriton where land was cheaper. Salters Bouverie Steam Laundry occupied two acres of land at Foord with good drying grounds and steam-powered dryers for wet weather. Clothes were washed in steam machines and moisture removed by extractors. Their methods of registering washing, the firm declared hopefully, made mistakes almost impossible. However, laundresses had not yet all disappeared as an advertisement of 1891 shows:

'One or two families' washing wanted, school not objected to, good drying ground. Mrs Hogben, 11 Spring Gardens.'

Dairymen also were ignored and roundsmen sold direct to the customer, filling jugs and bottles as required. Milk was sometimes watered down and, in May 1889 alone, there were four prosecutions for adulterated milk. Cleanliness, hygiene and good farm management were essential when tuberculosis and other illnesses could be passed on from infected herds. George Sharp supplied his dairy in the Sandgate Road from his Hawkinge farm, advertising

SHARP'S CREAMERY

special cows kept to supply children and invalids. He opened a tea room on the first floor which became very popular.

Another place of rendezvous was Gironimo's at 18a Sandgate Road, originally a baker's, with linen tablecloths, potted palms and stained glass windows. The largest and busiest restaurant in Folkestone was the Central, owned by Carlo Maestrani of Italian origin. He was a former cook, like another successful immigrant, Constantine Wampach, and had started in 1877 with a small establishment in South Street. In 1889 he moved to impressive premises in Sandgate Road, designed by Reginald Pope. He had the same struggle to achieve a drinks licence as the owners of the Grand, and it took three years before one was obtained. The business became a registered company in 1898 and expanded, catering to the Leas Cliff Hall, Leas Pavilion and Marine Gardens. But competition increased while business fell and the company was liquidated in the 1930s.

Wine merchants were noted for their longevity in commercial terms. The firm of J. H. & J. Brooke was founded at Hythe in the eighteenth century and came to Folkestone in 1851 with premises in Sandgate Road near the Town Hall. Underneath were enormous cellars full of maturing wines, later to be lit by electricity. They did a large trade with officers' messes throughout the country and exported wine to the colonies as distant as Hong Kong and Australia. Messrs. Underwood Penfold & Co. had a shop in the Sandgate Road and a bottling department at 28 Bouverie Road designed by Joseph Gardner. At the latter premises were living rooms and dormitories for employees with stables for the horses used in deliveries. When they were built in 1876 it was remarked that such proximity might be detrimental to the owners of West End mansions nearby. Both firms had depots near the harbour where bonded goods could be stored.

Brewing was always an important local activity. In 1812 a brewery was advertised for sale in Rendezvous Street. Ham Tite leased land from Lord Radnor in 1846 on which he built the Gun Brewery and Shakespeare Tavern. He and his son, who became an Alderman, evaded municipal regulations for years by using water from the Town Dyke to fill a capacious tank. The building was a familiar landmark and the beer judged to be excellent, but the premises were used only for bottling when taken over by Leneys in 1898 and were subsequently demolished. There was also a brewery in Tontine Street from 1855, illustrated in Russell's Guide, 1885.

Messrs. Oclee is the oldest business in Folkestone. John Holtom Oclee was a clock

and watchmaker, whose family connections with the trade went back to the early 1800s. He came to Folkestone in 1878 and started a shop by the pillar letter box in George Lane, later moving to more spacious premises in Sandgate Road, where he also sold jewellery. Cyril and Walter were the next generation, to be succeeded by Cyril's son Brian. It is now Brian's sons John and James who direct the firm.

OCLEE & SON

Photographers had been operating nationally in the early 1840s. There is a report in the Kentish Gazette of 1852 that W. Cooke would come to Folkestone on Saturdays to take Coloured Daguerreotype Portraits. At this time photography was a time consuming and dangerous business involving a mixture of chemicals, including cyanide. William Venables in Sandgate Road allowed an itinerant photographer to use his premises and then took up photography himself. At the same time he was an auctioneer and valuer, secretary to the Folkestone Savings Bank and a journalist.

Other photographers were Walter Blackall (later Hawksworth Wheeler) and the brothers Jasper and Lambert Weston, who set up separate businesses. Lambert's shop survived till 1982 and all have left valuable photographic records of the town.

The manufacture and sale of cycles was another expanding business. The Gun Cycle depot in Bouverie Road East, which had a staff of cycling instructors, also sold prams and mail carts. A popular line was the 'Fixit' dress holder, quantities of these being sold in windy weather. Harbour Street was the headquarters of 'The Wheeleries', Messrs. Hillsdon & Hillsdon, cycle engineers and manufacturers.

Coal came in by boat and with low transport costs could be bought cheaply. In 1896 the merchants were wondering if they would eventually be supplied with Kent coal. The longest running firm was Courts in Tontine Street, started in 1835, which had customers in many country districts. Francis Anderson & Co., established in 1844, kept coal and coke, hay and straw and every kind of animal provender down to canary seed. Coal was an important item of consumption and W. H. Pearson of Grace Hill was another fast growing coal business. The Dover Road sawmills produced 10,000 bundles of firewood daily using a machine with a gas engine.

Gas and steam were being used as power sources for a variety of purposes. John Dunk made a list of the 33 power supplies in use between 1885-95. They were to be found in the cement works; the brickfields; at the Bathing Establishment to heat water; at the Bradstone Mill; in laundries and printers' works; at the parish church for organ blowing and to drive the sausage machine at William Major's shop; there were dynamos producing electricity at the Pavilion Hotel. Steam engines were also used for road transport of heavy items, such as bricks, and there were complaints that these, travelling at speeds of up to 6mph, were not preceded by a man with a red flag.

There had been seven mills in the hundred of Folkestone according to the Domesday survey. In the nineteenth century mills were used for a variety of purposes: grinding corn and bones, sawing timber and making paper and silk. The waters of the Pent stream provided motive power for the Bradstone mill , which still stands in a yard at the back of Bradstone hall less its top storey. Shown in the 1698 estate map, it was probably rebuilt by William Stace. The first Baptist meeting is said to have taken place here and the first chapel and burial ground were near. The mill, which had five pairs of stones driven by a large overshot water wheel, passed into other hands in 1858. It continued to work until 1894, when William Marsh relinquished the tenancy. From his other property, William Stace sold to the South Eastern Railway Company a small wooden mill which stood at the top of what is now Bellevue Street. That mill disappeared soon after the opening of the railway, because either the viaduct deflected the wind or it was set on fire by sparks from the engine. He also sold some land on which part of the railway viaduct was built.

The Millfield flour mill was the best known of Folkestone mills, a picturesque feature on many postcards. It was built for John Claringbould before 1821 and went on working till 1885. At this time it was sold for £30 to George Jarvis, who removed it to Bethersden, where it was used as a sawmill until being demolished in 1921. George Jarvis bought also the Sandgate sawmill, visible in some prints, which came originally from Great Chart. It was put up in Sandgate before 1878, but the sweeps were blown off in a storm and caused great damage. There were four other mills in Cheriton parish: two on the Seabrook stream; one in Risborough Lane (which burnt down in 1856) and another in Ashley Avenue/Tile Kiln Lane. The latter had been built in Hythe in 1813, and re-erected in Cheriton in 1877 by Mr Brissenden, a Sandgate builder; it ran until 1919, powered first by wind then by gas.

Tile and brick making were flourishing industries in a rapidly growing town. In 1808 the Kentish Gazette advertised a well-established tile and chimney pot manufacturing business for sale near Cheriton, capable of producing two million tiles a year. The area

THE OLD BRICKWORKS

between Cherry Garden Lane and Tile Kiln Lane was the site of at least three brickworks. Mr Gambrill's Broadmead brickyard was on the junction of Bournemouth and Radnor Park Roads. A tramway led from the clay pit which had two level crossings and a bridge over the Pent Stream. Kingsnorth Gardens was the site of John Kingsnorth's clay pit from which much of the clay to make the ten million viaduct bricks was taken. There were complaints of *"unhealthy exhalations"* in 1870. The cement works on the East Cliff started by John Pope the builder were also thriving. Chalk was taken from the cliffs, carried by a light railway.

Transport within the town was solely a matter for private enterprise. There were regular horse-bus services to Sandgate and Hythe, but at first only one bus which waited outside the Town Hall to pick up passengers and made six journeys a day. Gradually bus numbers increased and there were several competing owners, so that by

PILCHER'S HORSE BUS 1880

1900 the number of journeys had risen to 90 a day. Buses were given names, like Michael Valyer's 'Victoria' or Henry Laker's 'Tally-Ho'. It was Michael Valyer, and later his son, another Michael, who became the most powerful figures in the Folkestone horse world. In 1855 he advertised ponies for riding and every sort of carriage for hire - clarences, landaus, britzskas and phaetons, cabs by the hour; he

offerred a large hearse with four horses travelling to the new cemetery for four guineas or an economy turnout for eight shillings. His was the sole right to supply cabs and buses to and from the stations and hotels, a right maintained with difficulty against interlopers. On one occasion an unfortunate customer saw her carpet bag torn in half by rival cabbies. His livery yard was at the side of the King's Arms, where horses for sale could show off their paces in front of the Town Hall. He had been riding master to the Queen and the Prince of Wales and it was suggested that noblemen, gentlemen and ladies about to purchase horses should commission Mr Valyer to examine them as to their age, soundness and warranty.

There were of course other livery stables - the increasing number of visitors and the fact that only a few outlying houses kept stables meant good business for all. The Osborne Mews and livery stables in Bouverie Road West, convenient for the hotels, had a large coach yard and specialised in elegant wedding carriages. Holman's stables in Christ Church Road provided accommodation for the coachmen of visitors, as well as their horses and carriages.

There were traffic accidents. The driver of a Valyer omnibus, going at 16mph, knocked down a little boy and was accused of furious driving. The defence elicited the fact that the constable came from a farm, where he would be more accustomed to the slow pace of the farm horses. A farmer invited Sergeant Alldridge from the camp and three lady friends for a drive in his pony carriage. Matilda Collier, a bonnet maker,

LADIES IN A CARRIAGE, BOUVERIE SQUARE

testified that the pony shied and the women squeaked and hollered. *"Ho'eavens,"* she said, *"We shall be killed immediately"*. A barrel of tar was upset and her dress was ruined. Captain Sawbridge, driving his four-in-hand too fast round a corner on the Leas, collided with and bruised the Countess of Winchelsea who was taking an outing in her bathchair. Michael Valyer sued another officer when his hired horse dropped dead on the way home from Barham races. He said that the officers were his worst customers, but the horse was found to have been suffering from heart disease and the case was dismissed.

By the end of the century, smart roomy horse-drawn charabancs with good horses were making excursions into the surrounding countryside for two shillings and sixpence, but their day was nearly over. Felix wrote in 1899, *"I don't want to alarm the bus proprietors but I hear that two or three motor charabancs will be driving into the rural areas from Folkestone. Hills will hold no terrors for them and fares will be reasonable"*. The age of the motor vehicle was dawning.

MOTOR CARS 1902

Susannah Toes was a shopkeeper and postmistress in 1782 at a salary of £8 a year. John Boxer, watch and clockmaker took over in 1811 at his shop in Rendezvous Street. Letters sent from Folkestone at 6.30pm arrived in London at 7.30am the next day. In 1845 Graffy Punnett was appointed postmaster in his little linen-drapers shop in Jenny Pope's Alley on the corner with Beach Street. The penny post had been started in 1841. Fish traders and harbour agents - accustomed to paying eight pence for letters between Billingsgate and Folkestone - seized the advantages of the new rate with eagerness. Graffy and his wife were overwhelmed by the pressure of new business which forced them to neglect their shop. Customers knocked on the window to attract attention and Graffy, spectacles on nose, would transact affairs with an angry growl. Small boys would torment him by asking for a penny stamp when he was making up the mail. Those were the days when postman Boorn, too hospitably entertained on Boxing Day, fetched up in a helpless condition outside the Apollo Rooms. The letters were distributed by passing pedestrians.

A new era opened with the appointment in 1857 of Thomas Spearpoint, who was both courteous and efficient, and a post office was opened in Tontine Street; the telegraph came to Folkestone in 1869. As trade shifted towards Sandgate Road, there was a general feeling that there should be a post office there. Large and commodious red brick premises, still standing, were opened in 1886. Thomas Spearpoint transferred there, Tontine Street being kept as a branch office. There were now four postal deliveries daily. In 1889 Miss Annie Spearpoint succeeded her father.

As was the case in other resorts, libraries were not particularly profitable and the bankruptcy rate was high. William Roden started one in 1806 but he went bankrupt in 1811, like Purdays in Sandgate, and had to sell his stock of 2,000 volumes. William Tiffin was in business in the High Street, Hythe, when he produced his Hythe and Sandgate Guide. By 1848 he had a library and fancy goods shop in Kingsbridge Street, carried on by Mrs Tiffin after his death in 1855. A library offering also stationery, heraldic engraving, bookbinding and fancy goods was founded by W. E. Cross. The shop, now specialising in stationery and office machinery, moved a few doors down Sandgate Road in 1986 and lost its ancient shopfront. A library and printing business fitted in well with the publication of guide books and newspapers.

The main newspapers of Folkestone and district were:

> The Folkestone Chronicle and Visitors' Guide: July 21st 1855-June 2nd 1906.
> The Folkestone Observer, Shorncliffe, Hythe and Sandgate News: December 8th 1860-September 29th 1870.
> Sandgate, Shorncliffe and Hythe Advertiser: March 14,1868-June 29, l940.
> Holbein's Visitors' List and Court Directory for Folkestone: May 21st 1884-December 28th 1899.
> Folkestone Up-to-Date: January 7th 1894-December 31st 1904.
> The Folkestone Herald: January 3rd 1891-still running.

Some of the above changed names, but were essentially the same paper. In addition there were seven other papers, which ran only for a few months or years, existing on advertisements, local gossip and a list of holiday visitors.

Henry Daniel Stock had the field to himself when he brought out the first issue of the Folkestone Chronicle in July 1855, the duty on newspapers having just been abolished. He promised the paper would speak impartially, redress grievances, stand up for the right and put down humbug. In addition he issued a Folkestone guide book which ran into many editions and had a large library and fancy goods shop in the High Street. The paper ran to eight closely printed sheets, later to be enlarged. Three sides only were devoted to local news and advertisements, the rest being given over to national and foreign news, share prices, proceedings in Parliament and at Court, book reviews and court cases. The latter were chosen for their human interest value, so that one could follow the Ripper murders, the case of the Tichbourne claimant, infanticide by servant girls or starvation in the Metropolis. A well-informed family needed no other newspaper.

STOCK'S LIBRARY

Local affairs were closely related to national issues during the first two years of the Chronicle's existence, a time when the British German Legion was stationed at Shorncliffe Camp during the Crimean War and the soldiers' frequent crimes made news. For local affairs there was an editorial column, readers' letters, court cases and Council reports. Added later were train and boat time-tables, and reports from the Elham Board of Guardians who controlled the workhouse. Advertisements, used by shopkeepers and employers, cost one shilling and sixpence for six lines.

The Express and the Observer - the Chronicle's rivals - kept to the same format, the difference lying in their politics and the general tone of the papers. The Chronicle was magisterial and conservative, on the side of the established church and against non-conformists, sceptical about school boards and universal education. All papers devoted a great deal of space to questions of religion and a sermon was reported at length each week.

John English of the Express had started originally as Stock's partner. He later opened his own library and fancy goods shop at the other end of the High Street, and published a guide to Folkestone and district. A Liberal, he was a fierce opponent of the Rev. Matthew Woodward, using such intemperate language that a libel action was threatened. Both editors enjoyed a position of power, rebuking Council members, the South Eastern Railway Company or local business men and adding spice to affairs generally. John English went bankrupt in 1870. Retiring in 1886, Henry Stock prophetically observed that *"future local historians will find recorded controversies, reports of meetings and information of every character upon which much of the future history of Folkestone will depend"*.

Logan's Folkestone-up-to-Date (see Chapters 10 and 14), campaigned for better conditions in the Elham Workhouse to which paupers had to walk, footsore and hungry, and opposed a penny rate to provide bands for public entertainment.

> *"What is a penny rate? Ask a corporation drainer at four*
> *pence an hour, a policeman on twenty-two shillings a week,*
> *a cabby on ten shillings a week who has not turned a wheel*
> *for the past fortnight or the man we saw begging for a job at*
> *the harbour."* (Folkestone-Up-To-Date)

The 1880s and 90s brought a different sort of paper, devoted to local news, incorporating many pages of advertising on which no doubt their existence depended. There were still extensive lists of visitors. The best-known of these was produced by Ambrose Hans Holbein, who had started life as a railway clerk, and eventually went bankrupt. Holbein's Visitors' List ran a series of articles on local history by E. Dale, containing valuable memories of the old town.

The Folkestone Herald was started In 1891 by Messrs. Thorpe, who were printers, stationers and booksellers, with a library and reading room next to the General Post Office in Sandgate Road. Thorpe's business was taken over by F. J. Parsons, who already published The Hastings and St. Leonards Observer. Shortly he transferred the printing works to the Bayle. The paper ran up to 16 pages of a tabloid size, sold for one penny and was strongly Conservative. The old Chronicle changed its views to become Liberal and supported Gladstone; regular readers were warned that they might be surprised by the tone of future editorials. Stock's works, now on Grace Hill, were acquired by Mr Kentfield to become the East Kent Printing Works, with modernised machinery, executing all kinds of printed matter for the Corporation, churches and banks.

Illustrations were beginning to appear in the papers, at first only stock engravings used for advertising. The Herald reproduced a smudgy photograph of Sandgate's Beach Rocks Convalescent Home, to be followed by frequent pictures of local worthies, beauty spots and special occasions, such as the Diamond Jubilee and the Kaiser's visit to Shorncliffe in 1902.

THE GAS WORKS, DEMOLISHED 1976

Pall Mall in London was lit by gas in 1807. It was to be thirty five years later, on December 29, 1842, that the Folkestone lamps were switched on. This was thanks to the initiative of Ralph Thomas Brockman, the Town Clerk; he had launched the Gas Company with

£2,500 shares which had been difficult to sell because of considerable local prejudice. With 60 private subscribers, William Stears had dug up the roads and laid the pipes to provide 30 street lamps. The grimy works with their tall chimney, which figured in John Leech's pictures of the town, were situated near the town's bathing place, now Marine Parade. In 1866 the works were moved to the village of Foord, which necessitated making an approach road and the destruction of Viaduct Villas, a pleasant group of houses. Mr. Sampson, the Company Secretary was prosecuted for stealing £2,000 from the funds he collected, but the Company grew rapidly and in 1868 there were 228 lamps, lit and cleaned by two men and a boy. It was a great step forward when lamp-lighting could be done by a man with a lantern on a pole, instead of using a ladder. There were threats of a rival company being started because of rising prices, but in 1876 a larger gasholder was installed. Gas shares fell when the Paris Exhibition was seen to be lit by electricity, but at this time there were cookery lessons in the Town Hall using gas cookers. By 1956 gas was supplied from Dover and the gas works were used only for storage.

The costs and operating methods of gas were well known and easy to understand. By contrast the installation of electricity gave local authorities many headaches and councillors felt out of their depths with the technicalities involved. They debated as to whether it should be left to a private company or municipal enterprise and which firm should be chosen to install it. The Board of Trade gave some guidance on possible agreements and insisted on the installation of approved systems.

Several hotels took the plunge and installed their own generators. In 1882, when a military band concert was lit by electricity at the Westcliff Hotel, several people remarked on the sickly and unnatural appearance it gave to their faces. Mark Parker of Stroud reported to the Council that electricity would cost 16% more than gas but was well worth it for the sake of convenience. The installation would cost £73,000 which could be borrowed. He was to advise it should be done as a municipal enterprise, with a refuse destructor included. Radical ratepayers strongly disagreed on account of the expense which would fall on the rates, sensing that the money would be better employed building artisans' dwellings. A questionnaire sent to possible customers, quoting six pence a unit as the cost, indicated 84 acceptances and 41 refusals. The Pavilion Hotel envisaged 400 lights, the London and Paris 20. The Council meetings were dominated for months by the electric-light question and accusations of jobbery abounded.

Private enterprise won the day. The Folkestone Electricity Supply was founded with a proviso that the Council could purchase the enterprise after fourteen years, an option never taken up. Land was purchased at Morehall for the works and by 1901 £93,000 had been spent from the pockets of shareholders at no cost to the rates. Mains were laid by the harbour and as far east as Earls Avenue. There was a siding for coal at the back of the boiler house, of which the smokestack towered 150 feet, making it a landmark.

The old town had no shortage of water, every well-to-do house possessing a well and a pump. The most popular supply was from the Town Dyke, which crossed St. Eanswythe's miraculous stream. Whilst there were public dipping places, the water was not meant to be drawn off for any commercial use. Even so, Ham Tite took water for his brewery and Alderman Gambrill for his brick works. Martha's Dyke supplied the East of the town from springs at Bowles Well and flowed finally into the Pent stream. The copious Pent carried offal, rubbish and sewage through a warren of narrow streets. Constable visited Folkestone twice in 1833 while his sons were at Parson Pearce's school and made a number of sketches. In the little village of Foord an enterprising developer hoped to establish a spa at the chalybeate spring which contained iron salts, and put up a sham ruin in support.

The Folkestone Water Company was founded in 1848, the moving spirit being Richard Hart. The first reservoir, the 'Bateman', was dug at the Cherry Gardens and was fed by six springs. Demand was continually rising and wells were dug, powered by a steam engine. Then came the second reservoir, the 'Hart', also uncovered. Although the water was hard it was clean, but ducks floated on the surface and sheep grazed in the fields, making pollution possible.

The Water Company had no obligation nor was it able to provide a continuous supply. The supply was on for eight hours, often less, so water had to be drawn off in each house and kept in cisterns, which could be dirty or rusty. In case of fire, the police had to ring the Company to re-connect, A major row over the purity of the water lasted for several years and resulted in a libel action; the judge said in former years it would have been settled by the sword.

Sandgate had its own supply, drawn from the Enbrook stream. Following a cholera outbreak in 1854, everyone affected was listed together with the source of their water supply, Folkestone or Sandgate. There was no clear distinction, the fault being found rather to lie with the drains: recently installed, they had been jointed with clay, allowing sewage to contaminate the water pipes. Holiday makers often consulted health statistics before planning their visits, so clean water and effective drainage were absolutely vital to resorts.

The Company was paying comfortable dividends of 7- 9% when the Radicals proposed it should be bought up by the Corporation, a demand which continued for several years. In 1897 there were two bills before Parliament, one to enable the Council to buy the enterprise because of its insufficient supply, which entailed an expenditure of £3,000 in legal fees and failed. The other, to authorise new sources of supply, was successful in spite of opposition from Dover, worried that their own sources were to be plundered. At last by the end of the century a continuous supply was achieved, when a third reservoir was made.

The Company is still independent and serves Folkestone, Hythe, Lydd, New Romney, Elham and other districts. The Cherry Garden and the Alkham valley areas remain the main sources of supply . The water obtained is pure and needs little treatment.

Because the drains in the old town emptied into the harbour, it grew very offensive. A plan for a new system funded by the Radnor Estate was made by Joseph Bazelgette, with the pipes routed to the east and tested to make sure sewage did not make its way round to the harbour bathing beach. There were regular reports from the Sanitary Inspector after 1875, with special attention paid to schools. In 1895 914 houses were inspected and 136 nuisance orders issued, requiring dirty houses and blocked drains to be cleansed. Some old wells were still in use as their owners did not have to pay water rates, but these were gradually condemned.

In 1846, the first dispensary was founded in Rendezvous Street by Dr. Donnelly, a retired naval surgeon. It was intended for the poor, who had to bring their own bottles, and was not for servants whose employers could afford to pay a doctor. Sandgate had a similar institution. The Folkestone dispensary was so successful that it moved to larger premises in Dover Road and some beds were provided. The Victoria Hospital was founded in 1890, funded by private contributions and bazaars, but it was a continual struggle to provide for rising costs. When the main building was enlarged by the addition of two wings, it became the Royal Victoria. Nurses and servants were recommended to obey the Matron as their mistress and to behave with tenderness and civility towards the patients.

Two sanitoria were built for infectious cases, mostly scarlet fever, cholera and small pox. St. Andrew's Nursing Home on the East Cliff (now flats) was founded by the Clewer order of nuns to serve the poor from London. At the present time the main hospital for the area is the William Harvey in Ashford, whilst the Royal Victoria is used for geriatric care and outpatient clinics.

Offenders in the old town were dealt with by the officers of the watch. They could be sent to a grimy cell under the Town Hall or to the Dover gaol where they would be put on the treadmill or set to picking oakum. The situation was revolutionised by Sir Robert Peel's reforms; policemen had a regulation uniform and were put at the service of the public. Crime in Folkestone, except for those connected with the military,

FOLKESTONE POLICE, UNDATED

was not a cause for great concern. There was a steady stream of drunks; thefts in most cases involved no more than a few shillings and the unfortunates found without any means of support were locked up for a week. The police - charged with duties under the licensing laws - laid information about the landlord of the 'Gun', whose clock had

TWO YOUNG CRIMINALS WHO HAD
DAMAGED A DOOR

unaccountably stopped and who was found serving drinks to a large company after hours. The force had its heroes such as the intrepid Councillor Lewis who broke up a brawl involving some fifty soldiers and citizens. It had been started when a peaceful Swiss legionary said he did not want to box with the British. At this a drunk citizen announced he wanted to kill all soldiers, but he was lugged outside by his collar into Radnor Street, followed by his comrades and the threatened riot was prevented.

In the 1850s there were, however, complaints of the excessive cost of policing the town, which amounted to some £500.The five constables and one inspector were each supplied with a frock coat, trousers and a felt helmet. Burglaries were held to be the fault of the police, since they shunned the less frequented parts of the town in favour of the High Street and the Sandgate Road. The two most serious crimes were the Great Train Robbery and two murders committed in 1856 by a young Swiss legionary from Dover, Dedea Redanies, He suspected his sweetheart of infidelity and, distraught with jealousy, killed her and her sister, leaving the bodies a little way off the Folkestone-Dover road. Executed at Maidstone, his last words were:

"In a few moments, I shall be in the arms of my dear Caroline."

11

BUILDERS AND ARCHITECTS

The boundary between municipal and private enterprise is fluctuating and often contentious. Both systems have deficiencies; the extravagances of the former could be compared with the self-interest of the latter. Our forefathers did expect provision of

essentials from their local government, though it was often of a limited and inefficient nature – drains, street lighting, provision against fire and crime, rubbish collection, road upkeep and in early days control over the prices of essential foods, such as bread and meat. Seaside resorts needed more enterprises than most towns in order to attract visitors, but these were to be provided from private pockets and therefore

FOLKESTONE PANORAMA

needed to make a profit. The establishment of the harbour, railway, pier, lift, theatre, baths and even piped water, gas, electricity, telephones and transport were all due to private companies, generally backed, except for the railway, by local money. These were risky businesses and those who invested in them, and especially the builders, were regarded as public benefactors rather than capitalist bloodsuckers. As one local

newspaper remarked of the speculative builder:

"It is he who puts up our houses from the workman's cottage to the patrician mansion, running the risk of loss by their remaining empty and unsold. He is the best of philanthropists for he provides work for the major part of our artisan and working population."

Speculative building was indeed an important element in the growth of Victorian towns. In an age of stable prices, many householders were content to rent rather than buy their homes and house property was a good form of investment, safer than railway shares and offering a higher rate of return than Government bonds. In 1860 a block of five houses let at £75 p.a. was sold for £980; a house and store in Dover Street, let for £19, brought in £300 when sold. Many of these

EAST STREET

properties were subject to a small ground rent payable to the Radnor Estate, but it did not seem to affect their value. Working class cottages, subject to visits and orders from the Sanitary Inspector, fetched a still higher return, with rents of £10-£14 p.a. and a sale price of £30-£40. Nos. 1 and 2 Clouts Alley, used as tenements, produced £66 p.a. Aldermen Banks and Sherwood, who owned many dwellings of this kind, were caustic in the Council over the proposal to build model artisans' cottages at an economic rent. An interesting survey of 1858 gives details of 176 houses with defects in the typically run-down areas of Fancy Street, Dover Street, Saffrons Row and Back Street. Of these, only 21 were owner-occupied and the rest were in holdings of two to thirteen cottages. There was never any shortage of tenants and demand far exceeded supply.

But the well-known builders rested their reputation on the mansions of the West End, as land for building was gradually taken up. The first two houses on the Leas were built by Robert Boarer, the 'Leas Mayor'. Bouverie Square was built from 1852, Pleydell Gardens from 1853 and Castle Hill Avenue gradually spread down from Langhorne Gardens in the 1860s. Holbein's Visitor's List in 1896 praised the two houses recently erected by Daniel Baker as models of what comfortable modern houses could be. The rooms were large and lofty with electric bells and speaking tubes in the sitting rooms, broad oak staircases and oak floors, a perfect system of ventilation, heated conservatory, hot and cold water in the bathroom, housemaid's closet, butler's pantry and extensive kitchen. Such houses, and those put up by William Saunders and Mr Holden in Clifton Gardens and Clifton Crescent, were designed to be rented unfurnished by wealthy families at £200 p.a., though sometimes they suffered the indignity of being let by floors in the season. There were boom and slump years and in 1859 a risk of failure:

"Far and wide modern villas, built to sell and fade, speckle the cliffs like mushrooms, a new street, half-built, leads to a dissenting chapel planted in a half-waste, its tall houses are but partially let and it seems even now prematurely old, the bold projector having repented to his rashness before his scheme was half carried out and carried his daring genius over the sea."

But on the whole builders were solid respected citizens and large employers of labour, often risen from humble beginnings. Daniel Baker's father was a plumber living in North Street. The younger Baker set up as a builder in Tontine Street, built part of Copthall Gardens and later the Manor House for Lord Radnor, the Burlington Hotel, some fine terracotta embellished houses around Grimston Gardens and Earls Avenue and many of the Riviera houses in Sandgate. His greatest achievement was the Grand Hotel which he both designed and built and, as he said at the time, *"I shall either be a man or a mouse"*. He was also physically daring and had to be forcibly held back from swimming out with a life line in the stormy seas when the 'Benvenue' was wrecked off Sandgate.

John Dunk, carpenter, living in North Street, married Daniel Baker's sister as his first wife. Enriched by subcontracting work on the viaduct, he set up as a master carpenter in Tontine Street, where his son William was an apprentice. Eventually he became a master builder and put up the original Catholic church in Lennard Road. William bought the business from his father in 1883 with the aid of family and bank loans. In his earlier years he advertised an undertaking service, a useful sideline, especially in winter,

THE MANOR HOUSE, BUILT FOR THE 5TH EARL OF RADNOR 1890

for carpenters and bricklayers. This side of the business was sold to Hambrook (later Hambrook & Johns).

William disliked speculation and preferred repair work or building to order, executing such commissions as St. Saviour's Church, the Woodward Institute, Church Street, and Spade House, Radnor Cliff Crescent. In those days a contractor would hold a large stock of materials, timber, cement, white lead in barrels for paint making, large ladders, planks and poles for constructing scaffolding. Lime was fetched by horse and cart from the lime kilns opposite Sugar Loaf Hill, bricks from the Park Farm Brick and Tile Co., generally taken straight to the site. A typical promoter of local enterprises, William was a director of the South Eastern Railway Co., the Folkestone Lift Co., the Pleasure Gardens Theatre and the Folkestone Waterworks Co..

Another interesting builder was John Pope, son of John Isaac Pope, an early Folkestone builder. (There were only two builders listed in the Universal British Directory, 1798.) John Pope was connected with the building of the Pavilion Hotel and built the Customs House, Marine Crescent, Longford Terrace, Bradstone Hall and the Bradstone Estate. H. M. Moody built the Catholic church in Guildhall Street, houses in Grimston Gardens, Earls Avenue and Broadmead Road.

ALFRED CAMBURN FOLKESTONE BUILDER

Older houses were needing bathrooms, basins and water closets, and plumbers were greatly in demand. As houses grew more lavish, new skills had to be learnt, such as the painting, graining, gilding and construction of conservatories offered by F. Franklin of 21 Rendezvous Street. E. J. Holden, whose father took over Tolputt's business in 1853, could put in electric bells, incandescent gas fittings, enamelled tiles, parquet floors and every sort of hot water and sanitary work. Alfred Camburn of Dover Road, established 1879, employed from

50-80 men on the erection of villa residences, large dwelling houses and shop fittings, personal supervision being a speciality.

Work for the builders meant also work for architects, some local and some with a national reputation. There are a few memorials to old Folkestone left standing, some handsome houses in the Bayle and by the churchyard, Ingles Barn, the Coolinge and Broadmead farmhouses, the Battery house overlooking the harbour, houses in Harbour Street next to a handsome Victorian terrace and some cottages on Sandgate Hill. The town is however a living museum to nineteenth century building styles, at last becoming appreciated at their true value. Most houses were put up by builders according to their own stock patterns, from the small artisan cottages of the east end of the town to the red brick, bay-windowed villas surrounding Radnor Park, and from mid-century stucco to terracotta, mock Tudor, gables, turrets and the cult of the picturesque.

The Radnor Estate employed two outstanding architects. The first, Decimus Burton, 1800-1881, tenth son of the architect James Burton, built the Calverley Estate at Tunbridge Wells, the Palm House and the Temperate House at Kew and the Athenaeum. No particular buildings can be traced to him, though Littlebourne Lodge and Frenches on the Sandgate Esplanade are very similar in design to a house he built in Regent's Park, London. He was succeeded by Sydney Smirke, 1798-1877, another architect

BOUVERIE SQUARE

well-known in London for his designs for the Carlton Club, Pall Mall, the portico and dome of the Imperial War Museum and the British Museum Reading Room. Such advice cannot have come cheaply and is a proof of the importance placed on good design when a resort was being planned. Smirke had general superintendence over new buildings and laid out the streets surrounding Bouverie Square. Marine Parade and Tontine Street are very much in the style he preferred, if not actually designed by him. The Marine Parade houses are particularly attractive, with rusticated blocks on the ground floor, columns with elaborate capitals around the first floor windows topped by iron canopies and decorative urns on the roof. Marine Terrace followed in 1860 and Marine Terrace in 1870, the work of John Pope. A pleasant early development of 1843-4 was Albion Villas overlooking the sea, three large stucco houses, two classical and one Tudor style. The Radnor Cliff houses were built in 1847, with gardens descending to the shore, heavy and dignified, almost Italianate. Many of these houses were originally finished in a mournful, greyish-brown stucco, rather than the light colours one sees today.

Much money was to be expended on church building from the pockets of the faithful and the Lord of the Manor. At the time of Folkestone's period of rapid growth, there was no argument as to which style was most suitable and the most calculated to draw the soul upwards towards Heaven. It was Gothic with traceried windows, soaring arches and wooden interior roofs. Sidney Smirke designed Christ Church in 1850 of Kentish ragstone roofed with slate, a fairly plain building with a nave and two side aisles, given more consequence with the later erection of a church tower. School design also followed the vogue for all things Gothic. Smirke designed Christ Church school at the corner of Cheriton Road and Bouverie Road East with attractive gables and a miniature belfry on the central roof

CHRIST CHURCH 1850. THE TOWER (STILL STANDING) WAS A LATER ADDITION THE MAIN BODY WAS DEMOLISHED BY A BOMB IN 1942.

ridge. The well-known architect S. S. Teulon built St. Paul's, Sandgate, in 1849, its four tall traceried windows looking down the hill and polychrome brickwork inside. He was also employed by Sir John Bligh to build a new country house in Sandgate to replace the former family home of Bellevue. His individual style was evident in the large oriel window and the romantic tower built out over the porch, similar to one he designed at Shadwell Park for Sir Robert Buxton. The attractive ecclesiastical-looking building in Sandgate High Street facing the church, now restored for living accommodation, is the former Sandgate School by P. C. Hardwick, 1866, who designed the Great Western Hotel, Paddington and Charterhouse School. It has a dominating central tower, bearing four stone animals, now somewhat weathered by time. Another pleasant Gothic school of ragstone was St. Mary's in the Dover Road, 1854.

This was the work of Joseph Messenger, whose office was in Kingsbridge Street near the harbour, and who seems to have been the first local architect to design a distinctive building for the developing town. He used Bath stone for the window tracery

THE TOWN HALL, 1859

and Gothic buttresses on the corners. However, Messenger was also responsible for the prize bloomer of the century in architectural terms. By the 1850s Lord Radnor's former Cistern House was too small to serve the needs of the growing town as a town hall. It was decided to replace it with a purpose-built building, incorporating a large room where courts or meetings could be held and prison cells. Entries were invited for a competition to design the new building. This method of choosing a design was quite common and had been used to select Barry as architect for the Houses of Parliament. Messenger produced his plan with due regard for economy and the foundation stone was laid in May 1859, the Mayor and Corporation marching in procession from the Royal Pavilion to attend. The expected cost was £4,000 and the cheapest estimate, from J. Edwards, accepted. By September the internal walls appeared in danger of collapse and the Council was so worried that an independent report was commissioned. Mr Shaw of London found that the walls were too thin and that drains running underneath had caused settlement, the wide roof needed a horizontal tie for stability and that the foundations were not sufficiently deep. He also emphasised the magnitude of the work and that the Council had wanted too much for its money. The Building News was sarcastic as to the incompetence of the Council in selecting the design. Messenger resigned and Messrs. Whichcord & Blandford of Maidstone were called in to rebuild the ground floor, strengthen the roof and finish the building. In the end it cost over £6,000 and lent colour to the expression "a Folkestone job", meaning a task badly done. Another jibe was that it should be a place fit to entertain a sovereign, as it had cost so many. However, it still stands, though no longer the Town Hall, a handsome stone-faced classical building, with a clock presented by Baron Mayer Rothschild.

Church restoration in the nineteenth century was as much a source of work as new buildings. The only churches to preserve their old box pews, clear glass windows and irregular stone floors were isolated and poor, like those on the Romney Marsh. St. Mary and St. Eanswythe's, Folkestone's old parish church, neglected and storm damaged, was an obvious case for improvement by an energetic vicar. Matthew Woodward was

such a man and restoration continued for twenty years, mostly under the direction of R. C. Hussey. The old galleries were taken down, the nave rebuilt, the chancel enriched and the south transept restored. It is difficult now to distinguish the medieval original from the nineteenth century restoration, a proof of its success. Hussey's four light west window was replaced by the large window designed by Spencer Slingsby Stallwood as a memorial to William Harvey. Stallwood is

RESTORATION OF THE THE PARISH CHURCH. THE ALABASTER ARCADING ROUND THE ALTAR BY SPENCER STALLWOOD

also responsible for the elaborate alabaster arcading round the altar and the mosaics are by Cappello. Hussey was commissioned by Woodward to design Folkestone's second neo-Gothic church in 1862, which replaced the temporary Mariners' Chapel. St. Peter's is built on a cruciform plan with a neat spirelet over the central crossing. Stallwood added a north aisle, porch and belfry, in all a picturesque addition to the skyline when seen from below.

Joseph Gardner, who practiced in Folkestone for thirty years and became consultant to the Manor Office, was a versatile and accomplished architect. His first commission was the Wesleyan chapel on Grace Hill (1866), built in the Early English Gothic style of ragstone with a soaring graceful spire, 133 feet high. In complete contrast was the

Baptist chapel (1873), still standing, which has an imposing classical façade with heavy Corinthian columns. Gardner's last church was the Congregational chapel (1897), now the United Reformed Church, which returned to a Gothic style, perhaps a trifle old-fashioned by the turn of the century. An architect's achievements are limited by the taste of his patrons and Gardner could also provide buildings to order in the brick Renaissance style, such as the Bathing Establishment (1869) and the Royal Victoria Hospital, both of which must have entailed a mass of technical requirements to be incorporated. Another different and interesting commission was the building housing the National Art Treasures

CLIFTON GARDENS

Exhibition. It had a long barrel vault on an iron framework roofed in glass, flanked by two towers, somewhat resembling the Crystal Palace. He was also responsible for Clifton Gardens (1865) and the imposing terrace of Augusta Gardens. The fashion for Nash-style stucco palaces was to wane, giving way to the Queen Anne style and the use of polychrome brickwork, as may be seen in Westbourne Terrace and the Westbourne Hotel, again executed to the designs of the versatile Mr Gardner.

The most impressive of the nineteenth century churches is Holy Trinity designed by Ewan Christian, described as *"a Pugin man in the 1850s, muscular in the 1860s and Tudor Old-English in the 1870s."* It is a solid and satisfying church with a wide nave, a semi-circular apse supporting an octagonal belfry and a spire covered in green slates. Use is made of arches, buttresses and stone columns, yet it is more individual than traditional Gothic. The interior is spacious and light, the chancel richly decorated. A less elaborate but attractive church is All Souls at Cheriton (1894) which he also designed. His other work in Folkestone was St. Andrews Convalescent Home on the East Cliff, a large utilitarian building of red brick (1881) with a chapel added eight years later. The other three Folkestone churches were all Gothic, perhaps St. Michael's in the Dover Road (1875) by F. Bodley was the most determinedly so, with a decorated tower surmounted by a spire. The stone weathered badly and it was demolished in 1953. The two still standing are: St. John the Baptist (1877-8) by A. Rowland Barker, built for the hamlet of Foord, grey ragstone outside, red brick inside and St. Saviour's (1891-2) designed by Micklethwaite & Somers Clarke. The latter holds a commanding position on the Canterbury Road and is an unusual and attractive church with a contrasting red brick and terracotta exterior, a commanding gable on the west front.

As the century drew towards its close, there were indications of a new spirit in architecture. Our Lady Help of Christians (1899), the Catholic church in Guildhall Street, was designed by Leonard Stokes as a young architect for his first commission. He was to design many Catholic churches and schools, including Downside, and twenty telephone exchanges. With the construction of the new road it can be better seen, a hint of Gothic in the lancet windows but also a hint of modernism in its shape and uncluttered interior. H.G. Wells commissioned C. F. A. Voysey to build him a house which he wanted to be a complete contrast to the usual pattern of seaside red brick villas. Voysey was one of the most influential architects of the early twentieth century and it is almost impossible to believe that Spade House was built in 1899. It seems to be a house of the 30s with its deep roofs and mullioned windows in a simple and striking style which he was to repeat elsewhere. The Public Library (1886-8) was by Brightwell Binyon, winner of an open competition. It is in the Queen Anne style of ornamented red brick and terracotta, perhaps a trifle fussy. The Technical and Art School next door by Frank Newman (1895) is a more original and interesting building. Newman was Secretary to the Art and Science School, originally started in the High Street. In 1895 he persuaded the Council to build a structure befitting the new opportunities in education with science laboratories. The building makes the most of a limited space, three tall stories with a pyramidal roof and a decorative band of Art Nouveau inspiration. He gave his services as architect free.

The most striking monuments to the late Victorian era are the great hotels still standing on the Leas, the Metropole by T. W. Cutter (1895) and the Grand (1899-1903) by Daniel Baker, the latter an immense feat for a man who started life as a jobbing builder. Here we are in a world of fantasy, of Kubla Khan palaces, where customers could wander through the Metropole, its Louis Quinze style conjuring up visions of

Mesdames Pompadour and du Barry, or frequent the Hispano-Moorish billiard room designed in the rich voluptuous manner of the Alhambra. This was strictly for the clients – the lifts and kitchens were of the most modern and labour-saving design. The exteriors reflected the trend towards brick and terracotta, exemplified also by Lord Radnor's Manor House and the Burlington Hotel. Lewis Cubitt's somewhat stark Royal

THE COMPLETED SPADE HOUSE IN 1901

Pavilion was remodelled in 1898 by Col. Edis in red brick and yellow patent stone reminiscent of a Loire chateau.

CHURCH AND CHAPEL

This chapter deals with the outward manifestations of religion, the services, congregations and church buildings, not with the deeper motions of the heart and intellect. Much of what is recorded is unedifying in Christian terms. There were internal dissensions and rows and accusations between one sect and another. Perhaps these were the tensions of people who quarrelled because they felt strongly about spiritual matters. So far as the newspapers were concerned, religion took the place of politics,

VICAR AND COOK, PUNCH.

occupying the headlines week after week. But there was a positive side, expressing itself in practical terms in the care of the poor and the sick and the building of new churches.

Class had a bearing on the choice of the church attended or indeed whether one attended at all. The upper class had always been supporters of the established church, particularly in country areas and were influential in the choice of clergy. The ideal was *"a gentleman in every parish"*. In large towns among the craftsmen and shopkeepers of the middle and lower-middle classes, the picture was very different. Here the Church of England had never exerted much influence. Here dissent and non-conformity took root and flourished, partly because the old parish churches simply could not cope with the increasing population. Amongst the respectable middle classes Sunday church going was a beneficial habit - a blessing on their hard work, self discipline and worldly success, even of the most modest kind. Folkestone being primarily a trading and shop-keeping town accounts for the strength of non-conformity.

The gentry in Folkestone were mainly those who came in search of health or for retirement, who were not deeply rooted in the area as they would have been in country parishes. It was something of a reproach to the High Church party that its appeal was to the weaker sex, emotional women, whereas non-conformist congregations had a preponderance of good solid men. The Church of England made great efforts to remedy the situation. Funds were raised by the Church Commissioners and even given by Parliament to endow new parishes. Missionary churches were built in poor areas, to be replaced by more elaborate edifices when funds allowed, as with St. Saviour's and St. Michael's.

ST. EANSWYTHE'S WITH THE WEST END RESTORED

The physiology of the sects was described by the Folkestone Chronicle in 1873:

"There is a pleasant excitement in High Church life which is attractive to many. It is Protestantism playing at Catholicism, like walking close to the edge of a precipice where a single false step may be dangerous. The chief characteristic of Low Church men is their unctuousness. You feel it in the shake of their hand, see it in their placid piously gleaming faces and that peculiar intonation with which they also address the Deity. They have an earnest conviction that they are completely right and others hopelessly wrong that makes them vigorous if not discreet, incessant if not charitable in their efforts to convert others to their own belief."

But persuasion, entreaties and reminders of their latter end fell upon deaf ears when it came to the labouring classes. They took each day as it came without troubling or being able to make provision ahead, spiritually or materially. Sunday was a day of rest after the week's work and many simply did not have the clothes in which to appear decently clad. As one workman put it, *"I would feel out of place amongst the rustle of silks and satin in the parish church"*. It was not until the 1880s and the arrival of the Salvation Army - noisy, non-intellectual, active and combative - that the working class really had their own brand of religion.

ST. EANSWYTHE'S REBUILT AFTER THE STORM OF 1703

In 1818 Thomas Pearce took up his duties as Rector of Hawkinge and Perpetual Curate of Folkestone (a title bestowed by Lord Radnor who was Lay Rector of the town). Parson Pearce was an old fashioned, comfortable, easy going cleric, ready with a cheery greeting for his parishioners, by whom he was well liked. He was reputed to ignore their little offences in the smuggling line, even finding the odd present of tea or keg of brandy left at his front door. If not a zealous clergyman, he was an extremely good business man, speculating with success in 37 small house properties and the Sandgate brewery. These were bequeathed to his daughter and fetched the enormous sum of £42,000. He lived at the Priory on the Bayle, where he had a school for the sons of gentlemen, and for several years he even contracted for the town's rubbish collection. He resigned in 1851, somewhat under a cloud, having officiated at the marriage of a runaway couple without complying with the marriage licence regulations.

His successor, Matthew Woodward described the church as being entirely devoid of colour, whether on wall or

THE INTERIOR OF ST. EANSWYTHE'S 1818 - 1851

window. Whitewash and plaster were everywhere. Even the ancient pillars of the tower were defaced by hat pegs and by large blackboards on which were inscribed in gold letters the particulars of various charitable bequests. The pews, which were of the old-fashioned box variety, were appropriated by a limited number of families and guests from the Pavilion Hotel, to the exclusion of the poor. The services, limited to two on Sundays, were of the slovenly and dull type known as 'Parson and Clerk duet'. The singing gallery housed instrumentalists as well as the choir - clarinets, flutes, fiddles and bassoons; the performance left much to be desired.

Under Woodward's leadership, a completely new era in the church's life began. Woodward had worked in a business in Manchester for five years where he was also a lay reader. He found his vocation and went to St. Aidan's Theological College. His first appointment was as vicar of Hythe and he was so popular that it was said the Mayor offered him a bag of golden sovereigns for each year he should remain. The new incumbent was fervent and earnest in his approach, but convinced in his opinions to the point of obstinacy, perhaps even relishing the opposition he excited. He was Vicar of Folkestone for 47 years and for at least half of that time his opinions caused

controversy, not only among non-conformists but among members of his own flock. After a short phase as a low churchman, he became a fervent supporter of the Oxford Movement, which had begun in Oxford with the publication of the first 'Tract for the Times' in a sermon preached at St. Mary's Church. The Movement sought to reawaken fervour in the English church by emphasising the sacredness of Anglican orders descended from the Apostles, its links with the Universal Church, and the adoption of practices used by Roman Catholics: frequent communion, preceded by confession; the appearance of statues, flowers and candles in the church; even adoration of the real presence of Christ after the consecration of bread and wine.

THE REVEREND MATHEW
WOODWARD, 1860

His ideas affected not only the parish church, but his own new foundations of St. Michael's and St. Peter's, which in their turn were accused of ritualism and extravagance. Some liturgical experiments which could not be permitted for reasons of prudence at the parish church were carried out at St. Peter's, whose vicar, the Rev. Ridsdale, had married Woodward's eldest daughter.

The first signal of Woodward's changing opinions was his introduction of the new hymn book, 'Hymns Ancient and Modern' in 1862. This was against the wishes of some in the congregation, who described the hymns as doggerel verses and *"tinsel Puseyism"*. (Many of these same hymns, however, are much used and loved today.) Woodward's high handed attitude and his indiscreet, imperious and intemperate manner were noted. He now fell foul of the popular organist, William Tolputt, of 23 years standing in the church, who refused to play a tune of which he disapproved. Was this defiant disobedience or a legitimate difference of opinion which should be respected? A lively correspondence ensued in the local press. One correspondent called Woodward's behaviour quiet and gentlemanly throughout. Another asked, *"Is it quiet and gentlemanly to stride up to any person with face paled and hands clenched and, with ill-concealed passion, to repeat his commands in a most offensive manner?"*. Tempers had been lost, the choir split and many members resigned.

Local newspapers seized on such incidents which filled the news columns, the correspondence columns and the editorials for weeks on end, together with reporting of lengthy sermons. The Folkestone Chronicle was wordy but fairly restrained in its comments. The Folkestone Observer called Woodward *"The Incumbrance"* and *"Loathsome Vermin"*. These hard words he brushed aside, but the same paper also accused him of misappropriating funds given for the poor. At this Woodward brought a libel action against the editor, William Ellis, for his repeated attacks. At first damages of £1,000 were suggested which would have bankrupted the paper, but eventually the action was settled for 40 shillings - a derisory sum - but at least Woodward's name was cleared.

By 1862 Woodward was well advanced in his liturgical innovations: intoning the services; holding processions at Easter and Christmas; decorating the church with floral crosses, a velvet altar cloth, a lectern and footstool embroidered with the keys of St. Peter. Opposition from the congregation grew more vocal. There were two ways in which parishioners could make their disagreement known. They could present a petition at the Archdeacon's annual visitation; although this was done several times, Woodward defended himself skilfully and no action was taken. They could also speak at the vestry meeting which came to be known as the annual Vicar-baiting. All who paid church rates could vote and, because the old parish boundaries still applied, this included those who belonged to other parishes and dissenters. An anti-Woodward churchwarden, Mr Coules, refused to pay the gas bill and the church was left in darkness. Woodward sought to pay church expenses, now about £200, from sources independent of the rates, such as pew rents and regular weekly offerings from the congregations. He was a superb fundraiser.

These petty local squabbles were but symptoms of the hectic fever which was infecting parishes in many areas of Britain. It was feared that all these crosses and genuflexions, flowers, candles and invocations of the Blessed Virgin, would lead congregations into the embraces of the Scarlet Woman, the harlot of Babylon, Rome itself. Those at risk were described as *"wholly inexperienced and impressionable young persons. Rome likes to fish for perverts amongst those who are already half perverted."*. Nationally, the Protestant Alliance was formed, which supplied speakers and funds and was responsible for many letters in the newspapers. The High Church Union entered the fray, using the same methods. There were meetings at the Town Hall to warn of the dangers lurking in the confessional. The whole debate took an offensive turn, judging from the description of the foul and licentious addresses of Mr McKay and the circulation of a pamphlet about the revelations of Maria Monk and Sister Lucy. *"Parents, brothers and husbands have had their feelings most grossly outraged at the tenderest point by finding papers in the hands of their wives and daughters scarcely fitting for the lowest of the low in the Ratcliffe Highway."*

Woodward had personal and family difficulties and one can only imagine the pressure he must have been under at times. He had married Rosamund, daughter of Sir George Barrow, and had eleven children of whom nine survived. His wife's mental instability took the form of religious mania. John Oakley, a friend and visitor, referred to episodes of actual physical violence in the night of which few, other than servants, were aware. In 1871 she was received into the Church of Rome at St. Augustine's, Ramsgate, followed by the baptism of the five youngest children in the Folkestone Catholic Church. This was during a mission about which Fr. Morrissey, the parish priest, knew nothing. This step was not a positive proof of mental instability, but it was one most calculated to harm her husband. The ultra Protestants in the town rejoiced that the danger to weak and feeble women had been most abundantly proved. Woodward was near despair. He considered a legal separation and his wife spent some time with her parents. Archbishop Tait, though hostile to Woodward's ideas, did not wish to spread the scandal further and refused to move him. This must have been the lowest point in Woodward's life, but things were to improve gradually. Mrs Woodward was able to return home and his daughters acted as hostesses on special occasions. In 1879 the family moved from their cramped dwelling in Victoria Grove to a newly built and spacious vicarage near the church.

It would be a great mistake to think of Woodward's career in Folkestone in terms of conflict and opposition. There were 27 services weekly which were popular and sometimes full to overflowing, particularly on Sundays. It was so crowded that the procession could only make its way round the church in single file. A feeling of devotion was heightened by the brilliant spectacle of the altar, covered with flowers and lit by fifty candles and a hundred gas jets. People came there to pray, not just to be seen. There were over a thousand communicants at Easter.

One of the tasks in which he took the most pride and pleasure was the restoration and decoration of the fabric of the church. This had to be combined with fundraising but the task inspired the generous donors. There was much to be done. The old galleries were taken down, to the consternation of the fishermen who used them. They were to be compensated with their own church dedicated to the fisherman Peter. There had been problems about an offensive smell. The fifteenth century roofing was exposed and R. C. Hussey rebuilt the arcades of the nave and widened the north aisle. There was a splendid new organ, a rood screen, stained glass windows and a complex scheme of wall paintings. This comprised paintings of the life of St. Eanswythe, the

Stations of the Cross and Gospel scenes. All these were surrounded by the hieroglyphics, as they were described, executed by the ladies of the parish. Elaborate decorations were common in the nineteenth century but the patterns have now been obliterated.

THE HIEROGLYPHICS OF THE LADIES OF THE PARISH, ST. EANSWYTHE'S

Harvey, the discoverer of the circulation of the blood, is Folkestone's most famous citizen. An official appeal was launched in aid of erecting a statue on the Leas. However, the way the church appeal was worded caused many to subscribe under the misapprehension that this was to be the sole memorial in the town of his birth. The elaborate alabaster arcading around the altar was criticised by Lord Radnor, still nominally Lay Rector, that he had not been consulted. Woodward replied that he respectfully declined to adopt so ridiculous a course as to seek the approval of his Lordship's architect. At this juncture, Heaven took a hand. A leaden casket was found within a plastered cavity containing some bones and a tooth of a young woman. Surely this was the lost remains of St. Eanswythe. The Times and other publications cast doubt on a positive identification, but Woodward had no doubts: *"Now she had made her appearance at this juncture to give her seal of satisfaction to the work they had just completed."* Mr Chapman, another anti-Woodward churchwarden, said that, after a good dinner, he had dreamt of the Saint sitting on his chest and demanding her tooth back.

One further change in the church and its surroundings came in 1895 when a handsome stone cross was placed in the churchyard where once an old cross had stood, the traditional place of the Mayor's election. Richard Hart, a well known Folkestone solicitor, had put up a sundial on the original plinth. There was some feeling it should not be touched and Woodward offered to abandon his plan. In his later years he was mellower and less inclined for a fight, but public opinion came round to his side and the cross was duly erected.

A duty Woodward took very seriously was the Church's task of educating the young. St. Mary's schools were opened and supported by voluntary contributions until State funds became available. Woodward often visited and gave religious instruction, being against the establishment of school boards. He felt that the church schools would be starved of funds as no one would wish to pay twice and that the board schools would not give proper religious instruction. However, when it became obvious that church schools could not keep pace with population growth, he changed his views and supported the new establishments.

Another project dear to his heart was to bring back nuns to Folkestone, the ancient site of the first nunnery in Britain. In 1864 a small party of Anglican nuns, the Clewer sisters, came to live on the Bayle. The Community of St. John the Baptist had been started at Clewer near Windsor by Mother Harriet Monsell, who had dedicated her sisters' efforts to assisting the poor, founding orphanages, homes for the elderly, schools and a hospital in Folkestone. They helped in the poorest districts, with the establishments of St. Peter's, St. Michael's and St. Saviour's churches; they worked in the schools and the soup kitchen, they started a crèche on the Bayle and collected clothes and dispensary tickets from well-off visitors. They took charge of their own mission chapel, St. Augustine's in Mill Bay, built in 1886. Their most lasting achievement was the building of the convalescent home of St.

ST. EANSWYTHE'S CASKET

Andrew's on the East Cliff, originally on the corner of Guildhall Street and Victoria Grove. With six floors, a hundred rooms and a lift, it was run on the most modern lines. A few beds were kept for Folkestone residents, but the care was mostly for the poor from large towns who needed sea air and good food to recover from debilitating illnesses, for which there was no speedy cure. The building is now converted to flats.

Woodward was also a trustee of the Royal Victoria Hospital and helped to raise money for it on Hospital Sunday. There was a host of other activities connected with the parish church, including St. Mary's football and cricket teams, Bible classes and the

Friendless Girls' Home in Tontine Street. The parish-organised district visitors were the only reliable source of help for families unable to cope because of sickness or unemployment and who did not wish to enter the workhouse. The only people Woodward failed to reach were the men of the working class. He did try, holding open-air meetings and services for men only, but perhaps there was an undue emphasis on their prevailing vices of impurity and intemperance. There was a church institute in Tontine Street with a library and games room and a club in the Sessions Hall in the old High Street; the club did well - permitting the sale of drink - but the services

THE CLEWER SISTERS, 1864

badly. In one service, he even advocated opening pubs on Sundays, which earned him a round of applause.

Towards the end of his life, Woodward became the grand old man of Folkestone. Controversy had died down and the innovations he had introduced were taken for granted. He gave an interesting sermon on his thirtieth anniversary as vicar when he was presented with a musical box and silver table decorations. He described the awakening of the church after its slumbering condition in the eighteenth century and the importance of the sacraments administered by a clergy descended from the apostles. A

very few had gone over to Rome, but this was nothing to the number of those who left the fold for the innumerable sects. By then, if the congregations had been deprived of 'Hymns Ancient and Modern', their grief would have caused a commotion as great as that at their introduction.

ST. ANDREWS

Woodward was created a Canon and Folkestone was host to the Church Congress in 1892, when vestry meetings were peaceful. He died in 1898 a revered, respected and much-loved figure. At his funeral, his coffin was laid in state in the parish church and three thousand people filed past it. Tributes poured in and the Mayor called a special meeting of the Council to testify their sympathy. During his lifetime Woodward had collected £200,000 for the church. He died a poor man, his family ill-provided for. There could be no doubt about his zeal and devotion to his flock and his last message was to send them his undying love.

Notwithstanding, by the 1880s the current of popular interest, the enthusiasm and also the bitterness and anger had shifted from religion to politics. In the polemics of the Radical newspapers and town hall meetings it is possible to hear an echo of the Low Church brigades of three decades before. It attracted those who were anti-establishment and believed that a reversal of the existing order would lead to a spiritual or material Utopia.

The history of the Church of England in the rest of Folkestone was one of continued expansion. In 1862 the church of St. Peter was opened on the Durlocks for the fishing community, which was later to have its own school. It was described as successful and filled with those for whom it was intended, but the forms of service used by Ridsdale were even more ritualistic than those in the parish church. There was already a report to the Archbishop of crosses, flowers and candles at services, the elements were consecrated as in the Roman service and water was mixed with the wine. Legal proceedings were threatened. Whilst it was ironic that religious practices were subject to the law of the land, this was the price for being an established church. The Public Worship Regulation Act of 1874 was intended to curb such practices and the case against the Rev. Ridsdale, who was Woodward's son in law, was the first brought under its provisions. The complainants were three so-called members of the congregation, a baker, a shoe-maker and a beer-house keeper. In fact they were not regular church-goers, but had the Protestant Association behind them. Ridsdale was supported by the

English Church Union and both sides employed eminent lawyers. The case attracted a great deal of attention nationally as well as in Folkestone itself. It formed the subject of a book, 'The Folkestone Ritual Case'. It was first heard before Lord Penzance, Dean of the Court of Arches. The main causes of complaint were: the screen with a crucifix on top, the wearing of vestments, communion practices and the Stations of the Cross. The crucifix and the stations, especially the wiping of Christ's face by Veronica, were said to be unscriptural. Lord Penzance found for the complainants and Ridsdale appealed to the Judicial Committee of the Privy Council, consisting of the Lord Chancellor, the Archbishop of Canterbury and four bishops. Some of the practices were still held to be unlawful and the crucifix was to be taken down.

Ridsdale submitted – indeed, he could have been sent to prison if he had not. The whole affair may now seem to be a storm in a teacup but its importance lay in defining the extent to which ritualism could go before being checked by law. It was a small consolation that the costs, which must have been considerable, were borne by the complainants and their backers. However, if you go to St. Peter's now, you will find the crucifix and screen together with the stations - which had languished in storage for twenty years - peacefully in position. No-one knows what the simple fishermen made of it all.

Another church founded in 1862 to serve the eastern end of the town was St. Michael and All Angels. The first church was temporary, made of wood and known as the Red Barn. It was not endowed and the first incumbent, Rev. Burridge, found it extremely hard going. He had a poor congregation and had to canvas the wealthy west end for funds. The Rev. Watson of Christchurch called him a *"clerical freebooter"* and the Chronicle said it was a reproach to the town that an educated and charitable man had to serve in a temporary church for £40 a year. In 1875 a permanent church was erected, a flamboyant Gothic edifice, since demolished. There was trouble with the Council about the building line.

Burridge's successor, the Rev. Edward Husband, was a Woodward protégé, a former curate of the parish church, but with no high church leanings. He was energetic and well-liked, perhaps something of a showman. He founded a boys' club with 200 members, a cyclists' club and an employment agency. His comic musical shows, accompanied by the choir boys and magic lantern at the Town Hall and the lectures about his travels, almost as funny as Mark Twain, were immensely popular. Because 160 of his boys wanted to go to sea, but their chest measurements were too small, Husband collected money to build a pool. He was also an accomplished musician, who designed for the church his great orchestral organ and published hymns and carols, songs and dances. He resigned from the Committee of the Church Congress in 1892 when a lady was put forward to speak, his grounds being that she would be assuming masculine responsibilities, detracting from the beauty and mission of womanhood.

In 1883 there was a grand bazaar in aid of St. Michael's. Such occasions were

common fund-raising devices but this one was especially elaborate. Lady Folkestone organised a polo match to cover the preliminary costs of a professional firm who decorated the Town Hall as a Swiss village with each stall as a chalet. The ladies of the parish had spent months preparing displays of knitted and embroidered goods, doyleys and slippers together with fresh food and cakes. Every husband and bachelor was urged to

ST. MICHAEL'S, THE RED BARN, 1862

contribute. If they refused, the reproachful glances from eyes moistened with tears haunted them for days afterwards.

Lord Radnor was not a sympathiser with the High Church movement and his two foundations - Holy Trinity and Christ Church - were refuges for those who disliked the Romanising tendencies in the parish church. Their clergymen were of the low or evangelical persuasion and they were also connected with his building plans, as visitors were attracted by having a convenient and sympathetic place of worship near their lodgings. Christ Church was consecrated in 1850 when there were few buildings around and the windmill was still standing to the west. Lord Radnor funded the building but did not endow the living. Unfortunately the first extensions had contributed to a debt of £2,000 and the only income was from pew rents and collections. The builder held the Rev. Watson personally responsible and a Town Hall meeting was convened, at which the accounts were found to be in a muddle. Watson

REV. EDWARD HUSBAND

died in 1873 and the next vicar, the Rev. Claude Bosanquet, an earnest evangelical, managed to improve the situation, when Charles Wampach, the well known Folkestone hotelier and Mayor was a churchwarden. There were two foundations connected with the church, Christ Church school, which started in 1850, and a mission hall in Victoria Grove in 1897, where fortnightly services in French were held. This subsequently became a parish hall when the church of the Good Shepherd was built. The tower of Christ Church is now the only portion left standing after the air raid of May 17th 1942, which destroyed the rest.

Holy Trinity cost over £13,000. At this time it was named the Church in the Fields. It had the same financial difficulties as Christ Church and Canon Baynes, on his resignation, was found to be £2,500 in debt. In 1890 he was arrested for theft, pleading a degree of mental confusion. However, the difficulties were surmounted. The congregation later became large and influential, with many substantial houses and private schools in the area and funding was easier. From 1885 the vicar was the Rev.

Frederick Woodhouse, a great scholar and an expert on the military orders and the Crusades. He and his wife presented six windows, the ceiling painting and the reredos to the church.

St. Saviour's was in a very different area. To the north of the town there were packed rows of dwellings, mostly occupied by railway workers. Woodward and Husband planned a mission there. With St. Michael's, two new parishes were to be formed. A former bakery in Sydney Street was adapted to serve as a chapel, Sunday school and cocoa tavern, an encouragement to teetotalism for the working man. The first Eucharist was celebrated on Easter Sunday, 1881, and the first missioner, subsequently to become the vicar, was the Rev. Claude Hankey. Unsurprisingly, given his two patrons, he had High Church sympathies and had been stoned in a previous parish because of his Popish practices. Distinguished visiting preachers of Catholic sympathies were invited to speak. He and his wife worked so hard amongst the poor that his health broke down. He was succeeded by the Rev. Alfred Day, who remained for fifty years.

From these humble beginnings rose a large and impressive church, still standing. First came the temporary 'Iron Church' on land given by Lord Radnor, at the junction of Black Bull and Canterbury Roads. It was hard work raising the necessary funds in a poor area but Mother Harriet, then living on the Bayle, took a special interest, so that two Clewer nuns made their home in Sydney Street. She canvassed her visitors for support, handing out collecting cards. Economy was to be the watchword – the use of the plainest materials to produce the most striking building. A good architect was chosen, Somers Clarke, pupil of George Gilbert Scott, and the builder was William Dunk.

The whole edifice, built in instalments, was not completed till 1913 and some projected features had to be abandoned - the 100 foot high tower was replaced by a gabled bell turret and the elaborate reredos by a plainer screen. It was built of brick with Doulton terra cotta facings rather than a stone exterior, but as an example of late Victorian brickwork it is extremely impressive. Social work was important, seeking to cater for every need. There was a working men's club, mothers' meetings, a library, day and Sunday schools attended by over a hundred children, a needlework society, temperance society, the Band of Hope and a charity shop.

There had been a mission in the small village of Foord and in 1877 the Rev. Claude Bosanquet founded a church there, St. John's, on land again given by Lord Radnor. It was built of stone in Gothic style and funded by donations and a bazaar, to be a working men's church in a growing area. Nearby was the chalybeate spring and, to the right of Black Bull Road, was the farm of the Pavilion Hotel with cows, poultry and pigs, fruit, vegetables and flowers. Three chairmen of the South Eastern railway - Watkin, Russell and Bonsor - were commemorated in road names. The area, originally Park Farm, then Foord Farm, was increasing rapidly with new houses and new roads.

One well-known figure should be mentioned in connection with Folkestone religious life - Father Ignatius Lyne, who had founded a monastery of Anglican Benedictines at Llanthony Abbey in Wales, high up in a beautiful but damp valley. He had been ordained by a schismatic Catholic bishop to ensure the apostolic validity of his orders, since Anglican orders were not accepted as valid by Rome. His father lived in Folkestone for

a year-and-a-half and his son came down to preach for funds wherever he could be admitted - at the Town Hall, St. Michael's and surprisingly, Christ Church. He spoke simply and informatively on monasticism, a picturesque figure in his long black robes, his hair cut in a tonsure. In the heated climate of the day, he aroused opposition, being stoned in Dover and libelled by Col. Brockman (who, on legal advice, apologised in a local paper). Many dissenters were interested in his talks, perhaps because he was an open Romanist and they objected to those who partially concealed their beliefs.

FATHER IGNATIUS LYNE

In spite of all the cries of *"No Popery"* directed at the Anglicans, the Catholics in the town progressed slowly and steadily, attracting little or no opposition. There had always been a Catholic presence along the south coast, because of the priests and nuns who had fled during the French Revolution, with a further influx during the religious troubles of the early 1900s. The old Catholics of good family, who stayed faithful during the years of fines and persecution, were scattered and few. The growth in Catholic numbers in the nineteenth century was due to the Irish labourers who dug the canals and constructed the railway lines. This grew to a flood during the potato famine of the 1860s when millions fled disease and starvation, arriving mostly in the large towns.

In 1850 the Catholic hierarchy was restored. The Times greeted the Pope as *"an Italian priest who is to parcel out the spiritual dominion of this country and who is to restore a foreign usurpation of the consciences of men."* The feeling of foreign dictatorship grew stronger in 1870 with the declaration of Papal Infallibility in matters of faith and morals. There was but one missionary priest in the Folkestone area, Fr. Costigan, whose parish in 1821 extended from Margate to St. Leonards. At one time it was considered that the upper part of the old Sessions Hall in the High Street might be let to them but public opinion was against it. In 1860 the first Catholic church was built in Martello Road, a long grey building holding sixty people. This was replaced by a larger building in 1869, supported by Mrs Woodward. During the week the sanctuary was screened off and the rest became a school. For a while this was staffed by Virgo Fidelis nuns, the Superior having been one of Florence Nightingale's nurses in the Crimea. They later moved to a building in Shorncliffe Road and took charge of middle-class education.

The first few priests had a difficult and lonely time. They served also the School of Musketry in Hythe but the Folkestone Catholics were few. Fr. Goddard who replaced Fr. Sheridan, the first priest, said he spoke to no one during the week except his old housekeeper and his dog. Nevertheless, a larger church was needed, the congregation now numbering 250, and one was built using more land. By 1879 St. Aloysius was again too small. Fr. Mooney, the new priest from the Isle of Wight, had not wished to come to such a small poor parish. In the first year he had six converts and the collection amounted to £2. He asked the Benedictines for a mission priest, but not the one who had caused confusion in the parish by receiving Mrs. Woodward. Finally a new and spacious church, school and presbytery were built in Cheriton Road in 1889 and are still in use. There was a popular and energetic priest, Fr. Denman, though even then the congregation was described as poor and the visitors, usually a good source of funds, were retired officers and aristocrats of swollen dignity but empty pockets.

Folkestone was such a popular centre for the Society of Friends (Quakers) that all East Kent meetings were joined to it for a time. The Friends specialised in helping the poor, they took in children and apprenticed boys. However, during the nineteenth century they were in decline and the meeting house was closed for a time. It was reopened and by 1895 Folkestone was again the largest centre in Kent.

The Baptists were opening their own Sunday schools in 1818 under the Rev. John Clarke. The old church in Mill Bay was coming to the end of its life and a site was bought in Rendezvous Street. The cost of £2,000 took fifteen years to clear, but the Nonconformists prided themselves on clearing their debts in an orderly fashion, unlike the Church of England in the wealthy west end. The Salem chapel quickly became too small. The minister at that time, the Rev. Mr Sampson, tried to sell the site but with no success. So in 1874 the new Baptist chapel, designed by Joseph Gardner, and still the most imposing classical building in Folkestone, was built on the same site, proving how the Baptists had advanced since the days of John Stace's parlour. It had room for 900 people and a basement school for 400 children. Here the first Baptist Mayor, John Fitness, took the Corporation to church on Mayor's Sunday.

Sampson joined enthusiastically in the debate surrounding Ridsdale and condemned him for his Romish practices. He was also an opponent of Woodward in the School Board controversy. The dissenters, who had their own thriving Sunday schools supported Bible teaching but not denominational or clerical influence. Sampson became secretary of the Baptist Union and was succeeded by the Rev. John Foster Jeffrey.

In 1898 the congregation gained an outstanding leader in the person of the Rev. John Carlile, a figure of national importance. He had worked with Cardinal Manning to settle the dock strike, became editor of the Baptist Times and President of the Baptist Union. He was known in Fleet Street as a good journalist and incisive thinker who wrote on social questions, national and international problems. During the First World War he wrote a book on Folkestone. He had come to Folkestone for a year for his health and stayed for 36 years.

One Congregationalist minister, the Rev. Smith, joined the Church of England. Woodward, somewhat tactlessly, addressed an open letter to the congregation, urging a

similar return to the church of their fathers, as they were now like sheep without a shepherd. His invitation met with no response. Their best known minister was the Rev. A. S. Palmer. The church was demolished in 1974 and the congregation is now merged with that of the United Reformed Church.

In 1852 the Methodists had a long narrow chapel next to the King's Arms and finally a magnificent Gothic chapel in Rendezvous Street, most of the money being raised by a bazaar.

The nonconformists were based in the east end of the town and here also in 1882 came the last and perhaps most contentious religious movement, the Salvation Army. William Booth, their founder, was a former Methodist who felt that any methods to win souls to God were

THE BAPTIST CHAPEL, NOW WETHERSPOONS PUBLIC HOUSE

excusable. The minds of the poor were not to be won, nor was the demon drink to be exorcised by quiet vigils. The Salvationists were organised as an army with uniforms, bands, banners and military ranks. But in nearly all towns where they gained a foothold they attracted the opposition of an unholy rabble calling itself the Skeleton Army,

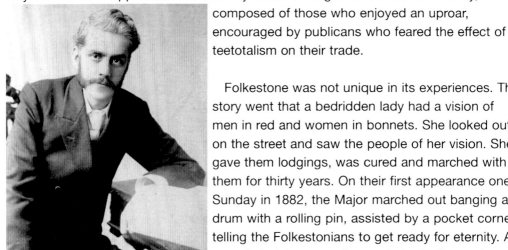

composed of those who enjoyed an uproar, encouraged by publicans who feared the effect of teetotalism on their trade.

Folkestone was not unique in its experiences. The story went that a bedridden lady had a vision of men in red and women in bonnets. She looked out on the street and saw the people of her vision. She gave them lodgings, was cured and marched with them for thirty years. On their first appearance one Sunday in 1882, the Major marched out banging a drum with a rolling pin, assisted by a pocket cornet, telling the Folkestonians to get ready for eternity. A crowded, riotous meeting ended with five seekers at

REV. JOHN CARLILE

the Mercy Seat. They rented the Bradstone Hall from John Pope. This had been built speculatively as a theatre and had a secret exit through the mill house out to Foord Road. One night Pope was stoned until he fell unconscious and there were frequent threats to burn down the hall. Sunday after Sunday all ranks would assemble in their uniforms in the long narrow corridor with their flag; they would march out to a hail of abuse, stones and rotten eggs. A special attack was promised one day and all were praying in the hall for fifteen hours without food or drink. Every window was smashed and the floor covered with stones. One Sunday the troops had to be sent from Shorncliffe and the Mayor read the Riot Act. Every week the peace of the town was disturbed by the noise. The Rev. Edward Husband, whose church was the nearest to the hall, issued a placard pleading to have the marches stopped as being incompatible with religion. The Salvationists

THE SALVATION ARMY BAND, BRADSTONE ROAD

answered that they were at war, fighting and suffering. They also blamed him for the attacks which was quite untrue. In the end things quietened down.

The nineteenth century was a period of experiment and expansion, both within the established church and outside it. With the advent of science and the Origin of Species the old certainties were fast disappearing. The world of H.G. Wells was to have little time for the niceties of faith and dogma and regular church going was not any more a badge of social acceptability. Many of the church buildings have been demolished, as being outdated and expensive to run for their small congregations. The days of conflict were over, the era of co-operation, but also of indifference was to come.

THE SCHOOLS

St. Peter's has the best school site in Folkestone, built on the Durlocks high up on the East Cliff with a magnificent sweeping view of the sea. Even today, a child may exclaim, *"There's my Dad's boat"*, as it rounds the jetty and comes into the harbour.

ST. PETER'S

In the early years of the nineteenth century formal education for a fisher lad would have been considered by many totally unnecessary. He would be needed to assist in cleaning the fish and making nets and later on would join his father on the boat. A lodging-house keeper's daughter would help her mother with the linen; an educated maid servant would waste her time reading her mistress's letters. The poor and sick had to be cared for and provision for them was an acknowledged duty of society. But the idea of universal education is a fairly recent phenomenon – many aspects of Victorian schooling may shock a twentieth century conscience, but in fact people were feeling their way towards the best and most effective ways of training both children and teachers.

Schools in Folkestone may be divided into three classes. It was not a question of free as against fee-paying schools. Until the end of the nineteenth century fees were expected even if they only amounted to a few pence a week. Admittedly the Grammar was also known as the free school, but even here we find small fees charged from a very early date. It is more a question of social status – schools for the poor, schools for the middle and upper classes and the Harvey Grammar which remained poised somewhat uneasily between the two levels, uncertain to which vocation it was called.

The two great local pioneers in education for the poor were Rev. Andrew Bell, an Anglican, and Joseph Lancaster, a Quaker. Their methods were similar and this may have sharpened the edge of competition. Disagreements between Anglicans and Nonconformists were to bedevil the cause of education up to the 1870s and 1880s when the State became the umpire. Both systems were cheap, costing from four shillings to seven shillings and sixpence a child per year. Older students taught the younger; everything had to be learnt by rote and repeated word-for-word. The children chanted in unison their tables, spelling and history dates. They used slates rather than pencils and paper. Schools of over a hundred were taught in one large room, children being divided into groups according to age; the air would be filled with the hum of repetitions and the squeak of slate pencils. There may have been disorder, since the young monitors were not always capable of enforcing discipline. Flogging was discouraged – it was the privilege of the middle and upper classes – and a system of rewards and punishments instituted. The Rev. Bell's school was the germ of the 'National Society for Promoting the Education of the Poor in the Doctrine and Discipline of the Established Church'. Readings were exclusively from Scripture. The British and National schools now flourished side-by-side, more National than British as it was considered the duty of each parish clergyman of zeal to start a parish school, often aided by a number of ladies who had few other outlets for their energies. British schools were undenominational in their religious teaching and more likely to be found in towns or where there was a strong dissenting tradition. Folkestone had examples of both. Larger workhouses did often have their own schools, not particularly good ones and with poorly paid teachers, but even so it was remarked that pauper children would be on a better footing than those outside.

When the paupers moved to Etchinghill under the provisions of the new Poor Law of 1834, Stewart Marjoribanks, the local M.P., bought the site for use by the British and Foreign Schools Society, to provide for 140 boys and 30 girls of the labouring, manufacturing and poorer classes. Scholars paid 3 pence per week; from 1862 the school secured grants and hence was inspected regularly. What was the Church of England doing? There was a National School in Sandgate in 1845 but the Vicar of Folkestone, Rev. Thomas Pearce, was presumably more taken up with his own private school. The National Schools started in Cheriton in 1847, Christ Church School opened in 1852 and St. Mary's in 1854. There is no direct evidence of their methods

ST. MARY'S

till school logs were started in 1862 but one can imagine them run on the lines already mentioned; the school plans certainly envisage large classrooms to be used by all ages. The Rev. Woodward took over the parish church in 1851 and must have started thinking of a new school even before the embellishment of the Church in 1856. A school to a clergyman of his fervent and enthusiastic temperament would be first priority to ensure the future spiritual development of the young minds in the parish. The education of the young was a sacred task, not to be entrusted into the hands of dissenters and non-believers. What the Church had built should be left in the control of the Church. Doctrine lessons were given regularly at St. Mary's and the children were encouraged to take part in services. Entrenched attitudes on both sides go far to explain the extreme bitterness with which the debate over the 1870 Education Act was conducted.

Meanwhile the national picture was one of progress. Previously all funds had been provided by private charity and fees. In 1833 the first government grant of £20,000 had been allocated for schools to help with costs of building; by 1846 it had risen to nearly

£100,000. It was given to both the National and British Schools and, to ensure that it was properly spent, a system of inspection was begun. These visits were of enormous importance – at last a common standard of instruction and discipline could be advised, though not enforced. A detailed questionnaire was proposed covering heating and lighting, discipline, the number and qualifications of the staff, finances, libraries and relations with parents. One can see from the log books the importance that all the school, staff and children, attached to the coming of the Inspector. More attention was being paid to teachers' training; by 1845 there were 22 colleges of education run by the Church of England. The award of a Queen's Scholarship meant that a grant could be made towards the expenses of training and in 1846 the pupil-teacher system was introduced. The pupil teachers were older and more efficient than the monitors and were even paid a small sum, as was the Headmaster for training them. This was a way upwards for the ambitious working class girl or boy who could earn £10 in their first year and, once they gained their certificate, have a house and salary worth £90 per annum. However, their duties were onerous, since they had to prepare lessons, take classes and prepare for their own exams.

Another way of increasing funds paid to schools after the report of the Newcastle Commission was the system of payment by results which lasted till 1897. Grants were paid from six shillings and sixpence a head on a combined report of good attendance and satisfactory test results. As may be imagined this acted as a spur to teachers to enforce both, though there were plenty of factors affecting attendance. The system bore

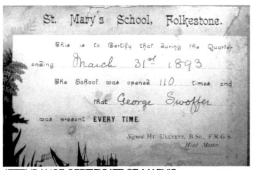

ATTENDANCE CERTIFICATE ST. MARY'S

hardly on schools in poor districts, such as St. Peter's, where satisfactory results could not readily be obtained. The best picture of schools in the 1860s may be gained from an examination of the log books: their difficulties regarding fees and attendance (which was not yet compulsory); the status of pupil teachers; the role of the Inspectors; the gradual enlargement of the curriculum and the varied incidents that go to make up school life. Here then are extracts from St. Mary's log signed by Mr. Norris, the Headmaster:

1863, January

The children are very restless today. I generally find them so after the holidays.

Most of the children absent last week have returned. Many of these have been kept at home from a mistaken supposition that the fees were raised. The charges at the British School are higher than they were last year, hence the mistake.

3rd division exam. Took the upper part in arithmetic and reading, the lower in arithmetic, writing on slates, making figures and difficult simple subtraction. The reading sheets seem too difficult for the boys.

All the pupil teachers have successfully passed their exams.

A school lesson is to be substituted for recreation till attendance at prayers is more satisfactory. (There are also notes on regular liturgy lessons from Rev. Woodward, evening prayers, and boys chosen to augment the choir at the Mariners' Church.)

The children had their monthly walk on the Warren.

Higher fees are to be introduced, the first child to pay three pence unless the parents give proof that they cannot afford it.

Several boys were punished for swinging during the time the bell was being rung.

A French boy was admitted in the room of one boy left who has gone to Boulogne to live with the French boy's relatives.

8 boys have left, some gone to work, some to small private schools, and 2 or 3 to the British Schools. This, I think, is partly owing to the change in fees, and partly to the strictness with which attendance at prayers is enforced.

March.

Tuesday. I received a note in very indifferent verse, although the writing was good, praying for a half holiday tomorrow on account of the steeple chase. I am afraid we shall have to disappoint them. Wednesday. Attendance 33. (A full attendance was 164. The steeple chases were held at Park Farm and were a great day out for many.) Several boys have made a habit of bringing peas to school and eating them during lesson time and they have been punished.

The bell rope broke and great numbers were late for school. Hugh Campbell has obtained a Queen's Scholarship.

Since Mr. Dryer left, the management of the Third Division has devolved for the most part on the two pupil teachers, but they seem scarcely up to it, though they seem to do much better than they did a short time since. (The total staff was now: Headmaster, an assistant master and two first year pupil teachers. Benjamin Dryer had gained commendation from the Inspector as "working successfully in a by no means easy place".)

July.

A printed circular has been sent round to the subscribers and principal visitors to appraise them of the coming exams and to invite their attendance. Everyone appeared satisfied with the discipline and attainments. (These visits and exams which consisted of questions and answers in class, together with the visits of the Government inspectors were the most important days of the year, both for finances and public support.)

August.

It is proposed to make various changes in the management, conduct and discipline of the school and a system of prizes has been instituted. Circulars have been sent to the parents and cards are to be printed on which marks may be entered for attendance, good conduct and cleanliness.

A LADY SUBSCRIBER

Many boys were absent on account of the circus.

The practice of repeating lessons is becoming more general. It is at present optional.

Though attendance is still down, those who do attend are more punctual now that there are marks for attendance.

The school was visited by the Inspector and examined in Scripture, catechism, reading, writing and arithmetic. He reported that: "The pupil teachers generally give satisfaction. A little more discipline however in their division is desirable. Reading lessons should be given by a qualified teacher."

1864, February.

The indentures of Thomas Cope are to be cancelled on account of the inability of the Committee to maintain the present staff of teachers.

Lessons in the Night School are irregular. (A tantalising reference which hints at an attempt at adult education. Night lessons were given to working men at St. Peter's from which they gained much profit. Of 22 men employed by the Corporation, 12 had to sign their name with a mark.)

Regular music and French lessons are to be introduced.

The fife and drum band is to play at the Parsonage.

The caps have proved detrimental to strict discipline, and the boys are told to attach tape so that they may hang from their buttons or belts.

One assistant teacher has left and there has been no replacement. The result is unsatisfactory and the boys seem to have retrograded.

September.

The school festival involving cricket took place in September and a comment after the event implies a certain amount of confusion with the arrangements. "Someone in future should go and see that the tent and hurdles are erected and that there is sufficient cricket equipment."

Many lads are leaving for situations in the small shops.

1866.

I took charge of the school – Henry Ulyett. He was a good and imaginative teacher who gave classes at the Museum and lectured elsewhere on a variety of scientific subjects. He was a strong contender for the Headmastership of the Harvey Grammar when it fell vacant in 1877. There was resentment in the town when he was passed over in favour of an outsider, Richard Stead, who edited "Bygone Kent."

1867.

Some subjects of Mr. Ulyett's lessons: birds of prey, cocoa palms, the brown bean, carbonic acid, cotton, the elephant, the rat.

Inspector's report: Mr. Ulyett seems a superior teacher and will, I hope, materially improve this school. The upper classes already exhibit more accuracy of work.

1869.

I was obliged to send a note to the British school, as several of their boys have waylaid ours and seriously ill treated them. 71 pupils sat exams, 87.3% passed. A total Government grant of £67.3.1 was given.

1874.

The drawing exams of the School of Science and Art are now regularly taken.

Arnold Ulyett, later to be Headmaster of Sandgate School, became a pupil teacher under his father.

1884.

No child should leave without a certificate, but several unqualified boys have left. No employer in the town ever asks for one and parents do not understand the value of it.

1886.

Poetry, history and progressive geography appear in the syllabus.
1893.

A contribution was given to the Sandgate Relief Fund. (The year of the landslide at the western end of Sandgate when 70 houses were damaged, but with no loss of life.)

The school was closed for 6 weeks on account of measles.

In the 1860s and 70s there was a feeling that sectarian differences in the field of education should cease. The Nonconformists were willing to hand control of their schools to the Government if they could be State-supported but they did not fancy public money being used for schools that would remain Church of England. The 1851 Exhibition acted as an impetus for technical education, as did the example of our great industrial rival, Germany. Grants now accounted for a third to a half of a school's

running costs. A survey was made of large towns; of 4 million poor children only one-and-a-half million were on the school registers, but still the question of denominational education blocked the way to further advance. Gladstone's Liberal Government, with W. E. Forster vice President of the Education Department, decided on a typically British compromise.

OLD LADY VOTING

For the first time it was recognised that the community should provide education as a right for every child. Councils could pass bye-laws to make school attendance compulsory, but did not have to do so. Where there were sufficient places in existing schools things could be left as they were, unless the inhabitants wished otherwise. But where places were lacking, a Board of elected members should be empowered to build the new 'Board' schools. The Boards, in number from 5 to 15 were elected by secret ballot; there were no property qualifications and women could both sit and vote. The report on School numbers in Folkestone, both actual and potential, reads as follows:

School	Maximum Places	Numbers attending
St. Mary's, C. of E	477	367
Christ Church, C. of E	243	269
St. Peter's C of E	300	199
British School, Dover Road	339	293
Harvey Grammar	77	37
Wesleyan	306	Sunday only
St. Aloysius, Roman Catholic	84	59

Christ Church was overcrowded but elsewhere there were places to spare. The Wesleyans, who wanted a School Board, refused to allow their schools to be used for day schools, which would have given a comfortable surplus. Once constituted, the Boards could levy local school rates from a halfpenny to three pence in the pound. The question was raised whether a Folkestone Board would be a heavy burden on 'maiden ladies and lodging house keepers who would be hard put to it to educate the children of others'.

By 1875 there were 99 School Boards, London leading the way. Compulsory bye-laws were eventually passed in nearly all areas. But in Folkestone the great debate lingered on till 1882. School Board supporters, mostly dissenters, compared their opponents with those who preferred oil lamps, cesspools and private wells to modern improvements in lighting and drainage. Compulsory attendance would involve severe hardship for the poorest families, ran the opposing argument:

"Children's earnings help buy bread and clothing for the family. The whole of the children of the working class will be thrown on the rates, and a much higher rate than three pence will be necessary, which we shall still be paying 50 years hence for the new buildings. It will destroy that spirit of independence which even the very poorest possess. Another evil will be the indiscriminate mixing

W.E. FORSTER SAYING TO CHILDREN "YOU *SHALL* LEARN"

of children, no division between those whose parents pay and those driven to school by the policeman's cane. And the 700 Folkestone children meant to be receiving their education in the gutters, where are they to be found? The dissenters are taking every opportunity to force a school board on this town against the wishes of the inhabitants. The hole and corner meetings in Tontine Street held by its supporters are now a matter of history." (Folkestone Chronicle, 1872).

The whole town seemed divided on the matter. In 1879 the Council advertised for a School Inspector who could persuade the poorer parents to forego their children's earnings and send them to school. Those who did not were then prosecuted.

By 1881 new schools were badly needed at Foord due to the rise in population and the Rev. Woodward invited subscriptions, but he met with public apathy as people felt no need to dig deep into their pockets to build a new school, since they would have to pay school rates anyway; let the Government do it. The Inspector had declared that 700 new places had to be found; in 1882 the new Board was elected of 9 members out of 12 possible candidates, mostly solid middle class with the exception of Mr. Pilcher - a shoemaker and red hot radical who had held office in the Labourers' Union, and promoted the strike of agricultural labourers in Kent. It was

ATTENDANCE ENQUIRY

said that sales of several good properties failed to take place because of the heavy school rate expected, but in fact it was not as bad as feared and settled at about one-and-threequarters pence in the pound. In 1885 came the first fruits of the Board's endeavours, the huge building in Black Bull Road, the North Board School, which cost £6,000 and took 700 scholars - boys, girls and infants. It was later to be named after

Mr. Mundella, the Vice President of the Committee on Education, who was present at the opening, as also was Sir Edward Watkin, Folkestone's M.P. and Chairman of the S.E. Railway Company. There was a banquet at the West Cliff Hotel and speeches were made. Sir Edward hinted at free education and free school dinners and a vote of thanks was passed to the Vicar, for the existence of the Church schools over the previous 30 years.

In 1886 the foundation of the second Board School was laid on the old site in Mill Lane Dover Road that had formerly been Hillside Elementary School. It took 833 children and was opened by Lady Watkin, whose speech had to be read for her as she was suffering from the effects of an accident. She again alluded to the possibility of a fund for one good meal a day. When in 1897 the third Board School was opened in Sidney Street, the Board Schools took 2,304 children and the voluntary schools only 1,389. The school rate had now gone up to four-and-a-half pence but the townspeople were used to the idea of paying it and felt it was economical.

The same debate went on in Cheriton about a School Board. There was a school connected with St. Martin's Church, but it became too small as a mixed school. A new girls' school was begun in 1883, the old premises being kept for boys. Sandgate never had a Board School, but kept its National School of which it was very proud. For several years it held the best attendance record for the whole of England.

A certain amount of log-book material still exists for the North Board and Sidney Street schools. It gives the impression that the pupils came from the lower end of the social scale: many children were being kept away for hop-picking, and the girls did work for the lodgers in their parents' boarding houses. Girls had lessons in needlework and cooking, while boys took elementary science. The Vicar explained these differences by remarking that girls did not explain themselves as simply and naturally as boys. There are records of pupils having to be sent home to be washed and some coming up from the Infant School who showed very poor results and had no idea of their letters. The grant had now reached twenty-one shillings and sixpence for each child per year – at last the long arm of the Education Department had stretched out to ensure some sort of education for all children in the town, however poor, dirty or backward.

Schools for the middle and upper classes were described as private adventure schools – the term being used in a commercial, rather than a scholastic sense. They came in all grades: some were small establishments in small houses where young ladies or young gentlemen - always described as such in the advertisements - picked up the rudiments of knowledge and the elements of gentility, enjoying the delights of clean sea air; others were large, efficient, well run establishments which continued for 30 years or so. Girls could stay till the age of 17 or 18 but the boys' schools were mostly for ages up to 11 or 13, preparatory for public schools elsewhere. One of the first fee-paying schools - which must have been successful as it is mentioned in guides between 1807 and 1839 - was Mrs. Cullen's Ladies' Academy on the Bayle. The Rev. Thomas Pearce, amongst his other business activities, also had a select establishment for 12 young gentlemen, terms from 100 to 150 guineas according to age, a lot of money for the time and rather more than for a rival establishment conducted by the Rev. Plater. The sons of John Constable were sent to Pearce's school. He came down to visit one boy when he was ill, to which we owe some sketches and studies of Folkestone and district. His boys were eventually removed, as his friends advised that the sole advantage of the school lay, not in its teaching but the healthy situation.

Another long-running establishment was that of the Rev. John Clark, Grove House School. He came to Folkestone in 1817, was ordained as minister of Mill Bay Baptist chapel, and started the school in 1822. It gave a sound commercial, mathematical and classical education, bathing three times a week in season and good religious grounding. His daughter, Mary Ann Clark, ran the prep school and he was succeeded by his son John. In 1871 there were 48 pupils, mostly from the London area, and 7 staff. In the same year, Fellenburg House School in Church Street, headmistress Miss Gittens, had 7 teachers and 49 students, one from Australia and two from India, the rest from Kent and London. In 1894 Grove House gave up, the Folkestone Herald noting that in its day the school had been busy and influential, but it closed at last, outdone by academies in the fashionable West End of the town. For girls, there was Kent College, a Methodist school, with 73 boarders and 61 day girls in 1889. The first headmistress was Miss de la Mare who opened her own St. Margaret's School in Clifton Crescent in 1890, later moving to Coolinge Lane, the school lasting till 1967. As described by one of her pupils, *"She was like the mother of a large and varied family, but I often thought there was something in her of a queen. Her mind was as straight and strong as her back; she had no use for slouchers and slackers."*

An unusual school was Praetoria House in Grimston Avenue, founded by Dr. and Mrs. Alfred Praetorius, of German extraction, with lessons in French and German on alternate days. Dr. Praetorius had the almost hopeless task of encouraging intellectual curiosity and youthful enthusiasm while attempting to produce English gentlemen of the public-school type. Ford Madox Ford, the novelist, went there and met his future wife, as girls also were admitted. Another experiment was the British Floating College advertising in 1857. Whilst the headquarters were ashore in the Bayle, afloat was a frigate with auxiliary steam power which would cruise while teaching naval instruction and marine engineering to young gentlemen aged 12-25. Three years later a sale was advertised at Bellevue House of nautical and mathematical instruments, a superior teak flag-staff and a four-oared galley. The best social tone was undoubtedly that of Miss Pincoff's School in Westbourne Mansions, where Queen Victoria had a godson; the school list was printed in order of rank, the head boy being the son of a duke. The boys wore a replica of an able seaman's uniform. There were many other establishments whose pupils filed in solemn crocodiles across the Leas but of whose history we know little – Pembury House, Cheriton Place; The Misses Clark, 21 Alexandra Gardens; Mrs. Harrison's Seminary, 47 Guildhall Street; T. Coleman, Commercial Boarding Academy; Rev. W. Green, Classical School; The Misses Howard, 40 Sandgate Road; Thomas Davis, Prospect Row; Mrs. Donald, Preparatory School for Young Gentlemen, Briarley Cottage, Foord. Richard Stead, Headmaster of the Harvey Grammar, passed sentence on some of them: *"It would really be better for the town if some of its more inefficient schools, especially preparatory schools, ceased to exist."* On another occasion he described them as extremely and unnecessarily expensive.

PRAETORIA HOUSE, SCHOOL. CLASS IIB

The Harvey Grammar School was relatively unimportant through most of the nineteenth century – by the end numbers were only just over 100. The potential was there, with an able Headmaster wishing to extend the curriculum to take advantage of the new grants for science teaching and a greater willingness of boys and parents to envisage an extended education. The other schools, though catering for ten times the number of children, were no more than elementary schools. Although the Harvey had started for a younger age group, it was the only school in the town offering advanced education for those who could not afford high fees.

Harvey Grammar School prides itself on its connection with the famous Dr. William Harvey, (see chapter 3). His bequest bought Combe Farm near Lympne and part of the rent went to provide a school and school house in Rendezvous Street, Folkestone. The schoolmaster, given £10 every year, was to teach twenty poor children English and Latin without fees. The surplus of the first and second year's rent went to build fishing boats for poor fishermen. In the third year the schoolmaster received the surplus, but out of this he had to keep the school in good repair. Sometimes this was so burdensome a duty that the Trustees had to step in and do it for him, and indeed borrow money for the purpose. The duties of letting the farm and arranging the finances were to be left to the Mayor and Trustees.

Reading the records, it is difficult not to conclude that concerns over the fishing boats were at least as prominent as matters affecting the school. The masters were of variable quality and, even when unsatisfactory, were not adequately supervised. The Rev. William Lancaster (1805-14) was perhaps envisaging a different sort of school, as he advertised sea bathing, French and Italian lessons for fee paying pupils. He had to resign for discriminating against the 'free boys' in his care. He was followed by James Bennett and Henry Butcher who died in office in 1845. Before the next appointment was made it was decided to rebuild the old school on the same site, the architect being Edward Gotto who built Sandgate's first National School. Unfortunately, much of the work was defective, inferior bricks were used and it was badly planned. John Whichcord of Maidstone had to finish it off. It had a large schoolroom in which all classes were taught, till a small room was partitioned off in 1869. There was a playground at the back and two houses, one for the use of the master, whilst the other was rented for 17 years to the Folkestone Dispensary. Joseph Samson took over the newly-built school in 1846, by which time the curriculum was to include Latin, mathematics and navigation. Samson in turn was found to be unsatisfactory and unfit for his office. He resigned, leaving the school at such a low ebb that it closed for 18 months, the boys being sent to the National School. Samson subsequently became Secretary of the Gas Company and was declared bankrupt in 1864.

Henry Ramsey, the new Head, was of a different stamp. He was already an experienced Master, zealous and conscientious in his duties. For some time he took in boarders and encouraged the entry of tradesmen's sons who could pay their fees in groceries by arrangement. There was an emphasis on the skills of good writing and learning by heart.

THE HARVEY GRAMMAR SCHOOL FIRST BUILDING

Monitors were used and paid small sums, occasionally taking charge of the whole school, still only averaging 40 boys. The master sat at his desk in the middle of the large schoolroom - his cane prominently displayed - the pupils' desks being ranged round the walls and in the middle. Recreation areas were the playground, Guildhall Street, and the churchyard (about which there were complaints). There were walks on Wednesday afternoons, cricket on the East Cliff, and a school outing to Lyminge or Saltwood by Pilcher's van in June. Prizes were distributed at the end of the summer term with the Trustees in attendance.

Ramsey's task was made easier when the Trust arrangements were reorganised in 1858. It was made purely educational, except for the Tanlade, and no more boats needed to be provided or boys apprenticed. Fees of £1-£2 a quarter were recognised except for the foundation scholars. These were the former free boys - admitted on the recommendation of the Mayor and Aldermen - preference still being given to the sons of Folkestone Freemen and fishermen. There was to be a public examination of the scholars in June, and ages of school attendance were to be from 8 to 16, which made the Harvey the one school in the town empowered to provide secondary education for poor children. There were to be 10 Trustees, the majority of whom were retired army and navy men, or country gentlemen such as Thomas Papillon of Acrise, William Deedes, Sir John Bligh, Lord Radnor (who hardly ever turned up) and Canon Jenkins of Lyminge, a cleric and scholar who served for 38 years. The town felt itself to be slighted, but the Trustees replied that it was better the school should be administered by those free from local prejudice.

Ramsey was succeeded by the Rev. Edward Head (1870-77) who took his London B.A. Degree while Headmaster. He retired and started a school of his own, York House in Cheriton Gardens, being also appointed Chaplain to the Elham workhouse. The next Headmaster was Richard Stead (1877-1900) who really gave the school its commanding position in the town. There is plenty of evidence for his term of office: all the correspondence between the Headmaster and the Clerk to the Trust, Mr. Harrison; the bills, rent, rates, gas, printing, making thousands of documents in all. He had to live down a certain amount of ill-feeling in that Henry Ulyett, the preferred local candidate, had been unsuccessful. But he was a man of some culture who had written historical and school books, and was ambitious for the school. By the turn of the century he was able to declare its results as being among the best in Kent, though he feared they did not get credit for this in the town. *"We shall soon have quite a group of London graduates amongst our old boys, and these coming graduates were nearly all foundation boys or from poor families. A few years ago no one would have thought of a H.G.S. boy aspiring to a degree."*

The intake for the Foundation Scholarships came from the poor schools – St. Mary's, the Wesleyans, and the Board Schools, but the standard of such entrants was often fairly low. In order to attract a better class of boy, Mr. Stead started his own prep school, with the consent of the Governors, and at the express wish of many parents.

> *"My idea is that we should engage a well-trained young lady teacher who is a good musician and skilled in the management of little boys. Plenty of really clever refined young teachers are to be had at very modest salaries – alas for them. The lady teacher need never come into contact with any of the assistant masters. I may add that I believe the junior school would be self supporting from the very first."*

And, as Canon Jenkins said, the boys would have the same methods and aims throughout their school career.

Since there was no place for a prep school in the 1858 scheme, it was in fact carried on as a private venture of Mr. Stead's, from which it is to be hoped he was able to reap some profit. A constant grumble was the smallness of the salary offered to both Headmaster and assistants. The Head received about £200 per annum including his capitation fee, but out of that he had to pay for printing forms, notices and small bills for repair, until he could be reimbursed by the trustees. The three assistant masters in

1881 got £66 each, until Mr. Stead put his foot down and insisted on the appointment of Mr. Froggatt at the large salary of £100; he had previously enjoyed 12 years' experience in the excellent middle-class schools attached to St. Mary's College, Chelsea, and was strong in the subjects most needed - modern languages, science, drawing and English.

RICHARD STEAD

As Headmaster, Mr. Stead obviously wanted to get on with his teaching and the affairs of the school, but was still responsible for collecting fees from the parents. These now averaged between £6 and £8 per term – not much when compared with the private schools, but to get them was at times like drawing a tooth. John English the printer complained he was not given any of the printing work at the school and so would not pay. *"All this sort of thing worries me far more than my regular work of teaching and managing the school."* And if fees went up, he was abused like a pickpocket, as it was widely believed the extra went straight into the Headmaster's purse. There was also a rumour current in the town that the non fee-paying boys were treated differently or put in a special class. Stead asked that this should be refuted in the strongest possible terms, as there was absolutely no difference made between the boys. In fact the amount involved in running the school seems extremely modest; in 1887 the tuition fees and rent amounted to £516, against an expenditure of £15 coal, £11 gas, £18 cleaning, £405 teachers' salaries, £3 stamps and stationery, a total of £452. In the end Mr. Harrison took over fee collecting duties.

The role of the Governors, apart from the fact that they now had no boats to look after, was much the same as it had been at the time of the original foundation deed of 1674. The Headmaster saw to the day-to-day running of the school, and they had to approve the finances and hear his report. They still had the affairs of Combe Farm to consider, Major Kirkpatrick being their agricultural expert. They also made arrangement for the foundation scholarships and the examiner. The Grammar School was not of course subject to visits from Government Inspectors and Mr. Stead explained the difference:

"I am half afraid the Governors wish to appoint Canon Routledge, the Government Inspector of Schools, to examine the Harvey Grammar. The good canon is used to elementary schools who concentrate on mechanical proficiency in the 3 Rs. The aim of our exam is to find out if the boys are intelligently taught, enabling them to pass the Cambridge Local exam. To put it plainly, the Government Inspector is an official employed to keep down grants, and he will be unconsciously biased against our own middle class school in favour of the elementary schools."

In 1889 he was also noting that while the scholarships offered education of a more advanced character to boys of exceptional ability from the elementary schools: *"the boys entering this year are in nearly all cases of superior social standing, showing that the school is more and more meeting the wants of the respectable middle classes"*. He wished to see it at the top of the tree, both socially and intellectually. One of his great interests was in science teaching. England had at last woken up to its importance and, as he said, the best science teaching could now be found in the secondary schools, certainly not in the public schools, still heavily committed to the classics. The Science and Art Department in South Kensington held examinations, gave grants, exhibitions were loaned and scholarships awarded. Of course these were taken elsewhere than in schools; they were meant to be a means by which the industrious working man could educate himself. Draughtsmen and engineers could learn machine construction, joiners and carpenters, building; grocers and ironmongers took maths, and grocers and tailors inorganic chemistry. Classes were held in Folkestone at the Museum and then at the Technical Institute opened in 1896. Mr. Stead fought for all the available grants and resources for those of school age to be concentrated at the Harvey Grammar where a really good laboratory was to be built and a science teacher engaged. The County Councils were also empowered to give grants and he was worried in case the School Boards tried to monopolise these.

A great step forward for the School was the move from the crowded noisy premises in Rendezvous Street to a new building in Foord Road in 1882. Mrs. Payer bought the old site for £3,575 and the new school was to cost over £4,000. Even then numbers were growing so rapidly, 100 boys by 1892, that several classes had still to be taken in one room. It must have been something of a wrench for the traditionalists to leave the school after some 200 years of occupation. The new buildings were in Elizabethan style with a tower, a large schoolroom and two more classrooms, a master's house and dormitories for the boarders. There was a playground outside and again there were complaints from the neighbours. Day boys were not to come in more than 20 minutes early or linger after school was finished; stone throwing, toy pistols, fireworks and matches were forbidden, as were wall climbing and rough and boisterous games.

As well as the new premises, there were more changes in the administration of the charity in 1885. Instead of the old Trustees there were to be ten Governors, though the surviving Trustees were taken on as Governors for life. The Mayor was to be an ex-officio Governor and two more could be elected by the Mayor and Aldermen, thus returning to the town some measure of the control which it had lost over the centuries. The Governors might choose subjects of study, fix salaries and school terms and authorise building repairs. The Headmaster should control the choice of books, the methods of teaching, the arrangement of the classes and had the power to expel boys. The school was to be of a Christian character with prayers read regularly, but Mr. Stead was careful to avoid any entanglements with visiting clergy. *"Beware of the*

Denominationals", he said, "as if one is let in, the rest have to follow." The Rev.

Woodward's suggestion of a clergyman to join the Board was not accepted. Many of the old-established endowed schools were also coming under the control of the Charity Commissioners. Mr. Stead feared that between the Department of Science and Art, the County Councils and the Education Department - each of which expected some measure of control if grants were to be made - the school was in danger of losing its independent status.

He would indeed be proud of the school now, with its fine new buildings and playing fields and its high reputation in the town. It is still a true grammar school, an institute of higher education where other schools and parents strive to send their boys, which is what he had always wished for it. There is also a girls' Grammar School and two other excellent secondary schools; Pent Valley Technology College and The Folkestone Academy.

NEW BUILDING HARVEY
GRAMMAR SCHOOL

THE LABOURING CLASS AND THE POOR

"*Some persons lend blankets to the poor, in which case, on their being returned, they should be scoured well and baked in the oven before they are put by in brown paper bags with pepper sprinkled over them.*"

(Workwoman's Guide, 1840)

A working man was not one of the poor. Not, that is, if he was in regular employment at the average wage of twenty one shillings to twenty eight shillings a week and avoided long spells of sickness or unemployment, if he paid a reasonable rent of three shillings and sixpence. to five shillings a week, if he had a decent thrifty wife, competent with her needle, not too many children and was not addicted to drink. He could enjoy a reasonable standard of living and hold up his head amongst his neighbours, perhaps putting by a few shillings weekly with the Savings Bank or one of the Friendly Societies. During the last half of the nineteenth century his standard of living rose, drains and clean water were mandatory for every house, his food, clothing and furniture improved in standard and variety and his children were educated properly. The unfortunates starved in the gutters and garrets of London, Liverpool, Manchester and Birmingham. There was distress in Folkestone, particularly during hard winters when builders had to lay off their men but there were agencies to give help and relief. The hard cases and bad times attracted attention precisely because the inhabitants had not grown accustomed to the abyss of hopeless poverty as had those in the large towns.

Indeed, Folkestone was for most of this period a magnet for those seeking employment and men came from London, Scotland and Ireland to work as builders' labourers or on the railways. There were still some 450 men employed in the fishing trade but, even by the time of the 1851 census, they had been overtaken by the builders. Only in the streets immediately surrounding the harbour was there a preponderance of those describing themselves as mariners and fishermen. Mr Sanders who had erected some of the houses in Clifton Crescent said at a workmen's dinner in 1880 that he employed at times 500 to 600 men. In 1873 there were jobs for a hundred men in the East Cliff cement works or digging for coprolite at Newington and Cheriton, but there were no takers. (Coprolite was fossil faeces used as fertiliser and the works were known as 'the gold diggings').

Distribution of population in class and occupation varied according to geography. The town was split in two by the steep sides of the Pent valley, the East end and the old fishermen's quarters being for workpeople and the West end for the gentry, visitors and their servants. Mill Bay, a narrow street of tumble-down cottages whose entry can be seen at the bottom of Rendevous Street (now the centre for Folkestone's revival) was described in 1862 as a wretched slum, a complete mass of filth which might even deter the summer visitors. In 1851 out of 115 people, there were twenty-two labourers and thirteen servants (these would have gone out to work), four brick makers, two errand boys, three paupers, a blacksmith, a stone mason, a half pay captain, a plasterer, a Chelsea pensioner and surprisingly, a 'gentleman'. North

MILL BAY, 1862

Street was still predominantly for the fishermen and mariners. There were also eleven domestic servants, eight laundresses, a railway engineer, a plate cleaner in a hotel (probably the Pavilion), two dressmakers and a post office clerk. Occupations in the narrow crowded High Street (371 people in 73 houses) were various; many shopkeepers as one would expect, some with apprentices living with them; three butchers; three drapers; three bonnet makers (one French); two tea dealers; a tailor employing six; a basket maker; three ironmongers; two greengrocers; twelve domestics; a coach maker; a hammer man in a forge; a gasfitter; six labourers; a pauper schoolmistress and a monthly nurse. This may be compared with the elevated social climate in the Upper Sandgate Road with twenty-four houses and twenty-five living in domestics, eight lodging house keepers, a solicitor, a clergyman, three annuitants, four landed proprietors or gentlemen, a J.P., a solicitor, a barrister and an architect. There were still sixty-five agricultural labourers in the farms surrounding the town, such as Walton Farm, Coolinge Farm, Manor Farm, Park Farm (pictured earlier in Hasted's History of Kent), Ingles Farm and Broadmead Farm.

BUILDERS

One has only to look around the magnificent mansions of the West End, the Town Hall, the schools, churches and chapels to admire the monuments to the brick makers, plasterers, carpenters, painters and labourers who worked on them. They were fine buildings made to last, put up by men who took a pride in their work; the men were paid decent wages by employers, such as Messrs. Dunk, Hoad, Baker and Moody, who did their best to keep them on in cruel winters. William Dunk put his men on to making coffins at such times. Wage rates in 1894 were: plumbers eight pence an hour, carpenters seven pence, painters seven pence and labourers five pence. For the other side of the coin, small builders who skimped their work, used bad materials, overworked and underpaid their employees, one has to read Robert Tressell's 'The Ragged Trousered Philanthropists', a fiercely partisan account of the building trade in Hastings in 1911. Perhaps it was the prototype of Mr Oily Sweater, cringing to the customers and harsh to the men, who sent Daniel Rawlings, aged twelve, up a 40 foot scaffold with a load of cement to the plasterer working on a house in the Upper Sandgate Road. He fell and was killed. It was his second day at work.

The plight of the fishermen when there was too much wind or no fish was revealed in 1825 by the overseers of the poor in evidence given to the Poor Law Commissioners. There was little money to give them, some five shillings a week, and little work available, only some fishing net braiding. They needed larger boats and a system of apprenticeship. No wonder that many of them took to smuggling to supplement their income.

The streets around the Stade were full of evidence of a busy marine trade – fish hung up to be cured in the many herring hangs, nets stretched on poles or hanging up to be mended. By the 1851 census, fishermen outnumbered builders only in the streets immediately surrounding the harbour. North Street had 28 mariners and fishermen and 8 labourers, but in Mill Bay there were 5 fishermen to 22 labourers, 4 brickmakers and a plasterer. An

FISHERMEN

estimate of 1874 gave the number of 160 boats and 450 men engaged in the fishing trade. Mr. Cullen, chief clerk in Messrs Rothschild's bank gave a list of 180 nicknames used by the fishermen such as:

Old Sharper, Old Buck,
Old Tippo, Old Muck,
Old Charity, Dillo and Proctor,
Old Pork Ears, Old Sir,
Old Graffy, Old Parr,
Tommy Newbolt and Old Piker Boxer.

The men were described as many figures wearing knitted guernseys, great sea boots and often the typical headgear, the Phrygian cap.

There were many pubs frequented by fishermen in the harbour and High Street area; in 1905 these were reckoned by the Chief Constable to number one to every hundred inhabitants. Often their names had maritime connotations – The Three Mackerel, the Hovelling Boat (later the Packet Boat) and the Folkestone Lugger in the Sandgate Road. The North Foreland was purchased by the Edinburgh Castle Company to be turned into a coffee house and later became a fisherman's Bethel. A typical pub of the 1850s was described;

"The fishermen having enjoyed a game of ninepins in the cellar, found their way upstairs to the sanded floor parlour where a 'free and easy'

was at once started. A strong smell of herrings, oily and pungent,
filled the room and almost hid the light of the tallow candles on
the table in the overcrowded cabin-like compartment. Fishermen
filled every corner of the room and puffed away at their long clay
pipes behind their pots of beer, as the wind began to howl outside
and whistle through the closely compartmented windows, from
whence the men occasionally glanced to see if their boats in the
harbour were safe at their moorings. Nanny Widdy made a skirmish
into the room and brought out her son, Squashy, before he became
hopelessly immoveable. Discourse took a practical turn. All the
herring hangs were said to be full of fish. The harbour master came
in for an uncomplimentary share of the conversation, the steam boats
were voted a nuisance and the tan copper needed mending."
(Holbein's Visitors' List, Nov. 19, 1890).

But life is always uncertain for fishermen and their families. The loss of two vessels in the 1880s, the 'Sprightly' and the 'Eliza Jane' and the plight of the widows and orphans left without support, save for the funds raised by the Mayor and clergy, made the fishing community seriously consider an effective scheme of insurance. The Folkestone Fishing Boat Insurance Company covering 35 boats was started in 1884 with funds of £500 and encouragement from Sir Edward Watkin, who was a great believer in self help. The True Blue Club of the 1890s also made provision for sick pay.

The large hotels provided employment for both men and women. The Pavilion had thirty-eight staff in 1851; three cooks, three porters, seven waiters, thirteen maids, two bath attendants, four linen women, an upholsterer, two clerks and the housekeeper. Of these only four were born in Folkestone, the rest coming from other parts of Kent and London. They waited on twenty-eight guests of whom five were titled, accompanied by ten valets and ladies' maids. The census was taken out of season and in 1871 there were only eighteen visitors to thirty-eight staff. A waiter would earn £1 a week and could also count on generous tips. Many of them had been employed for twenty or thirty years and there was an annual servants' ball, as also at the Westcliff Hotel. Below stairs in the hot and steamy kitchens, conditions were different – mountains of washing up, saucepans to scrub, silver to polish, and food to prepare. At the Grand the staff day began at 6am and ended at 8pm. If there was a ball, they could finish at 1am A kitchen boy would get board and lodging for the first six months and two shillings and sixpence per month thereafter. There was a long dormitory over the carriage houses with one room for males and one for females.

There was no class of men more vilified and unpopular than the cab drivers. Their number of 52 was restricted by the Council under the powers of the Folkestone Improvement Act and each cab was numbered. Byelaws also specified the fares, one shilling minimum and two shillings per hour. Drivers were exhorted to be sober and not to smoke. Complaints of insolence and extortion echoed down the years. The drivers in most cases did not own their cabs, and hoped to make up their money by

CABBY

overcharging, hiding their number plates under the seat in case of complaints. The Mayor said that in 1866 there had been 20 cases of overcharging in journeys made from the Royal Pavilion and several families testified that two or three times the legal fare was commonly charged, any demur being met with a torrent of abuse. In the same year William Bird and three ladies hired William Hammond's cab. Hammond was drunk and drove the wrong way, swearing at his passengers. The ladies left the court so that the obscene language could be repeated. A constable was called and Hammond kicked him in the shins. The judge declared that Folkestone was notorious for its bad cab drivers, often not the regulars but saucy men hired for the season.

Sites for cab stands were also regulated at the harbour and railway station, on the Leas and several residential streets. These too were a cause of complaint among residents because of the smell and bad language. But one may spare a thought for the unfortunate drivers, patiently waiting outside in all weathers, protected only by a rain shield and large black hood. A fund was opened in 1900 to provide a shelter outside the Cheriton Arch station and the men themselves agreed to light it.

Horse welfare was not forgotten. Owners could be prosecuted if horses were ill or cruelly treated, often on the initiative of the Society for the Prevention of Cruelty to Animals. One horse had a tight collar causing discomfort and another had influenza. Both were unfit to be driven and the owners were fined 10 shillings each. Horses had to be under proper control, unless munching peacefully in their nosebags. Shopkeepers would often send a driver to make deliveries and the animal would be left unattended in the roadway. One horse was making its own way back to the stable: the driver, found in the taproom of 'The Swan' said only: *"I dare say the old mare got home all right"*.

The Corporation did not have a very good record on employment, chiefly because of the low wages paid, 4 pence an hour instead of the 4 1/2 pence usual in private employment. Their men were engaged in laying drains, paving the streets and watering them in dry weather. Some jobs, such as rubbish collecting, were initially under contract to private scavengers. Several men amongst the carriers requested an extra halfpenny an hour. One, accused of being the author of a round robin, was dismissed in spite of his ten years service together with four others whose names were on the list. This built up into a full scale row and Councillor Logan went to consult Tom Burns M.P. The Corporation's defence was that the men were dismissed because there was no work for them, whereas one man's cart was already being used by someone else. In the end the men were reinstated.

Till 1898 and the Workmen's Compensation Act there was no redress for injuries due to accidents at work. Folkestone Herald readers were asked to subscribe for a man named Wessell whose arm had been amputated by the lift. The Company had done what it could but it was not sufficient to support him. Reduced payments of wages might be made in cases of illness. The Council agreed to pay a man fifteen shillings instead of twenty five shillings till he had recovered from bronchitis. There were no pensions and the elderly who had not provided for themselves could be given a small dole from the poor rates or go into the Union workhouse, though pride prevented many from requesting assistance. Some of the more active elderly became crossing sweepers. They touched their caps rather than soliciting tips but, when the crossings were paved, there were complaints that this was becoming a nuisance. Children, if in good circumstances, were expected to contribute to the

COUNCIL WORKMEN BUILDING THE PROMENADE, 1905

support of their parents. John Pope aged 84 had four sons, one a pleasure boat proprietor, one a hall porter and one a captain in the Merchant Navy. His relief had been disallowed and it preyed on his mind. He crawled to the window and fell out: *"Speak to the Mayor"* were his last words.

Life as a shop assistant varied from those working in the cheap shops at the East end of the town to the large, elegant and brightly lit emporia stocking the latest Paris fashions, bonnets, fancy work and gents' suits in the High Street and Sandgate Road. Unmarried assistants often lived with their employers and had very little freedom. Hours were long and a twelve or fourteen hour day was normal. In 1863 an 'early' closing hour of 5pm once weekly was suggested for drapers and grocers. After the Shop Hours Regulation Act of 1873 this was reduced to 2pm The Chronicle felt this to be a retrograde step. *"Our streets will be filled with fast young people, the spirit of idleness will be encouraged and in later life the assistants will look back upon what they now regard as a boon, as a decided injury."* The young people looked forward to a delightful free afternoon walking, and later cycling, in the countryside with perhaps Bible or singing classes in the evenings. Folkestone was the workplace of the most famous fictional shop assistant in all Britain, George Arthur Kipps. H.G. Wells, his creator, had worked in the Southsea Drapery Emporium and well knew the frustrations and pettiness encountered by a lad of spirit. He wrote the book in 1905 while he was living at Spade House in Sandgate. The indentures he described are identical to those of Frances Annie Underwood who bound herself apprentice to learn drapery to Messrs. Plummer Roddis and Beecroft in 1892.

"The indentures that bound Kipps to Mr. Shalford were antique and complex; they

made him over, body and soul, to Mr. Shalford for seven long years, the crucial years of his life. In return there were vague stipulations about teaching the whole art and mystery of the trade to him but as there was no penalty attached to negligence, Mr. Shalford being a sound practical business man, considered this a mere rhetorical flourish, and set himself assiduously to get as much out of Kipps and to put into him as little as he could in the seven years of their

SHOP ASSISTANT, PUNCH

intercourse. What he put into Kipps was chiefly bread and margarine, infusions of chicory and tea-dust, colonial meat by contract at three pence a pound, potatoes by the sack and watered beer. He was also allowed to share a bedroom with eight other young men and to sleep in a bed which, except in very severe weather, could be made with his overcoat and private undergarments, not to mention newspapers, quite sufficiently warm for any reasonable soul."

Apprenticeship could be a useful way of teaching young people a trade or it could be, as when Oliver Twist was bound from the poorhouse, an excuse for minimal wages and poor conditions. Lewis & Hyland were prosecuted in 1890 for working three young women beyond the permitted hours of 8am to 9pm. Agreements were enforceable by law. William Bromley, bound to Newmans the builders for six years, was taken to court for absconding. He was receiving ten shillings a week in wages and had to find his own tools. On the credit side the large firms usually had an annual day out for their workers. In July 1898 Lewis & Hyland took their thirty tailors by train to Ashford, then in charabancs drawn by four spanking horses to Biddenden and a good time was had by all. Other jobs for young people were as fisher boys on the boats, generally an occupation which ran in the family. There were the ubiquitous errand boys, some of whom were noticed in Pleydell Gardens, exchanging the packages and tasting the eatables, carefully rewrapping them afterwards. Others were seen reading such horrific publications as 'The Dashing Highwayman' or 'The Pirates of the Deep' in which vice and thieving were associated with romantic daring, seeds of wrongdoing sure to bear full fruit in the prisoner's dock. The butchers' boys were renowned for driving their gaily painted carts through the streets to the alarm of the inhabitants.

Employments open to women were more limited. For gentlewomen, opportunities were few. Most went to work as governesses or music teachers, conditions depending very much on the family with whom they lived. Belonging neither to the gentry nor the servant class, they could find themselves either as an honoured friend of the family or an overworked drudge, in charge of a large household of fractious children with spare time spent in mending clothes. Wages were poor, £10 per annum as against £25 expected by a good cook and there could be as many as a dozen applicants for each place. Intelligent and determined working class girls could rise to teacher's posts via the pupil teacher system and, with the aid of grants, go to teacher's training college and gain their certificate. By far the largest category was that of domestic service, from skilled cooks, ladies' maids, parlour maids to chars, laundresses and maids-of-all-work. The latter were often employed for a pittance by families far down the social scale. Jobs were found through newspaper advertisements:

GOVERNESS

> Groom wants place in gentleman's family. No objection to looking after a cow.
> (Folkestone Chronicle July 29th 1865).

> Lady wishes to recommend ladies' maid, no objection to travelling. She does not profess hair dressing, but can get up fine washing and light dishes. Wages £14.
> (Folkestone Chronicle July 28th 1860).

> Plain cook as general, no washing abstainer. Small house, no family. Wages £18.
> (Folkestone Chronicle November 1st 1890).

The advertisements for the better paid and more skilled jobs were in for a week only, indicating a satisfied client. Those for general maids would often run for a month. Working in the basement kitchen of a lodging house, often infested with cockroaches, involved trips to answer the bell, coals and hot water to be carried up to the lodgers' bedrooms, blackleading the grate and scrubbing the front doorstep. In 1883 the Folkestone Society for Friendless Girls at 4 Westcliff Gardens provided a registry office for jobs and a place to stay while out of work. By the 1890s there were also registry offices at Grace Hill and 33 Guildhall Street. Ladies who could train competent servants were considered to be doing more good than if they distributed hundreds of tracts amongst the poor. But employers felt the incompetent were more frequently

DOMESTIC STAFF, FOLKESTONE HOUSE

encountered. *"Who is sufficient to describe the sulkings, skulkings, gossipings, impertinences, holidayings, sly scribblings and Sunday evening dodgings of so many of our modern educated Mary Annes?"*

(Folkestone Chronicle October 4th 1884).

A small vignette of domestic life is provided by the case against Captain Wale, R.N., brought by his maid, Lucy Fellows, claiming wages in lieu of notice. She had refused to attend family prayers, sulking because she had been spoken to about her chemise in front of a young man. The Captain marched into the kitchen to find her boiling a large saucepan of clothes on the range. ("An indecent and nasty habit," interjected the judge). Her mouth full of bread and cheese, she refused to stand up on his arrival, so he promptly sacked her. *"A man must be master in his own house,"* he explained but would not agree that a record of eleven cooks in eleven months indicated excessive strictness. A year later Mrs Wale was in trouble, having employed a wet nurse who proved to have an insufficient supply of milk, and attacked her, calling her a murderess and impostor. Such scenes were, fortunately, rare.

A more independent source of jobs arose from the steam laundries in Cheriton, mainly established to deal with the linen of the growing number of hotels and lodging houses. Independent laundresses were gradually becoming superseded. The work was heavy, hot and steamy, but once it was over the girls were free – perhaps too free as in 1884 a block of cottages was built in connection with the Broadmead Mission for the girls of Mr Foster's steam laundry exposed to the temptations of Cheriton. There was a complaint that the homes were not cheerful and the girls sermonised over too much.

The oldest profession was indeed doing well, Folkestone and Sandgate between them having both a barracks and a port. There was a well-known brothel in Dover Street where the owner brought an action for breaking and entering against two soldiers who had spent a night with her girls. There was the sad case of Elizabeth Hart aged fifteen, found sheltering in an outhouse. Her father was a railway porter and her mother had left home eleven years before. Her bed was in the bushes near Military Hill where she regularly slept with the soldiers from Shorncliffe.

There was a refuge in Sandgate at Compton House where the girls could be housed and found work. The Matron, Mrs Jones, dealt with 42 girls and was instrumental in good works, persuading one to leave a local beerhouse, arranging the marriage of another and reuniting one with her soldier husband; she had lapsed into her old sinful life while he was away on foreign service. In all 31 were rescued though some had to be treated in reformatories or at the Lock hospital in Shorncliffe.

Tramps and beggars came into the category of the undeserving poor. Seven days hard labour was the usual penalty for begging. From the 1870s onwards the flood of such persons increased and became a positive nuisance following a nationwide trend. Between 1866 and 1871 the number of vagrants went up from 77,000 to 172,000 as the unions became lodgings for men looking for seasonal work. They had a hard bed, oakum to pick or stones to break and a breakfast of bread and hot water. There was difficulty in sending a tramp, footsore, hungry and penniless all the way to the poorhouse at Etchinghill. The police had no funds for food but provided shelter in cells set aside for the purpose in the Sessions Hall in the High Street These were grossly overcrowded and seventeen tramps were crowded into one cell.

It was felt to be a grievance that Folkestone, although it provided nearly half the poor rates and half of the inmates of the poorhouse, had only two representatives on the Elham Union Board of Guardians. The tramps' ward also was grossly overcrowded and at times they had to sleep in the stables where the hearse was kept in one corner, a scandal exposed in the national newspapers.

A Folkestone branch of the Kent Mendicity Society was founded in 1871 with bread tickets to distribute instead of money which could be spent on drink. It was not unknown to find the bread tickets torn up and scattered on the Leas. There was also a Travellers' Rest on Grace Hill where the men could have a cup of coffee and something to eat.

OLD POORHOUSE BEFORE 1836

The deserving poor were mostly the elderly whose conditions in the Union gradually improved over the years. They had at first been deprived of many little comforts, sitting on backless benches and not allowed visitors, books or newspapers. Gradually more privileges were provided together with tea for women and tobacco for the men. Going outside the walls needed special permission, in case the old men found their way to the nearest pub; it was felt that drink had brought them there in the first place. Private rooms were not provided for married couples until the end of the century. Finally the old ladies were freed from their uniform of black coal scuttle bonnets and shawls. In 1888 cottage homes were provided for the children, releasing them from the taint of pauperism.

A TRAMP LEAVING ELHAM WORKHOUSE

According to the strict letter of the Poor Law Reform Act of 1834, there should have been no more outdoor relief, as any family in distress had to give up all their goods and enter the workhouse. This provision proved in practice to be uneconomic and unworkable even in the early days. In November 1835, there were ninety people a week on relief, fifty-one from Folkestone and Cheriton. Sums given varied from one shilling and sixpence to five shilliings a week.

It was generally expected that men in work should make their own provision against hard times. There was a burial society and in 1863 the Folkestone Savings Bank had £6,000 on deposit from 888 investors. The Friendly Societies were strong in the town; in May 1876, there was an expedition to Boulogne which filled four boats, with members of the Oddfellows, the Foresters, the Druids, the Prussian Hermits and the Good

OLD LADIES, ELHAM WORKHOUSE

Templars wearing the scarves and collars of their orders. As well as help in sickness and unemployment and the provision of a doctor for their members, the Societies had a social aspect *"to afford to the industrial classes the means of social intercourse, mutual helpfulness and to provide refreshments and rational recreation"*. (Folkestone Chronicle December 16th 1876, meeting at the Foresters Arms.) Dickens described a pleasant picnic on the downs. But there were times during the winter when self help was not enough, poor law aid was not forthcoming or not sought and private charity might have to fill the gap.

Those affected were mostly builders out of work during a cold winter, who could number up to a hundred, and of course their families were also affected. At such times the labourers were described as tramping the streets in vain looking for work, while their hungry families crowded round the scanty fire and the children cried for food. *"Old, careworn, drooping and emaciated creatures pass us by without even lifting their eyes from the ground."* (Folkestone Chronicle December 16th 1871). One of the most popular and long lasting charities was the soup kitchen on the Bayle, whose accounts date back to 1821, and money was regularly collected for this purpose. *"Who is there who has not had his eyes gladdened by the beaming smiles of the hungry little ones as they trudge down the street with all kinds of describable and indescribable utensils full of steaming hot soup?"* (Folkestone Chronicle December 11th 1869). The spirit of independence was preserved as it had to be paid for at a penny a quart. Rev. Burridge in his poor parish of St. Michaels provided forty hot dinners three days a week in 1870.

There were dinners served at the Congregational Schools in Tontine Street in the 1890s. In addition there was often a special appeal from the Mayor at a Town Hall meeting to collect money for coal, food, warm clothing, and sometimes appeals for the poor elsewhere, such as the cotton operatives in Lancashire and Cheshire badly affected by the American Civil War. Some workmen were about to enter the Town Hall and were waved away by the Town Sergeant in his loftiest manner, observing: *"We are about to relieve the poor".* It was suggested at the meeting that the Radnor Estate might like to have the Undercliff path made up to assist employment. This was refused but Lord Radnor sent a personal donation of £25 and Baron Rothschild contributed £200, amounting to two shillings per head for the needy, as an ungrateful recipient observed.

Handouts were all very well but a more structured and long term means of assistance was needed, particularly for those who dreaded the poorhouse. There were the Church of England district visitors who could supply coal and food and also collect savings. They divided the poor areas into thirteen districts and each street - such as Fancy Street, Mill Bay, Caroline Terrace, the Narrows, New Zealand and Saffrons Row - had its lady visitor who knew the circumstances of each family. It was said however they could be imposed on by old stagers in the art of living on charity, who stood more chance of being considered favourable cases than the independent man who considered his house his castle. The Folkestone Charitable Organisation was founded in 1885 and a diary in the Library records the particulars of those seeking relief in 1885-6. Some claimants were outside the scope of the Society and were recommended to apply to the relieving officer or to enter the workhouse. Such were poor old Tom Cockett, the former Town Crier, living at 49 Rose Cottages, Foord, a disreputable drunkard and a nuisance to his neighbours, and William Sherwood and his wife living at 6 Mill Bay, he a drunkard and she totally depraved. Relief was given to the deserving - Mrs Cuffley of 23 Grace Hill with six children to feed and household goods in pawn but her house was clean. John Flower, aged nineteen, was unable to work through illness and lived with his brother, a labourer at the cement works on eighteen shillings a week. He was given four shillings a week. James Ward of 4 Nelson Place had only partial work, a sick wife and four children. He lived in wretched quarters and everything was pawned. John Rutland, a cab driver, employed by William Peden of the Pavilion Shades, had subscribed to the Prussian Hermits for fourteen years. He met with an accident and found that the club had gone bankrupt. Mrs Catherine Reed, aged seventy-two, lived with her daughter who had eight children and a husband earning eighteen shillings a week on the roads. Help was small - a few shillings a week, the redemption of the family boots or a workman's coat from the pawn shop, the purchase of a hawker's licence - but advice and regular visiting helped many just to keep their heads above water.

For those hardy souls who could stand the distance, the separation and the journey, there was still the chance of a new life in the colonies. Before the Poor Law Amendment Act parish funds could be used to pay for tickets for families who would otherwise be a charge on the rates. In 1835 two Cheriton families went to Upper Canada, one with six children and an unemployed father. There was a bachelor also who had contracted idle habits. A year later Folkestone sent six adults and five boys. In 1879 there was an advertisement for farm labourers and domestic servants in New Zealand, the category of working people who had the worst wages at home. They were offered free passage and bedding on the ship and £20 - £40 a year on arrival.

There does not seem to have been much resort to strikes as a means of gaining higher wages. The only large scale strike recorded during this period was that of the carpenters and joiners in 1866, who asked for sixpence a day more because of the high price of food. The masters threatened to bring in workers from outside and the men met incoming trains in order to dissuade others from taking their places. A

EMIGRANTS' FAREWELL

subscription list was opened in Dover for their support. The Amalgamated Society of Carpenters and Joiners must have had a militant reputation as in 1876 it had to be denied that the purpose of the Association was solely to foment strikes; it also provided sickness benefits and a superannuation fund. There was a Folkestone branch of the Agricultural Labourers Association which met in the same year and in 1884 the walls were placarded with invitations to join the union. Exhibitions are notoriously strike-prone; in 1886 John Sims was trying to get the men working on the National Art Treasures Exhibition building to strike but without success. He applied to the Charitable Organisation for relief and was refused, not because he was a striker but because he was living with a woman who was not his wife.

However, the last decade of the century did see a marked increase in the growth of radicalism. Councillors Logan, Payer and Jones, all coming from the East end of the town, were elected to the Council as Radicals. In Folkestone-up-to-Date, Logan promised to fight injustices such as distraints for rent, servants' boxes being kept back until they paid out money in lieu of notice and distress levied on bath chairs worth £25 for a rent of two shillings left unpaid. The paper ran for a few months in this vein, attacking the Council and the Radnor Estate, claiming a readership of five thousand. Although the advertisements were at first exclusively for Logan's outfitting - tailoring, boots and shoes and hats - other advertisements started to appear and the political tone changed, becoming fairly mild and more like the other papers. From 1893 the Municipal Reform League was holding weekly meetings at the Tontine Street Assembly Rooms and demanding: trade union rates for council workers (now five pence an hour); the use of English rather than German bands; compulsory purchase of land for allotments; the electricity and water undertakings to be purchased by the Council, and the development of the East end of the town. Councillor Jones stood as Labour candidate in the 1894 parliamentary election and made a rousing speech:

> *"The interests of the poor working man is better served by one as*
> *poor as themselves, not by a purse proud and satisfied politician,*
> *his wealth enabling him to subscribe to church and chapel and*
> *to football clubs. Such have never known what a hard day's work*
> *is and their life has not been an endless struggle of toil and anxiety."*
> (Folkestone-Up-To-Date. August 12th 1894).

Another fiercely debated topic was that of housing for artisan families. The pressure on housing and shortage of small houses to rent was in part a measure of the town's success in attracting new employment. Expectations of what constituted acceptable housing was also rising. Since the Folkestone Improvement Act of 1855 there were more powers to deal with unsatisfactory housing and Superintendent Martin of the police force was appointed the first Inspector of Nuisances. There was also a Building Inspector with powers to enforce proper standards for drains, roofs, water closets and thickness of walls for new buildings. Plans for new buildings had to be submitted and houses under construction were inspected. Action could also be taken against overcrowding. George Major was brought to court in 1877 for living with his wife and seven children in a shed formerly used as a fowl house and measuring 12'6" x 11'. He was fined 10 shillings a day and it would be surprising if he had paid, as no alternative accommodation could be found.

There was a shortage of houses in the East end of the town and the Radnor Estate was fiercely attacked for asking £1,000 an acre for building land. It was eventually reduced to £700 because of the protests. The Artisans' Dwellings Act, a measure passed by Disraeli's government, gave councils the power to borrow money at 3% in order to erect working class dwellings. They were also given the power to pull down unsanitary cottages, such as those in the Narrows, a well known slum area, described by the Lancet in April 1875:

> "They are two storey buildings of brick and stone, drained and supplied
> with town water. They have closets, about one to every six houses.
> The courtyards are paved with brick and are filthily dirty, the gutters
> are full of refuse. The interiors seem unsavoury. They are inhabited by
> the lowest class of population, chiefly Irish, and the bad condition of
> the quarter depends more on the class of people who inhabit it than
> the buildings themselves."

Typical inhabitants were Mrs Madden, a hawker and her daughter, who had not been considered for assistance because of the dirt. She did eventually make an effort to clean things up. At No. 9 were Mr and Mrs Owen, a decent couple paying four shillings and sixpence a week rent. He did odd jobs at the pier and fishmarket.

It was levels of rent that caused difficulties in council housing. Aldermen Banks and Sherwood - both of whom as owners and agents had many small houses on their books at three shillings and sixpence. and four shillings and sixpence a week, though conditions were often unsatisfactory - were eloquent in the Council chamber as to the impracticability of the new houses. Forty of these, let at rents of ten shillings a week, had been put up in Penfold Road by 1897. These rents could only be paid by the superior class of artisan, or the houses had to be sublet and the overcrowding started again. The question was partly solved by the development of the Shaftesbury estate and the growth in the suburb of Cheriton. Land, and hence rents, were cheaper and some agreeable streets of small houses were erected.

The lower classes needed intellectual stimulus. The Working Men's Educational Association was founded in 1850 and the Sandgate Literary Institute in 1855. These provided access to books and lectures. Women were admitted to the Folkestone Society, which in 1855 had 400 members and some marriages followed. Lectures were held in the Guildhall, the National Schools and in the premises of the Harveian Institute, the old wooden theatre on the Bayle. The Harveian had at first a more upper class

THE NARROWS

membership, but was a similar cultural association. Charles Dickens read extracts from 'A Christmas Carol' on October 5th 1855, in a carpenter's shop on the Dover Road, a function to which the working men were admitted at the special price of three pence. The Harveian had an annual dinner and a reading room but suffered from declining membership in the 1870s, the premises falling so low as to be used as an auction room for unredeemed pledges left at the pawnbrokers. It revived, with an increased salary for the secretary, to be opened as the Folkestone Free Library in 1878 and served as such with the provision of daily newspapers till the opening of the Public Library in 1866.

But the favoured place of recreation for the working man was the pub. In 1847 41 licences had been granted in Folkestone, which rose to 85 by 1855. Sandgate was considered to be almost swimming in beer - with the many beershops which served the soldiers from the Camp - and their influence on its moral character was notorious. But on the whole the pubs were peaceably conducted and could lose their licences if they were not.

Some family men spent more on drink than they could afford, and it was considered essential to provide them with places of refreshment that did not serve alcohol, such as the Edinburgh Castle coffee house on the Stade, formerly the North Foreland pub. The Rev. Edward Husband ran a club for working boys with gymnasium and billiard table to keep them out of mischief. But some earnest souls went further and sought powers to close pubs altogether on Sundays and, in line with the Permissive Bill before Parliament in 1872, to close many altogether if two thirds of the ratepayers voted against them. A dignified and sensible comment came from a working man employed by the South Eastern Railway Company:

> "The working man does not care to be lectured to, preached and scolded as if he were different flesh from other mortals. Grimy with dirt, I come home. I have a good sousing with water, my tea and my pipe afterwards. Then comes bedtime for the children and my wife's company. This becomes rather flat after a while, and I think she would rather have a chat with her neighbours while she does the mending.

> "No one respects the parsons more than I do, but they are always moralising at us. Don't Sir Edward Watkin and the parsons enjoy going out to dinner, a glass of wine and a good cigar? If it is not wrong for the gentlemen of the Radnor Club to drink the high priced liquors at their place, it cannot be wrong for the working

man to have a drink at his club. Oh! that those above us who so earnestly lecture to us and talk about us, would recognise us as men of like passions to themselves. They like a smoke, so do we. They like a dance two or three times a year; I have my shilling hop at the Town Hall. They don't like doses of tea and coffee mixed with perpetual advice, and sometimes they think to leave the company of wife and fretful children for the pleasant company of their fellow men – only they have spacious apartments upstairs to fly to and I like a little recreation in preference to remaining all evening in my crowded dwelling".

(Folkestone Chronicle. November 25th 1876)

15

Oh! I DO LIKE TO BE BESIDE THE SEASIDE

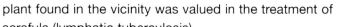

FrHe mid-eighteenth century up to the great explosion of holiday traffic from the 1850s onwards, a trip to the seaside, which had now taken over from the spas, was valued as much for promoting good health as for holiday making. Treatises, such as Dr. Russell's published in 1752 - A Dissertation on the Use of Seawater in the Diseases of the Glands, particularly the Scurvy, King's Evil, Leprosy and the Glandular Consumption - advocated sea-bathing and even the daily drinking of sea water. Sandgate was an earlier resort than Folkestone, having a genteel company from the officers at Shornecliff Camp and a good position below the cliff, sheltered from sea breezes. A small marine

plant found in the vicinity was valued in the treatment of scrofula (lymphatic tuberculosis).

"This is a pretty little village, exactly halfway between Folkestone and Hythe which has suddenly started into notice...lodgings may be obtained here on reasonable terms and of late there have been erected some very good houses."
(Guide to all the Watering and Seabathing Places, 1806).

The great actress Mrs. Siddons came to Sandgate for the bathing in 1790, finding 'little neat lodgings and good wholesome provisions' and William Wilberforce spent some family holidays there. A visitor suggested:

THE SANDGATE NYMPH

"What opportunities are here. The town can boast the most clean,
safe and best calculated shores for that purpose in the kingdom.
Have you no public spirited moneyed men to forward so likely a
scheme to benefit the town and its environs by expending a little
on buildings and other necessary accommodation?"

A sailor replied, *"Moneyed men, oh yes Sir! Many, some worth twenty or thirty*
thousand; we have men of spirit too but, as the devil would have it,
they are two distinct beings with us. The money has gone into one
and the spirit into another so that we and our bathing scheme may
go to the D. for what the money'd care."

This story may be apocryphal, but the writer obviously considered it a charitable duty for men of means to build Assembly Rooms, to promote baths and circulating libraries, since this would ensure prosperity and employment for one's native town. The same idea is found in Jane Austen's 'Sanditon'. Folkestone did not have the advantage of cheap steamboat communication with London, as did Gravesend, Herne Bay, Margate and Ramsgate. From 1814 - when the first steam yacht, the 'Thames', arrived in Margate Harbour - such boats brought in swarms of London passengers. However, the crowds and cheap fares meant these resorts were destined to be patronised almost exclusively by the lower and lower-middle classes.

THE CHERRY GARDEN RESERVOIR

In the old town amusements were simple and infrequent. Tiffen's Guide of 1816 mentions a cottage half hidden among fruit trees called the Cherry Garden where refreshments were served and young people on fine evenings enjoyed a sprightly dance upon the turf. Badger baiting took place in the vicinity (where now the reservoirs of the Folkestone Water Company are situated). A popular story was that, during the Napoleonic Wars, a press gang advertised the sport and captured the participants for service in the navy.

There was a wooden theatre on the Bayle opened in 1774, having boxes, a gallery approached by a steep ladder and backless wooden benches in the pit. It was used by the company of Mrs Sarah Baker who ran several other theatres. In 1775 she presented 'Miss in her Teens', 'Cupid's Revenge' and 'The Beggar's Opera'. John Jonas and Sampson Penley applied for licences for theatrical performances in 1804/5; Penley's company acted also in Tenterden and Lewes. In 1825 B. Rooke presented 'Venice Preserved'. The old theatre was described by Dickens in a way which recalls his account of the Crummles family:

> *"I went at night to the benefit of Mrs. B. Wedgington at the theatre*
> *who had placarded the town with the admonition, 'DONT FORGET IT!'*
> *I made the house, according to my calculation, four and ninepence*
> *to begin with, and it may have warmed up, in the course of the evening,*
> *to half a sovereign. There was nothing to offend anyone – the good*
> *Mr. Baines of Leeds excepted. Mrs. B. Wedgington sang to a grand piano.*
> *Mr. B. Wedgington did the like, and also took off his coat, tucked up his*
> *trousers and danced in clogs. Master B. Wedgington, aged ten months,*
> *was nursed by a shivering young person in the boxes and the eye of*
> *Mrs. B. Wedgington wandered that way more than once. Peace be with*
> *all the Wedgingtons from A to Z. May they find themselves in the season*
> *somewhere."*

While the railway was being built the theatre was used by the Rev. Thomas Pearce as a chapel for the navvies. Theatrical performances were revived in 1859 with the visit of the Grand Opera Company performing Italian opera, but it was not well advertised and the company played to almost empty houses. After this the building was used for educational lectures.

For visitors, the activity above all else which is proper to the seaside is that of bathing, whether for health or recreation. Unlike walking, riding or listening to the band,

A BATHER, PUNCH

bathing for the Victorians could be morally dangerous, the garments worn being less voluminous and more revealing of the figure than was customary. For the sake of decency, regulations had to be made, the sexes kept separate and a certain amount of concealment was necessary. Bathing machines were the solution. First used in Scarborough in the 1730s, they were cold, wet, draughty cabins with canvas or wooden hoods, to be wheeled down to the water's edge; thereafter, a flight of steps allowed the bather to descend with comparative privacy into the water. Even this protection was not enough; the Folkestone byelaws of 1851 decreed that no person should approach within 100 yards of any machine in a boat and no machine used by a female was to be within 20 yards of that used by a male. In 1865 it was noticed that:

> "snobs and blackguards poke about amongst ladies' bathing machines. They go in as close as they can and stand there glaring at the women with newspapers in their hands on the pretence of reading while they are gloating over the often half-exposed forms of the bathers."
> (Folkestone Chronicle, September 2nd, 1865).

By 1857 in Sandgate William Henry Willis had licences for 11 machines from the Council and James Taylor 5. Willis had 15, in 1860, and 27 in 1865, the maximum number until they passed into the control of the Bathing Establishment in 1869. A notable improvement in machine design was the invention of Walter Fagg, who displayed a model at the Bathing Establishment, where he was manager. Twin carriages ran on rails across the beach, with basins and room for 15 cabins on each side and a corridor down the middle. At the end was a diving board and an area caged in for safety. It cost £250 and was drawn up by 12 men working windlasses. A suggestions book reported approving comments: *"Great improvement"*, *"Fagg, thy fortune's made"*, *"Ripping idea, takes the cake"*. By the 1890s tents were taking the place of machines. Hire of machines cost sixpence for half-an-hour, towels provided. This was a sum beyond the reach of the working classes who would swim before 8am without the use of machines. Surprisingly, before that time there was no power to compel the wearing of costumes. Many were the complaints of a sad lack of decency, especially from early-rising inhabitants of Marine Parade and long-sighted ladies walking to early service along the Leas. Amongst the fisherfolk, bathing was known as 'pulling-off' and the dialogue would run as follows;-

"Hallo! Where you bin, Bob?"
"Pullin'-off down the 'shene (machine) beach."

In 1871 the Mayor suggested that bathers might rent drawers for a halfpenny as they did at Hastings, but the Town Clerk replied that there was no power to compel this. There were also complaints during the 1890s of the attenuated nature of men's costumes, as being no more than a pocket handkerchief. During the early morning period the Council provided a man and a boat for safety, after which the responsibility passed to the Bathing Establishment which controlled the beach and its amenities.

For those who could not face the cold waters of the Channel, hot and cold seawater baths were a necessity, as in other resorts. Ramsgate had the splendid marble Isabella Baths, built in 1816 after the pattern of the warm baths of Naples, and Margate the spacious Clifton Baths built in the 1820s. Folkestone had three small sets of baths in the 1860s: Mr Willis's, some in Beach Street and some at the Pavilion Hotel. There had been rumours of a large-scale bath enterprise for some time and its expected profitability.

The minutes of the Bathing Establishment provide an interesting example of the 'money'd men' providing a local amenity, with somewhat indifferent success, which later would be felt to be the duty and risk of the municipality Shares were priced at £100 each, a large sum. The 38 original backers included the cream of the tradespeople: John Fitness, grocer, Mayor 1877; John Holden, plumber, twice Mayor; John Sherwood, grocer and estate agent, four times Mayor; John Gambrill, who farmed Park Farm; Dr Bateman, Medical Officer of Health, twice Mayor; William Henry Willis, former bath and machine owner who was compensated for his machines on surrendering them to the Establishment. Joseph Gardner, who took two shares, was appointed architect to

THE BATHING ESTABLISHMENT 1868

the enterprise and was also to oversee the engineering portion, for which specialist assistance was needed. The builders were Messrs. Holden & Powell. The old Earl and Viscount Folkestone, after a little persuasion, took two shares each. It was envisaged that £4,000 could be raised on shares, a further £3,000 on mortgage, but the sums raised were never enough and the enterprise remained undercapitalised. Further investment in the baths would have been desirable, but dividends were low or nonexistent and not all the existing shares had been taken up. Lord Radnor had to be asked to reduce the mortgage rate by 1% in 1876.

However, at the outset, all was optimism and Julius Thompson was appointed manager. The building was going ahead, with six dozen iron chairs and four settees being sent from Paris. A concert was arranged with the Glee Club of Magdalen College, Oxford, and two page boys were hired, to be dressed in jackets with silver buttons and silver cord down their trousers. The crowds were out on the opening day, September 8th, 1868. In his opening speech the Lord Chief Baron of the Exchequer, Sir Percy Kelly, said he remembered when there were not six houses between the Town Hall and Sandgate. The imposing red brick building was cut into the front of the cliff. There was a large plunge bath, 178 feet by 98 feet, on the ground floor; the first floor had small private baths and the next floor a large saloon for concerts or balls, a reading room and a billiards room. Though opened at the end of the season, it was the idea of the Directors to make it a year-round centre or club, the main income coming from subscriptions. There were to be balls, flower shows and concerts during the summer. Yet it lacked support, especially in the winter:

> *"Empty chairs and uncut papers stare one reproachfully in the face.*
> *The billiard room is the scene, night after night, of an exciting contest*
> *between the purveyor of refreshments, which no one is there to partake*
> *of, and the boy in buttons, who has seldom any play but his own to mark."*
> (Folkestone Chronicle, March 22nd, 1873.)

Water heating was expensive and wet weather reduced the profit on the machines. In the 1870s although there were surpluses over expenses as high as £130 per week in the short season, this was not enough to pay the interest on the mortgage. Page boy Rawlinson was dismissed. In 1878 the manager's accounts were in confusion. He wrote to the Directors: *"I cannot possibly meet you this evening, as I have got into disgrace in the town and cannot show my face again."* He also was dismissed.

The salvation of the Bathing Establishment was to be the lift. The first plan, made at the beginning of January 1875, was to build a pier and lift together. Councillors were in favour of the scheme, though it was pointed out that, from the pier, bathers would actually be seen in the water. The project was slow to take off, partly because the Establishment's lack of success had made investors wary. Eventually the combined scheme was shelved in favour of the lift alone, a much less expensive undertaking. It was to run on a simple and ingenious principle: the weight of a carriage, plus passengers and water ballast descending from the top of the cliff, would pull up a carriage with passengers from the bottom.

The Folkestone Lift Company raised £3,000 in £5 shares. Promoters included John Sherwood and the two prominent hotel keepers, Mr Wedderburn and Mr Hart; a lease of the land was obtained from Lord Radnor in September 1885. The carriages ran on rails secured into the cliff by timber baulks set in concrete. At the lower end there was a waiting room and ticket office, tickets costing one penny. The lift was used for Regatta Day and formally opened to the public on September 21st, 1885. To the relief of investors the enterprise, which had cost £3,244, proved an immediate success. At the end of the first financial year a 15% dividend could be paid. Queues formed at busy times and a second lift was installed by the side of the first in 1890. Reginald Pope was the architect, Messrs. Waygood of Southwark, the engineers, whilst it was

THE LEAS LIFT 1885

built by Newmans, a local firm. A pumping engine saved water and avoided delays due to the inability of the Water Company to deliver a constant supply.

A third lift was to be built at Sandgate, where the Folkestone, Hythe and Sandgate Tramway Company had contemplated a long lift up to Shorncliffe, but had abandoned the idea. This lift - under the same management as the Folkestone lifts, though a separate company - ran from the top of the Leas over the footpath that was to become Radnor Cliff Crescent. Opened in February 1893, the lift had a substantial waiting room and ticket office facing Sandgate Hill. Since it was at the wrong end of the town for the crowds and motor buses were soon to run up Sandgate Hill, it was never a financial success. The Metropole lift of 1905 owed its existence to the new popularity of the western end of the Leas and the two large hotels. There were too many lifts for the resort to support as its fortunes waned. Ultimately only the 1885 lift remained, under the control of the Council, but that, too, closed in 2009.

The success of the lift had been an encouragement to the pier enthusiasts. The 1886 prospectus envisaged year-round usage, with a projected tramway from Hythe passing the gates. Military bands and balls would bring in revenue, as would entrance tickets, chair hire and advertisements. An 8% dividend was hoped for but costs at £28,000 were on a different scale to those of the lift. In May, 1887, the foundations of the Victoria Pier were laid, the builders being Messrs. Heenan and Froude. Mr Ridley, the engineer, had worked with Eugenius Birch who had designed piers at Hastings, Brighton, Blackpool and Bournemouth. The pier - opened by Viscountess Folkestone on July 21st, 1888 - was 700 feet long and 30 feet wide. It had a pavilion for entertainments with room for 700 people and two elegant bazaars at the shore

THE FOLKESTONE PIER 1887

end. There were bands, concerts and plays such as 'East Lynne' and 'Oliver Twist', but these were expensive to put on. Again, as with the Bathing Establishment, investors were in for a disappointment.

The pier made a pleasant promenade for a fine day. There would be ladies holding on to their large hats and fluttering skirts for dear life and small children clamouring for pennies to put in the slot machines, but receipts were seasonal. Not till 1891 was a dividend proclaimed, and then it was only 1%. When in 1893 Keith Prowse took over, entertainments included the D'Oyley Carte opera company in Gilbert and Sullivan; events were better attended, though the entry price rose from one penny to twopence. The switchback railway, also built in 1888, was a popular attraction in the 1890s but finally succumbed to repeated storm damage. At the beginning of World War II the pier was partly demolished, the remains being destroyed by fire in 1945.

There were pleasure boats to be hired at one shilling and sixpence an hour and sailing boats at sixpence per person per trip. An important day for fishermen and

yachtsmen alike was the Folkestone Regatta, held generally in September. This took place 15 times between 1859 and 1900. There were lapses because of bad weather or because the enthusiasm of the organisers, the Mayor and local tradespeople, had evaporated. Thousands of people lined the shore, the Leas and the pier. Excursion trains came from London, bringing also a fair sprinkling of pick-pockets on their day out and extra detectives to catch them. There

FOLKESTONE REGATTA 1860s

were special steamers from Boulogne. Three or four bands played, the harbour buildings and vessels were decorated with flags and shops closed at noon. On the beach was an Aunt Sally, a Punch and Judy, and legs of mutton on top of 50-foot high greasy poles. Cheapjacks moved amongst the crowds selling sweets, toys and watches for two-and-a-half pence. The proceedings ended in the evening with a display of fireworks and a ball at the Royal Pavilion Hotel.

It was a mixture of fishermen and amateur yachtsmen who provided the crews for the Regatta events. The fishermen had not forgotten the traditional skills learnt by their ancestors in the days of smuggling. 'The Pride of Folkestone', a four-oared rowing galley, became South Coast champion in 1871 and the crew were chaired round the town on their way home from Margate Regatta. In the same year they participated in the Folkestone Regatta, but the weather was so rough that two men only could row, the other two being occupied in bailing out the boat. Next year they won first prize at Boulogne, but, due to a dispute over the size of rowlocks, were only offered second place. The irritated Folkestonians refused the prize, saying they could afford to donate it to help in paying off France's war indemnity to the victorious Prussians.

"Among seafaring people a regatta is a great event. The fishermen don their best clothes, trim and oil their hair, polish their ear-rings and stand and gaze at the competitions in earnestness and excitement. They know the pedigree of the rowers, they talk with eloquence of the value of the boats, their shape and swiftness."

(Folkestone Chronicle, September 13th, 1873.)

The Regatta cash prizes were valuable, as much as £12 or £14 being donated by Baron Rothschild. A similar regatta was held at Sandgate. Crews and visitors from England patronised also the Regatta at Boulogne, Folkestone's sister resort across the Channel. By 1869 there were half-price day tickets, though smells and bad drainage occasioned some adverse reactions. John English published an illustrated guide carrying advertisements for hotels, cooks, tailors and governesses.

The Folkestone Chronicle had a Boulogne letter with a column of news from 1865, though this did not appear during the Franco-Prussian war when there were hardly any English visitors. There was also a resident English colony of some 3,000, consisting at one time of: families down on their luck, such as those ruined by the slump in railway shares; deserted wives; those who wished to live cheaply abroad, or who had made their native land too hot to hold them. There were many attractions – schools; good food and lively cafes; an English church; the Établissement des Bains with its casino; a statue of Dr Jenner; the Fete des Fleurs; the Concours Hippique, and of course rows and rows of bathing machines.

ESTABLISSEMENT DES BAINS, BOULOGNE 1851

Visits became easier when vessels could leave both ports at any stage of the tide in the 1880s.

Another enjoyable day out was a visit to Canterbury in an old-fashioned stagecoach drawn by four horses, now considered more as an excursion vehicle than a serious means of transport. (Pictures and prints of coaching scenes with snow and jolly landlords were on many walls.) Coaches drove through the winding lanes in style, the guard blowing his horn and people turning out to watch. The first coaches were promoted by the proprietor of the Royal Norfolk Hotel in Sandgate in 1870 and were run three times weekly in the season. But horses are expensive to keep in the winter; in October up to twenty would be sent to Aldridge's Horse Repository to be sold. From 1880 till the end of the century there were daily coaches - 'Old Times', 'Quicksilver' and 'Tantivy' - which started from one of the large hotels, the Westcliff or the Grand and were often driven by noted whips. A famous whip was Mr. J.P. Scott who accomplished the feat of driving to London and back in twelve hours with passengers, involving seven changes of horses. He was welcomed at the Brunswick Hotel, Jermyn Street, by Mrs.

A COACH AT THE GRAND HOTEL 1890

Wedderburn, late of the Westcliff Hotel, Folkestone. In 1896 he was involved in two accidents, the first when the horses were frightened by a traction engine and the second which resulted in his death, when the horses shied and he was dragged along the ground.

The provision of band concerts was also a product of local enterprise. The managers and proprietors of the Royal Pavilion, the Westcliff and the Metropole hired bands themselves for regular performances in the season; these were a great draw for visitors and, if one large hotel had them, the rest had to follow suit. There were public performances on the Leas paid for by public subscription, mostly from lodging house and hotel keepers. The costs amounted to about 10 guineas a week in the 1860s and it was often difficult to raise the necessary money. After the Folkestone Corporation Act of 1893, bands could be paid for from a halfpenny rate. Bandstands were erected: the site of the westerly one donated by the Metropole Hotel is now a flowerbed; the easterly bandstand put up by the Corporation in 1895 is still standing; there was also one in the Marine Gardens.

The band question was made a political matter by the radical Councillor Logan. He saw band provision on the West Cliff as yet one more measure which excluded the

FOLKESTONE TOWN BAND, 1890

working-class area of the East Cliff from amenities. Why should not bands play also on the East Cliff? The Band Committee, in its first flush of enthusiasm, overspent by £120, making the members themselves theoretically liable for the excess. When available, military bands with their high standards of performance and smart uniforms were always the most popular. In contrast, the artisans composing the band of the Artillery Volunteers - who did not have time to practice properly - came a poor second. There were also picturesque foreign bands: Hungarian, Italian, Bavarian, Austrian and German, as well as the Folkestone Town Band. The band of Herr Moritz Wurm was well known, and that of Signor La Camera from Naples cost £72 a week in 1898. In 1879 there were even rival bands playing each other down and making an intolerable noise.

Other summer attractions on the Leas were the sporting events held on Sandgate Plain - formerly the land of Plain Farm - where polo was played by officers from the camp. During the 1860s a cricket week took place in July, for which an entrance fee was charged and the London papers sent down cricket correspondents. By 1869 the

Folkestone Cricket Club held regular matches, including an occasional tradesmen's match. A dismal picture of the rising generation appeared in 1882, (Folkestone Chronicle, June 3rd):

> "Twelve years ago, the Club was highly respected and such giants as the Graces, Lord Harris and others came to play the members, even t radesmen, some greyheaded and middle-aged, were to be seen practising. Now gentlemen who do no sport, short-piped, light-suited Sam Weller gentry haunt the Leas and the Pier, read 'Punch', play billiards, sip gin and water, but never handle an oar, a tiller or a cricket bat to vary their dreary daily round."

Football also took place on the Plain, the club being founded in 1884. It afterwards moved to a ground in Cheriton where a stand for 300 people was erected; in 1896 the club were semi-finalists for the Kent Senior Cup. By 1889 a golf club had started, using land at Broadmead Farm. Cycling was a popular pursuit. An 1885 picture of the first

Folkestone club shows ponderous gentlemen on their penny farthings but gradually bicycles grew lighter and cheaper and ladies' cycling costumes were being advertised. The Rev. Edward Husband, vicar of St. Michael's, always anxious to encourage young people, was President of the Folkestone Cycling Club which met at the Bathing Establishment. From 1890 an annual Church Parade of cyclists was held at his church and

THE FIRST FOLKESTONE CYCLING CLUB, 1885

excursions were made to local beauty spots. His sermons on these occasions had a cycling flavour, referring to the joy of seeing hardworking young men, often badly paid, who were now able to enjoy their leisure bicycling to the countryside. He warned against the dangers of excessive speed and mentioned the Railway Company's exorbitant charge for carrying bicycles. Sunday runs should not be prohibited but participants should first visit their place of worship. After such a service, 169 cyclists trooped outside and mounted their bicycles, the ladies displaying perfect balance.

A demon cyclist was F. Lemuel Wale. His diary records his award-winning hill ascents, club runs in rain and wind when none but he turned up, and the purchase of a new, lighter Brooker Safety No.2 Model to replace his old Apollo. *"I can simply fly up the hills without blowing."* The Folkestone Express published 'Cycle Notes' from 1897, giving hints on how to keep the toolbag from rattling, bloomers for ladies and reports on people who scattered nails on the road to discourage Sunday outings.

There was a rowing club and a swimming club which met at the Bathing Establishment on Thursday evenings. The rowing club had lost its old premises and enthusiasm had waned, but in 1884 some gentlemen had managed to raise enough money to build a new boathouse near the Bathing Establishment. It attracted 150 members and had a good fleet of boats. Lord Radnor, who had given the site, was President. Sir Edmund Hay Currie's school also owned a boathouse on the shore to the west and two fours rowed across the Channel. In 1885 the Folkestone Piscatorial Society was founded with prizes for the best catch, salt or fresh fish. A skating rink was opened in 1875 in Ingles Park and became immediately popular. It had lamps and comfortable seats for spectators but, once the lower classes were seen there, it went out of fashion. Another rink opened in the grounds of the Pleasure Gardens Theatre did well, in conjunction with other attractions including a lawn tennis court.

From 1858 steeplechases were held, first at Terlingham Farm, then at Park Farm, much patronised by the military. In March 1863, 10,000 attended:

> "Along the high bank were pitched many tents and a double line of vehicles of every description from the coach of the aristocratic visitor to the humble cart of the huckster. The vivid green of the grass set off the bright uniforms and the ladies' dresses."
>
> (Folkestone Chronicle March 28th, 1863).

In 1897 a racecourse was planned at Westenhanger. A vast influx of the London sporting world was expected, including members of the aristocracy. £50,000 was raised, Leopold Rothschild and Lord Radnor being among the subscribers. Stands were put up, three separate courses laid out and the railway company provided a station. The first race in 1898 was, however, a fiasco, as there were only two runners. Although the first company went into liquidation, the course survived, being especially popular for military races when cavalry regiments were stationed at Shorncliffe.

Public entertainments were revolutionised by the building of the Town Hall in 1860. The large room could be hired for every variety of activity: concerts, plays, balls, pantomimes, political and religious meetings. In the 1860s the Christy Minstrels could always command a good audience, being 'funny without coarseness'. August 1865 saw the appearance of the four smallest beings in the world, Tom Thumb, his wife and two other midgets. They had played before Queen Victoria and seemed well fitted for the usages of good society. Mr Mobbs gave a course of Tonic Sol-fa classes. In November 1868, electric light was used for the first time and pictures of statuary were illuminated on a screen. Panoramas were popular events, a magnificent one appearing in February 1872, which showed 55 separate pictures of the Franco-Prussian war - including the battle of Sedan and the revolution in Paris, culminating in the burial of the murdered Archbishop - accompanied by descriptive lectures. Miss Annie Fay, sitting behind a curtain with her hands tied, played musical instruments, drank a glass of water and threw about heavy objects, the sort of marvels performed by spiritualist mediums. This, however, was acknowledged to be clever conjuring. In 1879, twenty Zulu warriors were to appear, advertised as having escaped from Cetewayo's army, but were found to be shams, being negroes imported from Whitechapel.

Some months later, Mr Brandram in Shakespeare imparted a welcome note of culture. A pantomime written by the editor of The Folkestone Express - 'Pharaoh's Serpent and the Mayor of Folkestone' - made several appearances at Christmas time. The original pantomime legend was from an early nineteenth century ballad, The Folkestone Fiery Serpent, concerning the appearance of a peacock on Jacob's Mount, which

THE FIERY SERPENT WITH SOME TERRIFIED RESIDENTS

was taken by the credulous inhabitants to be a terrible monster. The play starts with a mischievous small boy from Sandgate bringing news to a chorus of Indignant Ratepayers that a horrible serpent has been seen in the Back Street drain. They reply,

> "How dare you bring your foreign face
> Among us, the sons of the true guinea race.
> Beside all foreigners we truly hates,
> They are sure to be paupers and come upon our rates."

The drunk Town Crier was a portrait from life of Tom Cockett. The help of the Mayor of Dover is solicited and his response is far from courageous,

> "Oh! I say! Look here, come, come!
> Bring my welocipede, I'm going 'ome."

The end is a joke, the only serpent in the drain is – dirt; the Mayor turns into Harlequin, the Mayoress Columbine. The story, written by a Liberal, points the moral that the wealthy ratepayers in the West End were none too keen on paying for improvements to the drains in the East End, of which Back Street was a typical thoroughfare.

Sandgate had Rigden's Music Hall, afterwards the Alhambra, patronised mostly by fishermen and soldiers from Shorncliffe. There was a change of programme every week, with music hall turns such as nigger minstrels, comic singers, Mlle Lawrence in 'Poses Plastiques', and real Newfoundland dogs in 'The dogs of Montargis'. It closed in 1914 and reopened as a cinema in 1921. A soldier remembered the dashing dragoons seated in 'The Bricks', as it was then called, uniforms brushed and hair oiled, with their pipes and pints. Their evening was rudely interrupted by the sound of the evening gun signalling the hour for a general return to their comfortless barracks, which bore a close resemblance to the between decks of an emigrant ship.

There were many exhibitions of wild animals, described by Dickens as being in an unhealthy and malodorous state. Sanger's Circus was a regular visitor to the town in the

1860s, with Arabian horses, a giant elephant and a procession that stretched half a mile. One occasion that had sadly deteriorated in the nineteenth century was that of the annual fair. Fairs of ancient origin, such as those held on the Bayle, used to be occasions for a useful exchange of goods and services. They were now an excuse for petty thefts, drunkenness and fighting, all the more noticeable as Folkestone was generally such a respectable town. In 1877 the arrival of the fair was announced by musicians and groups of 'pikeys' (gypsies), followed by a procession of shabby carts. Tents and merry-go-rounds were put up; there was an African who swallowed boiling oil and a red-hot poker. The participants were dirty and bad language abounded. Young girls who attended were seen as taking the first steps on a path that led to degradation and ruin. After a woman was killed by a swing boat in 1880, Lord Radnor forbade the letting of the field. The fair still continued at another venue, the aptly named Folly Fields, much to the disapproval of the townsfolk.

There were many better attractions for visitors during the season: balls, concerts, open air fetes; church bazaars, flower shows, visits to Mr Meikle's nursery gardens in Shellons Lane; entertainments at the Town Hall, Pleasure Gardens, the Pier Pavilion and the Bradstone Hall - used for this purpose before it was taken over by the Salvation Army. The most resplendent season and the most outstanding attraction in the town's history - or so its promoters hoped - was to be in 1886. After the success of the Great Exhibition in 1851, instructive exhibitions were in fashion. Manchester and Leeds had a Health Exhibition, a Fisheries Exhibition and Art Exhibitions. Folkestone should have a great National Art Treasures Exhibition. This was the inspiration of Felix Joseph, a rich Jewish philanthropist, who had already presented the town with a set of Wedgwood, which is still in the possession of the Museum. He, well-connected as he was, envisaged approaching his aristocratic friends for loans of their remarkable treasures, leading to a grand opening presided over by the Prince of Wales. Half-a-million visitors would flock from London, the provinces and the Continent. A handsome building would be erected, to serve later as a Winter Garden. Of course, this would not be cheap: guarantees of £50,000 to cover all expenses were needed, but this was a mere formality as all expenses would be repaid by ticket sales. Great enthusiasm was roused in the town. In the course of several Town Hall meetings, £30,000 was raised and expectations of future trade and profits were high.

However, a difficulty arose over final control of the project between Felix Joseph and Somers Vine, a paid administrator appointed by the local Executive Committee. Felix Joseph resigned, but this in no way disturbed progress. The Committee felt that Somers Vine must know what he was about, as he was at the same time organising the prestigious Colonial Exhibition in London. The Railway Company offered £15,000 and a 9-acre site was provided by Lord Radnor. In December the foundation stone of the building was laid by Lord Granville, Lord Warden of the Cinque Ports. He was escorted from the station by a thousand working men, assembled under the banners of their various benefit societies and unions, including the Carpenters and Joiners. There were four bands - that of the fisher boys playing in a boat - and church bells rang out; all Folkestone watched the spectacle. Lunch for the notables was at the Royal Pavilion Hotel, where Sir Edward Watkin made a notably insincere speech, in view of his private opinion of Lord Radnor, praising his lordship's liberality.

NATIONAL ART TREASURES EXHIBITION OPENING DAY

Under the direction of Joseph Gardner, the architect, and Moody, the contractor, the great building began to take shape. The central hall was 210 feet long and 63 feet high with two side galleries. Lavatory accommodation was by Messrs. Doulton, electricity by the Electricity Power Storage Co. and catering in the dining room, bars and tea room by Messrs. Spiers and Pond. A strike of the 356 men employed was threatened but averted. There was a temporary railway line from Shorncliffe Station to take the exhibits. On Saturday May 22nd 1886, the opening ceremony was performed,

THE PICTURE GALLERY, NATIONAL ART TREASURES EXHIBITION

not by the Prince of Wales whom the local committee had approached unsuccessfully, but by the Lord Mayor of London, accompanied by the Sheriffs, other Mayors and all the local gentry. Displays included a large fountain, an organ, statuary, paintings, prints, books, manuscripts, costumes and jewellery.

The first sign of trouble was that season tickets which cost a guinea were being sold at half price to domestic servants. As the season wore on, the lack of visitors became apparent. Although local people thoroughly enjoyed it, using their season tickets and going there often, there were not many coming from farther afield. What had gone wrong? In retrospect, it had been disastrous to let Felix Joseph resign.

The time and attention of Somers Vine must have been given almost wholly to the Colonial and Indian Exhibition, with its exotic and fascinating exhibits from jungle and palace. Opened by the Queen herself, it made a profit of £35,000 and Somers Vine was given a knighthood. The Folkestone Executive Committee - composed of tradesmen, military men, vicars and local gentry - possessed none of the influence and knowledge of Felix Joseph. To see the art exhibits was simply not worth a long journey, since they were mostly Cinque Port antiquities, already known in Kent; many of the pictures were second rate, lent by the artists themselves, in the hope of publicity and sales. The exhibition lost money every week, and backers suggested closing it early to save overheads. Felix Joseph wrote from St. Leonard's, telling of his sad satisfaction, in seeing what should have been one of the greatest successes of the year turned into a gigantic fiasco.

The financial consequences for the guarantors were disastrous. £37,760 had been spent and only £18,000 was recoverable. There had been waste in advertising and entertainment and the building looked like being a white elephant. Most people paid up, but some writs had to be issued; those in humble circumstances suffered, such as the engine driver on seven-shillings a day wages, who had to find £15. The very word 'Exhibition' was anathema, so that when support was requested for a forthcoming Health Congress in Hastings, bitter laughter was heard in the Council chamber.

In March 1888, the Folkestone Pleasure Gardens Co. bought the building for £2,100, no more than the cost of the iron used in its construction. It was neither wind nor water-tight. Hayward & Paramour undertook the conversion to a theatre with stage, whereon inaugural performances of Gilbert and Sullivan were given by the D'Oyley Carte Opera Company. The grounds were laid out with skating rink, tennis courts and a gymnasium

THE PLEASURE GARDENS THEATRE

which were a source of profit, while the western galleries were let to Sir Edmund Hay Currie for his school. 'Boote's Baby' was a great success on stage and Lady Radnor brought down her Ladies' Orchestral Band. Though the building was still plagued by draughts, the venture was making a small profit by 1893 and, from then on, the Pleasure Gardens became established as Folkestone's major theatre. Plays were put on for a week and pre-London productions often appeared. As might be expected, the staple fare was comedies and musicals, with occasional doses of opera and the classics.

In Easter week, 1889, for example, there was 'Vice Versa' at the Town Hall, 'Robinson Crusoe' on the Pier and 'She Stoops to Conquer' at the Exhibition Palace. Against this the entertainments of today and the number of visitors look meagre indeed. Further additions to the amenities of the Pleasure Gardens by the turn of the century were a cycling school, used for badminton in the winter, croquet lawns and the marvellous military tournaments. These three-day events included mock battles, drill, competition in all varieties of military skills and a giant tug-of-war. After the end of the Second World War, the Pleasure Gardens Theatre was reduced to showing cheap cabarets and wrestling matches. It was a large and expensive building to keep up, the fabric was decaying and its closure surprised no-one. The site is now occupied by the police headquarters.

Many Folkestonians viewed with regret the end of theatre productions at the Leas Pavilion and made considerable efforts to save them. The building, still standing on the

Leas, was opened by Lord Radnor on July 1st 1902, as a restaurant offering light lunches at two shillings and sixpence and afternoon teas. Inside there were potted palms, fine Indian carpets, a large stained glass window and wicker chairs painted pink. Entertainment was provided by a ladies' orchestra and vocalist. A stage was built in 1906, on which concert parties such as 'The Gypsies and their Jester' and 'The Mad Hatters' performed. In 1928 plays were inaugurated and a year later Arthur Brough took over, not retiring until 1969, a record for the longest-running repertory company under one management; the tea matinees with choice of *"Buttered toast or teacake, sir?"* were famous.

From Stock's Library in the High Street - which in 1848 contained a thousand volumes - to Thorpe's spacious and up-to-date premises in the Sandgate Road, Folkestone visitors had ready access to the best of modern fiction, together with tales of romance, travel and life in the colonies. Available for purchase in the fancy goods shops were sketching tablets and watercolours; materials for Berlin Wool work or bead embroidery on cushions, purses and slippers, and cross-stitch patterns with a medieval flavour. The Prince Consort, who encouraged his children to make natural history collections, set an example to parents. Objects of study in Folkestone and district could be plants, fossils, insects and birds. Finding them meant healthy exercise, while cataloguing them and pressing flowers kept children and adults happy and amused for hours.

The North Downs and the Warren are rich in plant and animal life and were favourite spots for excursions and picnics. Tents for schools and parties could be supplied by T. Harrison of Dover Street and Warren Farm offered refreshments. There were local naturalists who provided guidance. Samuel Mackie, a customs official, wrote 'An Outline Sketch of the Geology of Folkestone' in 1860 and his fossil collection passed eventually to the Folkestone Museum. Henry Ulyett, headmaster of Sandgate School, lectured extensively in the town on scientific subjects, such as electricity, heat and magnetism. In 1880 his 'Rambles of a Naturalist round Folkestone' was published with exhaustive lists of the plants, butterflies, moths, birds and shells to be found within a six mile radius of the Town Hall, a challenge to a keen collector. He also wrote Simpson's 'Handbook to Folkestone'. William Glanfield, born in 1855, son of a later headmaster of Sandgate School, contributed articles under the pen name 'Felix' to The Folkestone Chronicle and The Herald, where he was on the staff, These included many suggestions for walks, historical rather than scientific in their approach. A selection of these was later published in book form in 1913 as 'Rambles around Folkestone'.

As in all seaside resorts, there was a profusion of guide books which ran into many editions, generally commissioned by enterprising local printers and illustrated with engravings. The earliest was from William Tiffen of Hythe, The Sandgate, Hythe and Folkestone Guide, first published 1816, followed by Purday's guide of 1823. Samuel Mackie wrote and himself illustrated, Folkestone and its Neighbourhood. In 1856 he went bankrupt - possibly because of unwise speculation in lodging houses - was dismissed from his post and moved to London. The printer, J. English, owner of the Folkestone Express, republished and updated the book in 1883; it eventually ran to 14 editions. Henry Stock, printer, owner and editor of the first Folkestone newspaper, The Folkestone Chronicle, published The New Illustrated Guide to Folkestone and its General Neighbourhood, which appeared first in 1848. These two guides were the most popular and enduring but there were also others, from R. Stace & Son, 1866; C. Creed, 1869; Russell, 1885; W. Simpson, 1870; W.E. Thorpe & Co., 1897, and Mates' Illustrated Folkestone of 1900 which made extensive use of photography. There were collections of engraved views, many taken from the guide books and of course a multitude of postcards of every picturesque spot: the Leas, the old tanhouse on the harbour, the parish church and the fleet of fishing boats. In reading these messages, like those scribbled on the walls of Pompeii, one is listening to authentic, and otherwise unheard, voices from the past.

This from a postcard with an image of the Beach and Lift:
Dear Mrs. Corderoy. We are having a fine time, weather is simply baking us. Do you miss tormenting Sid if so, you will soon have him back. He took me out in a boat and made me do all the rowing while he had a sleep. He has been bathing with all the girls, with love from Rose.

A concert party on East Beach:
Dear Mrs. Rands, Just a line to let you know I am having a party on ripping time and lovely weather and we go and listen to these every night. I have been to Dover and Shorncliffe beach. Yours Kate.

Marine Parade
Dear M and D. Just a card to let you know we arrived safe, but Eileen is alful (sic) she has cried every day since we have been here and wont speak to anyone I shall have to take her home if she keeps on love to all from us Nan.

Lower Parade and the Beach
Dear Clarkie simply grand down here we have just had tea and now taking a quiet rest before going to hear the band. This morning we had to dress up and parade on the Leas but this afternoon allowed to change and go and lie on the Warren and read. Presently we have to rig out again and go and hear the band. Grand place here.   Last night we walked to Sandgate and visited the Castle. Of course I had to write my name on about 5 times, just like me isn't it! Bye bye for the present love from Dollie the torment.

Parish Church
*Dear E. I arrived safely, I am afraid by the time you get this
I shall be thinking of coming home. I am sitting on the Leas
it looks very dull here hope it will keep fine love from Alice.*

Lower Sandgate Road:
*Dear M. Very many thanks for pc and Mary's letter. Have
been to St. Mary's Church then Church parade after, jolly
nice, are these pines anything like Bournemouth – with fondest love.*

The Tollgate:
*From 5 East Cliff. Dear Bee. Weather simply glorious also the place.
We are all very pleased, most comfy aparts – ome from ome.
Kind regards, hoping all are well sincerely Bob.*

The Golf Links:
*Dear Ada I hope this will find you all well. Folkestone doesn't
seem to be agreeing with me. I feel very seedy hope to be better soon.
Plenty of trippers about of course and the weather is very nice lately.
Glad you and M. like the little dog's photo, yrs with love Susie.*

The Warren:
*Dear Brother, we are happy to tell you have arrived quite safe
through God's mercy, and have spent a very happy time up to
the present although the weather is not very grand, we are very
thankful to you for your recommendations as the Capt. and his
wife are dear children of God and the dear Lord has been made
more precious to us since we have been here. You will be happy
to hear Mr. Hyder has confessed Christ asking still your prayers
we remain Yours in Christ Mr. and Mrs. G. Hyder.*

The Warren:
*Dear Ethel Here we are at Folkestone and ever so much better for
the rest and change. By jove, Auntie's ideas of rest and mine don't
coincide. She has literally walked me off my legs climbing all the
blessed cliffs we come near. Much love from Flo.*

A child, with bare legs, paddling near the pier
*Dear Florrie. I am sending you a picture of our promenade
pier. Is the little girl in the front of the picture anything like
you when you were paddling? I am stiff today not used to playing
rounders with a lot of lively girls. The one with bare legs was a child in the
picture. I don't think young women would have exposed their legs.
P.S. I hope you will not feel shocked about the little girl.*

16

THE RESORT

Imagine a fine summer's day in the 1890s, the golden period of Folkestone's prosperity, which lasted until the outbreak of the First World War. Viewed from an upper window of one of the stately mansions in Clifton Crescent, the crowd on the Leas must have looked like a flower garden set against the broad green expanse of turf. The blossoms were the ladies in their bright silk or muslin dresses, leg-of-mutton sleeves, flounced parasols and hats trimmed with every variety of flower and feather. They were set off to perfection by the sober attire of their escorts in frock coats and dark trousers, black

VIEW ON THE LEAS 1890

toppers and gloves for Sundays, straw boaters for weekdays. They stroll in groups, our great-grandfathers and great-grandmothers, chatting, admiring the view, the brief moment captured for posterity on the photographer's plate. Here and there an upright nurse led her charges, the boys in sailor suits and girls in starched pinafores.

Formality and decorum were preserved, and, to the very edge of the water, no item of clothing was discarded whatever the temperature. Protection against the sun was vital for females. In spite of repeated applications of Rowlands' 'Kalydor', a preparation for the skin much advertised in seaside newspapers, exposure endangered a delicate pale complexion causing it to become brown and peasant-like.

CHURCH PARADE

The thickest of the crowds gathered on Sundays, the Church Parade, after a sermon at the parish church or, for those of a low-church persuasion, a service at Holy Trinity or Christ Church. Viewing the ladies' hats and dresses (often changed two or three times a day) and listening to the band were the main diversions along this elegant promenade.

"On a fine breezy day 'The Leas' was covered with a host of the smartest of smart people in the smartest of costumes, making a blaze of various colour and beauty as they stroll up and down to the strains of the bright and popular music of our first rate bands …The maidens can display their daintiest frocks at the delightful function known as the Church Parade, where they were pretty certain of meeting a goodly number of 'swagger' officers from the adjacent camp at Shorncliffe."

(Mates' Illustrated Folkestone).

The hard upright wooden chairs grouped around the bandstand were now being replaced by more comfortable striped canvas deck chairs. A reminder of human mortality was provided by the bath chairs, black hoods pulled up against rain or sun, in which the elderly and invalids were being wheeled like so many large babies. A more

cheerful note was struck by the Town Crier with his bell and announcements of goods for sale and 'Lost, stolen or strayed'. The former Crier, loud-voiced Tom Cockett, whose visage was as red as the scarlet facings on his uniform and whose oratorical powers would have fitted him for a Shakespearean tragedy, was dismissed for intemperance and

A BATH CHAIR

disobedience in 1874. Lord Radnor's policeman in a peaked cap was also on patrol to collect the pennies for the chairs and to check any signs of disorderly conduct,

suggesting to obviously lower-class trippers that they might feel more at home on the Marine Parade below. Mr Punch had appeared on the Leas, for charity of course, but Brother Bones, the nigger minstrel, with his singing, dancing and jokes, was held to be vulgar and had been banished.

A pleasant place to sit was the Leas shelter, put up in 1894 at the joint expense of Lord Radnor and the Corporation. It lies below the Leas, which had to be excavated by the contractors, Hayward & Paramour. The central hall was sixty-two feet long and could hold five hundred people, with lavatory accommodation at each end. It opens on to a rustic veranda with a tiled roof, bright with hanging baskets of flowers.

TOM COCKETT

Below the cliff was all the fun. You could hear the shrieks of those hurtled along the Patent Gravity or Switchback Railway, watch the concert

177

parties or Punch and Judy, listen to an itinerant preacher, buy sweets and cheap toys or ices hawked by Italian vendors amongst the crowds. And crowds there were, numbers of holiday makers unimaginable today. There were rides on the donkeys waiting patiently along the Lower Sandgate Road and munching in their nosebags, the bad

language of their attendants being a continual source of complaint. You could watch the lifeboat being launched, marvel at the Camera Obscura or hire a so-called 'pleasure' boat and enjoy a queasy fishing trip amongst the sparkling waves. Even the *"West End lot"* were being lured down to sea level by the convenience of the new lift, to take tea in the Royal Pavilion's Winter Garden, to stroll on the

THE LEAS SHELTER

pier and enjoy the amenities of the Bathing Establishment. Of course children could paddle and their elders take a dip from Walter Fagg's bathing carriage or the rows of bathing machines strung out along the shore. By the late 1890s as these were being replaced by tents, there was even a notice, 'Mixed Bathing', by the pier.

A stroll to the Harbour to watch the arrival or departure of the tidal boat was popular. Here was the bustle of passengers, porters and luggage while the horses and carriages were hoisted on board. Several papers refered to the favourite pastime of disengaged Folkestonians in rough weather, which was to walk to the harbour and mock the pallid faces and forlorn aspect of the

Lots of people on the beach at FOLKESTONE
A FOLKESTONE POSTCARD

returning passengers as they tottered to the shore, an activity called disapprovingly by The Daily Telegraph *"systematic rowdyism"*. At the harbour one could also watch the passage of the fishing boats, the fish being packed for market, with tubs, nets and tackle in all directions. The swarms of rosy-faced urchins noticed in Stock's Guide, 1865, were now immured in school, during term-time at least. The picturesque alleys and lanes of the old town could be explored. There was entertainment of a more

dubious nature in the High Street; cards spun on a reel belonging to the Mutoscope Company depicting 'A mouse in a girl's bedroom' or 'How to serve the salad undressed'. The ladies wore fleshings but the magistrates decided the titles alone would lead to speculation and the material was destroyed.

A SKETCH OF FASHIONABLE FOLKESTONE

How did Folkestone become an aristocratic, fashionable and select resort in contrast to its early beginnings? It must be put down primarily to the influence of the Radnor Estate but also to the acute perception of the traders as to which side their bread was buttered. The situation was summed up by George Hart, the proprietor of Bates and the Longford Hotels:

> *"My houses are patronised almost exclusively by the nobility and aristocracy. The great inducement that they have in coming to Folkestone is that it is a quiet and select watering place. Any influx of cheap day trippers I should look upon as a disaster."*

The Folkestone Chronicle remarked in 1871:

> *"If we were patronised by the class who visit these places (Margate and Ramsgate) our reputation would decrease and we should find a diminution of those aristocratic and high class visitors who have so long made this town their resort in the autumn of the year. We cannot receive the patronage of the two classes and our experience teaches us which is the best to favour."*

The same article also looked forward to the growth of commuting by a resident mercantile class whose business necessitated a daily visit to the metropolis. It was clear the businessmen preferred quality to quantity. High prices, good hotels and the right people strolling along the Leas were preferable to the troops of East Enders, the 'Arries and 'Arriets who sprawled on the beach at Margate. Of 118 arrivals listed in the Chronicle in June 1856, over half were titled and there were no cheap-day tickets till the end of the century.

Although the trippers were ostracised, their numbers kept increasing like a plague of locusts. The Folkestone Herald recorded on July 21st 1884:

LOW TRIPPERS

"A more disgusting and disgraceful set of excursionists never put their feet into the town than those who visited Folkestone on Sunday last. Mad with drink, reeling about the streets as early as eleven in the morning, they filled the air with coarse oaths and insulted everyone who came their way. They pushed a young lady into the water up to her neck and stood and laughed and one laid hands on the rails of Fagg's bathing machine and nearly had his fingers chopped off."

As long as there were standards to be preserved, it was the Radnor Estate which would maintain them. The Estate owned the Leas and preserved it from commercial development, planting the Undercliff with trees and shrubs; it granted leases to builders who were going to put up sizeable houses instead of selling freehold land, thus preserving property values in the area. If one walks round the area of Victorian development - Albion Villas, West Terrace, Longford Terrace, Clifton Gardens down to Castle Hill Avenue and Grimston Gardens - one has a feeling of cohesion, not so much in architectural styles (which altered over the century) but in social attitudes. These are houses built for well-to-do families with large staffs, houses built to last. As well as holiday makers, a better class of residents was to be attracted, the retired, invalids and those of independent means who wished to live in a pleasant healthy town with many amenities. Hence also the prime importance of a winter season, so that the town should not seem intolerably dull after the diversions of summer.

With the railway, the harbour and the Estate developments, the town's future was assured and it could take its share of a rapidly-growing market. Many of the visitors, particularly those at the Royal Pavilion, were on their way to catch the tidal boats or to recover from the journey. Others were simply coming to enjoy a holiday - two or three weeks by the sea with the family was an amenity well within the budget of the middle classes, increasing now in numbers and economic power. Mothers could introduce their daughters into society, but sadly at the seaside there was always a preponderance of ladies over gentlemen. The officers from Shorncliffe were in great demand as partners at balls, though perhaps not considered great catches as husbands. Ageing spinsters without means were consigned to a hard and lonely struggle to preserve their status as ladies. They were often condemned to drudgery as governesses when posts were hard to find, or as useful poor relations in a family. For them any respectable husband was acceptable.

> *"When the shades of midnight spread*
> *Darkness o'er the Leas, girls rest,*
> *When the thought of years unwed*
> *Rack the heart and wring the breast,*
> *When the Flirts' last hopes are wrapped in*
> *Dreams of some old Shorncliffe captain,*
> *Lovely Alice, hear me then, Make me happiest of men."*
> (Folkestone Chronicle, March 11th 1871).

Folkestone was ranked high as a health resort. Then, as now, its chilly breezes were described as *"bracing"* and *"invigorating"*. It was rightly proud of its low death-rate; its reputation for clean water and good drains was jealously guarded, which explains the public excitement over the waterworks in 1874:

Visitors listed in the local press as resident in Folkestone in the first week in August over several years.

SOURCE AND DATE	MALES	FEMALES	TITLED	ESTABLISHMENTS
FOLKESTONE CHRONICLE 1861	73	48	11	WESTCLIFF, PAVILION
	137	244	4	OTHER
TOTAL	220	292	15	
FOLKESTONE CHRONICLE 1871	97	83	27	PAVILION, WESTCLIFF, BATES
	173	299	12	OTHER
TOTAL	270	382	39	
FOLKESTONE CHRONICLE 1881	129	88	4	PAVILION, WESTCLIFF, CLARENCE HOUSE
	133	219	4	OTHER
TOTAL	262	307	8	
FOLKESTONE VISITOR'S LIST 1891	81	105	3	PAVILION AND SELECTED BOARDING HOUSES
	294	648	9	OTHER
TOTAL	375	753	12	
FOLKESTONE HERALD 1901	376	717	15	ALL

"There is a class of people of a hypochondriacal nature who,
before going on their long vacation, purchased a blue book
for the purpose of ascertaining the town where there was
the fewest number of deaths and off they started for that place."
(Folkestone Chronicle, June 20, 1874)

Dr Bateman, the Medical Officer of Health, waxed eloquent on the subject of Folkestone's advantages and its drains and water, in an address to the Association of Sanitary Inspectors holding their annual meeting in the town in 1889. In this respect the town was thought to be superior to many foreign resorts which had suspect drainage and where bad smells were frequently encountered. In France, where tap water was never considered safe to drink, there were regular cholera epidemics through the century. In the summer of 1885 hundreds were dying daily in Italy and Spain. Precautions were taken in Folkestone - the import of rags from Boulogne prohibited and cautionary leaflets printed - but all this was fortunately unnecessary. There were political upheavals, such as the revolutions of 1848 in France and across Europe which brought many exiles to England's shores. Visitors who would have crossed to the Continent stayed in England during the 1870-71 Franco-Prussian war and its aftermath, as mentioned in Chapter Eight; the steamboat service was suspended with only one mail boat a week crossing the Channel. Folkestone was a good place to gather news of the ruined crops and the exactions of the advancing Germans. A bazaar was held in aid of the victims.

With few effective cures for disease, illnesses and convalescences were lengthy. Invalids stayed for weeks or months, some of them illustrious figures. Ruskin lived in a small house in Sandgate for nearly a year, recovering from a period of mental derangement. Lord Shaftesbury, patron of bootblacks and climbing boys, died at a rented house in Clifton Gardens in 1885. H.G. Wells came to Sandgate after a serious illness in 1898 and decided to settle there. Mr G. H. Cooper said his father saw Dickens

H.G. WELLS

drawn along the Lower Sandgate Road in a bath chair, though Dickens of course knew the town well from previous visits.

Both Wells and Dickens were of far more importance than as invalids or casual visitors. By their writings they brought the whole town to life. Dickens found that he needed to be out of London for several months during the summer when he could work uninterruptedly free from heat and the endless round of dinners and evening parties. He preferred staying by the sea and it was also good for the children. At first he chose Broadstairs but it became too noisy. In the 1850s Boulogne was his principal summer retreat; he had three sons at the Rev. Mr Gibson's

school there. With his other Continental travels he often passed through Folkestone and visited the town when staying in Dover or Broadstairs, walking much of the time. During these brief visits he observed life in and around the town: the new hotel opened for the benefit of travellers; the Royal George Inn with its wedding party and somnolent dog and *"the breezy hills and downs carpeted in wild thyme … the singing of the larks and the distant voices of children at play"*.

In 1855 while writing chapters 2 and 3 of Little Dorrit, Dickens decided to take a house in Folkestone between July and October. The house was a pleasant building facing the sea, 3 Albion Villas, *"always to be known by having all the windows open and soap and water flying out of all the bedrooms"*. When the news came that he was to be resident for some time, the Harveian Literary Institute and the Working Men's Educational Institute jointly approached him to give a reading. He said the two societies had not the slightest sympathy or connection and insisted that the working men should be admitted for three pence each instead of the general price of five shillings. The reading from A Christmas Carol took place on October 5th

3 ALBION VILLAS

in a carpenter's shop in the Dover Road; he described it as a far more alarming place in which to read than the Town Hall at Birmingham.

His days in Folkestone were spent in a standard routine, as he explained to Raikes Currie of Sandling Park whom he proposed to visit: *"I have lately fallen hard at work upon a new book, and, when I am so engaged, I am always by myself from 9 to 2. It is a part of my necessary habit to go out and walk afterwards till 5"*. These walks consisted in breezy expeditions in the Warren climbing the chalk cliffs, with the book always uppermost in his mind. *"He may generally be seen (in clear weather) from the British Channel, suspended in mid-air with his trousers very much torn, at fifty minutes past 3pm."*

DICKENS

He was also busy with the affairs of Household Words, the weekly magazine which he had founded and edited, reading and analysing contributions and making regular visits to *"the great oven"* of London on its account. His monthly article for the magazine in September was on Pavilionstone, followed several months later by 'Out of the Season', the two articles providing an inimitable Dickensian view of Folkestone and resorts generally. He portrayed the shops and the theatre; the harbour, with the perils of the Channel passage and attendant seasickness; the Royal Pavilion Hotel and the old smuggling town with its furtive ways. He described the new Pavilionstone: *"we are a little mortary and limey at present … we are not overfanciful in the way of decorative architecture, and we get unexpected sea views through cracks in the street doors. On the whole, however, we are very snug and comfortable and well-accommodated"*.

Albion Villas was full of children during the holidays. The young Walter Dickens seemed to be constantly jumping on the stairs with 150 pairs of double-soled boots, while Dickens found the elder daughter of Mark Lemon - editor of Punch and a great friend of his - *"makes too much noise (when my attention is rendered free by solitude) in eating biscuits"*. There were other congenial visitors, such as Wilkie Collins and John Leech, who drew for Punch a series of seaside pictures featuring the town, in which the tall chimney of the gasworks near the shore is always recognisable.

Others who passed through were Sir Edwin Landseer in 1855; Gladstone; Thackeray; Edward Lear on several visits to France; Ellen Terry in 1886, Max Beerbohm in 1898 and Queen Victoria in 1899. There was a host of titled ladies and gentlemen whose arrivals were duly noted in the local journals. In Trollope's The Small House at Allington, Adolphus Crosbie, who has jilted the enchanting Lily Dale in favour of an Earl's daughter, spends a disastrous, loveless and expensive honeymoon in Folkestone. Lily would probably have preferred the Lake District.

The quality and duration of the summer season were of vital economic importance to the town, from the good hotels downwards. 'Rooms to Let' signs appearing during an economic slump or a prolonged spell of bad weather were noticed as flags of distress. There were perpetual anxious questionings as to whether the town provided enough amusements for visitors in winter.

"No German bands disturb the morning's quiet. A few old gentlemen pace the Leas in quiet and content; dogs run about unmuzzled, sane and happy. Flymen stick their hands in their pockets and abuse the byelaws. Bathchairmen go home to dinner instead of indulging in a daily picnic on the Leas. Tradesmen give up charging visitors' prices for their goods."
(Folkestone Herald, June 26th 1897).

Dickens also described winter in a seaside resort in Out of the Season:

"All the houses and lodgings ever let to visitors were to let that morning. It seemed to have snowed bills with To Let on them. This put me upon thinking what the owners of all those apartments did out of the season, how they employed their time and occupied their minds. They could not always be going to the Methodist chapels, of which I passed one every other minute. They must have some other recreation. Whether they pretend to take one another's lodgings and opened one another's tea caddies in fun ... The chemist had no boxes of ginger-beer powders, no beautifying sea-side soaps and washes, no attractive scents, nothing but his great goggle-eyed red bottles, looking as if the drifts of the salt sea had inflamed them ... At the Sea-bathing Establishment, a row of neat little houses seven or eight feet high, I saw the proprietor asleep in the shower bath. As to the bathing machines they were (how they were got there it is not for me to say) at the top of a hill at least a mile and a half off."

The town was not known as a cheap place to stay. The Chronicle remarked in 1885 that the most economical visitor could hardly have a week in Folkestone for under £2. There were several ways of arranging accommodation - staying at a hotel or lodging house; renting a furnished house or floor of a house. Often in the latter case, a family would bring its own servants and provide its own food. John Sherwood, grocer and house agent, had long lists of these:

"Longford Terrace: Elegantly furnished, containing dining room, drawing room, library, 9 bedrooms, large attic bedroom, housekeeper's room, pantry and all other convenient offices. Good sea views from both sides of the house."
(English's Time Tables, August 1st 1889).

One of Mr Holden's mansions in Clifton Gardens or Clifton Crescent could command as much as 20/30 guineas a week in the height of the season, Augusta Gardens 15/18 guineas, Manor Road 5/10 guineas and Cambridge Gardens 4/5 guineas. The ownership and letting of houses, from rows of artisan cottages to larger dwellings intended for seasonal tenants, was a reasonably secure and popular form of investment. However, the sub-division of large houses could cause overcrowding and a confusion of servants who gossiped together. Washing was hung from the windows and could be seen from the Leas.

In Pigot's 1839 Directory seven lodging-house keepers are listed in Sandgate, none in Folkestone. Kelly's Directory of 1845 gives twelve in Sandgate, five in Folkestone. In both cases these numbers may be underestimated. In 1865 there were 151, of which 90 were female-owned. This was one of the ways a woman could earn an independent living, although it was a meagre and penurious one - if she had no husband's earnings to rely on, the profits of three

LODGING HOUSE

month's occupancy had to tide her over the rest of the year. There were bad seasons and complaining lodgers. On November 5th 1880, Mrs Wynne wrote to Mr Mackay: *"Twice I have had to toast my chop for proper doing and today I had to send it away as a mass of black. Half a pound of my London butter was made off with by someone and my own maid had made our beds."* At the top end of the scale were the establishments with sea views, such as Tresillian House, 24 Clifton Crescent, (Mrs Dell), with large and airy rooms charging in the season two-and-a-half to three-and-a-half guineas a week. Standish House, 30 Bouverie Road West, (The Misses Townsend), earned praise: *"The superiority of well-conducted boarding houses over hotels as temporary homes, especially for ladies, needs no demonstration. Apart from social considerations, the better class are always more refined, quieter and more select."*

Below the cliff there was perhaps a shade less refinement matched by lower prices, though the Victoria Private Hotel and Boarding House (Miss Pope), at the end of Marine Crescent, was a substantial building with a good reputation. Gentlemen, including many naval and army officers and churchmen, found a home-from-home at Waller's, 14 Manor Road, kept by Mr Waller, former steward of the Radnor Club. Complete respectability was essential when accepting visitors in one's own home:

'An officer's daughter, having two spare bedrooms, desires
to meet with two or three paying guests in her small private
house for the season or longer; every comfort, references
essential, M. F., Stace's Library, Guildhall Street, Folkestone.'

'A clergyman's widow offers board and residence in her private
and pleasantly situated house, either permanently or for a change.
Terms moderate, References exchanged. –B., 8 Kingsnorth Gardens,
Folkestone.'

'Folkestone (best part) good private Temperance Boarding House
conducted on Christian principles, home comforts,
42s. to 52s.6d. weekly, Miss Woodward (member of the
British Nursing Association), Haverstock House, Claremont Road, Folkestone.'

Of Folkestones hotels the oldest and best known was the Pavilion, called by Dickens 'The Lion of Pavilionstone'. Though it never welcomed Queen Victoria, the Empress Eugenie stayed there, and it later became the Royal Pavilion. The proprietors played a

large part in the life of the town. In 1856 the hotel was overtaken by scandal when the new manager fled with £1,500 belonging to a French customer. Then came Mr. Breach, an Englishman, followed by a Frenchman M. Doridant. In spite of his nationality, he was elected Mayor four times and in 1868 retired to Menton. His successor, J. B. Edwardes, took a prominent part in schemes for

THE PAVILION HOTEL

improving Folkestone's attractions. George Spurgen, a former cellarman, took over - first in partnership, then on his own - and was also elected Mayor. He sold out to Frederick Hotels in 1896, when the old Pavilion was completely remodelled to meet the challenge of the new Metropole Hotel on the Leas. It was furnished and decorated by Maple & Co., who employed six hundred workmen for the purpose. The refurbishment included an oak frieze depicting shipping from Egyptian times onwards.

The hotel had already been altered and enlarged from Cubitt's original plan, though the main T-shaped structure was preserved. A west wing was added with additional bedrooms for over two hundred guests. In 1885 a Winter Garden was built, with hot pipes and thousands of exotic plants, to make a popular out of season resort. There was a carriage and porters to meet passengers at the railway and harbour. It had its own farm and dairy situated at what is now Pavilion Road – a useful precaution in days when there were many prosecutions for adulterated milk. By the turn of the century, the old clock tower on the harbour was used as an annexe whenever necessary. The scale of charges ranged from two shillings a night for a small bedroom to three shillings for a ground floor room; wax candles were one shilling and sixpence, dinner four shillings and sixpence. The table d'hôte at the Pavilion, open to non-residents, was renowned for its good food and good company. Another great institution was the Pavilion Lawn, where the regular military band concerts and entertainments became a fashionable venue. Here the Crimean heroes from Shorncliffe and Dover were entertained at the end of the war and a toast was drunk: *"To Miss Nightingale, but not to Mis-Management."*

Dickens, who stayed there often, has described the hotel:

*"If you are for public life at our Great Pavilionstone Hotel, you walk
into that establishment as if it were your Club; and find ready for you,
your news-room, dining-room, smoking-room, billiard room,
music-room, public breakfast, public dinner twice a day
(one plain, one gorgeous), hot baths and cold baths …
Do you want to be aided, abetted, comforted or advised
at our Great Pavilionstone Hotel? Send for the good landlord,
and he is your friend. Should you, or anyone belonging to you,
ever be taken ill … you will not soon forget him or his kind wife.*

*"A thoroughly good inn, in the days of coaching and posting,
was a noble place. But no such inn would have been equal to
the reception of four or five hundred people, all of them wet
through, and half of them dead sick, every day in the year …
In our Pavilionstone hotel vocabulary, there is no such word as fee.
Everything is done for you; every service is provided at a fixed
and reasonable charge; all the prices are hung up in all the rooms;
and you can make out your own bill before-hand, as well as
the book-keeper.*

*"You shall find all the nations of the earth and all the styles of shaving
and not shaving, hair-cutting and hair letting alone, for ever flowing
through our hotel. Couriers you shall see by hundreds; fat leathern
bags for five-franc pieces, closing with violent snaps, like discharges
of fire-arms, by thousands; more luggage in a morning than, fifty years
ago, all Europe saw in a week."*

(Household Words, September 29th 1855).

The Queens Hotel, opened in 1885, was an establishment which ran into early difficulties. It had sixty bedrooms and was tastefully fitted out, but was perhaps too much in the busy centre of the town to be patronised by the upper class and was used mostly by commercial travellers. These less-affluent 'knights of the road' were also catered for at the old Rose Hotel, which was still in business in Rendezvous Street. For abstainers from alcohol, Clarke's Tontine and Temperance Hotel above the Albany Bakery in Tontine Street and Foster's Temperance Hotel in

MAID IN HOTEL

WESTCLIFFE HOTEL

Dover Street offered a warm welcome. The London and Paris, because of its easy access to the harbour, was used principally by those voyaging to and from the Continent. The Hotel Wampach under Charles Wampach, a former cook in a boarding house, was enlarged four times to become a spacious comfortable hotel with eighty bedrooms and bathrooms on every floor, famous for its good food and its commanding site on Castle Hill Avenue. It had to battle for a drinks licence, as did Maestrani's Restaurant in Sandgate Road. Hundert's Hotel, later Princes, 46 and 48 Bouverie Road, had the advantage of overlooking the grounds of the Pleasure Gardens Theatre. Two well known private hotels were owned by George Hart: Bates, later the Esplanade, and the Longford.

There could be no ambiguity about the status of the great Metropole, (which was to

THE METROPOLE (LEFT) AND GRAND HOTELS

become largely apartments towards the end of the following century). It exemplified the late nineteenth-century trend towards investment in large hotels. The first company, which gained the lease from Lord Radnor of three acres of land on the Leas (formerly the polo field), in August 1893, was the Folkestone Metropole Hotel Company; this was a syndicate of eight business men including James Bailey, proprietor of Bailey's Hotel, South Kensington, and Mr A. Smee of Smee & Cobay, hotel furnishers of Finsbury Pavement, London. None of them was from Folkestone, though the Cobay brothers were formerly in business in Hythe High Street. The total capital to be raised was £100,000. Application was made to the justices in September for a liquor licence which would obviously be essential for a hotel of such size. The cause of temperance was strong in the town, even among the justices themselves, so that the licence was opposed by the Church of England Temperance Society, the Nonconformists and thirty boarding-house and lodging-house keepers. At the hearing Daniel Baker, the builder, spoke of the proposed hotel as one of the best things that had happened to Folkestone, if not the best. The licence was refused and there was an outcry.

By the time of the Brewster Sessions of 1894, the opposition had died down and the application was successful. It was patently ridiculous that a hotel of this nature which would add greatly to Folkestone's prosperity should be compelled to bring drinks from outside for its patrons. (At the same time the Wampach gained a liquor licence, and

Maestrani's Restaurant one for beer and wine.) The imposing new edifice had 200 bedrooms, spacious grounds, and an electricity plant. The architect was James D'Oyley - his plans being amended by Thomas Cutter of London - the builders were Messrs. Jennings, also a London firm. The first company was bought out by Gordon Hotels Ltd, the new owners declaring the Metropole to be the most perfect modern hotel that had so far been erected. The mixture of decorative styles was reminiscent of a Hollywood extravaganza. The entrance hall had walls of *"Rose Vieux, Porphery (sic), Rouge Vert and Siena marble with onyx columns; the billiard room was in the Hispano-Moorish style in the rich voluptuous manner of the Alhambra, the library had a fitted seat like a canopied Medician throne while the drawing room was in the Louis Quinze style conjuring up memories of Mesdames Pompadour and du Barry"*. Those parts the patrons did not see, the service quarters in the basement, the drainage and kitchens,

were modern and efficient. Although there was a bandstand in the grounds, it was not successful due to the echo from the high walls and Gordon Hotels presented it to the town. It was the only bandstand on the Leas till a second, still standing, was erected to the east in 1905.

THE MONKEY HOUSE

The hotel opened on July 1st 1897, for the best of the summer season; it was immediately successful, so much so that a new wing was added in 1900. There was a resident orchestra which played daily. The Westcliff, the Wampach and the Pavilion were remodelled at the turn of the century, to meet the challenge of a new, affluent era with its higher standards. Grand Mansions, thirty suites of apartments with hot meals available in each suite carried up by lift, was the achievement of Daniel Baker, a Folkestone builder supported by local money. He visualised a large and magnificent building using the latest building techniques. The ground floor has a steel frame, making large windows possible with wide views of the sea and some floors were made of reinforced concrete from the cement works on the east cliff. All the decorative materials were of the highest quality, marble, oak and luxurious carpeting. Building was begun in 1895 and there was a grand opening in 1903. The chef, M. Dutru, came from the Savoy and the manager was Mr. Gelardi. Both were known to Edward VII and the King became a frequent visitor to the hotel together with the Queen, his mistress Mrs. Keppel and members of the court. They could be seen by the public dining in the Palm Court, the large glass verandah, also known as the Monkey House.

17

FOLKESTONE INTO THE TWENTY FIRST CENTURY

H.G. Wells spent thirteen of his most productive years in Sandgate, having

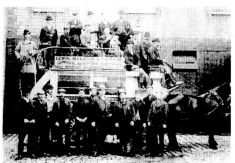

STAFF OF THE HYTHE, SANDGATE AND
FOLKESTONE OMNIBUS CO. LTD

arrived as an invalid and been cured. The design of Spade House, which was designed and built to his specification, is described in Chapter 11, Builders and Architects. Here he wrote 'Kipps', 'Tono Bungay' and many of his best novels. Although he lived as a respectable family man with his second wife and two sons - becoming a Borough Magistrate and welcoming many friends from the world of literature, including Conrad, Henry James, Arnold Bennett and Stephen Crane - he was in fact involved with a series of mistresses, though this was kept well hidden from the public.

The declaration of war on August 4th, 1914, marked the end of a golden era. The year had started on an optimistic note, with the inauguration of the first omnibus service between Folkestone and Hythe and the attractions of the Grand and the Metropole. It had been a fine summer and the Leas was packed with a record number of fashionable holiday makers. A straw in the wind was the unexplained disappearance of German and Austrian waiters who were rejoining their regiments; those who did not leave were subsequently to be interned.

The town emptied as if struck by the plague; hotels and boarding houses deserted. In two weeks Belgium was overrun by the Germans and an army of refugees fled to Britain via the port of Folkestone. They came in all sorts of boats from fishing boats to colliers, the majority terrified and destitute. Eventually some 100,000 refugees passed through the port. They were most generously received, in the first instance by fishermen's families, who provided lodging, clothing and food. A relief committee, set up with access to funds, made

GERMANS UNDER ARREST AT
FOLKESTONE HARBOUR STATION

available houses and church halls, while many people worked tirelessly providing winter clothing and babies' garments. The Catholic church opened a club and a hostel and funds were provided for Protestant pastors. Messrs. F.J. Parsons published a Belgian newspaper and it was rumoured that the Belgian Royal family were to stay at the Grand.

Some refugees could pay for themselves, many were sent elsewhere and many young men joined the army, becoming a useful source of information. The Belgians felt very grateful for the *"wonderful kindness"* of the Folkestonians; their tears were dried and they felt they had found a new home.

REFUGEES ARRIVING IN FOLKESTONE AT THE OUTBREAK OF WORLD WAR I

Folkestone's menfolk of military age - 3,500 of them - were joining up drilling on the Leas and in Radnor Park in their civilian clothes, before enlisting in the Buffs. Some young men were so eager to go to France that they stole a boat. The notabilities were not far behind: Sir Philip Sassoon, MP, served in France and became Haig's private secretary; Captain Viscount Folkestone was wounded near Jerusalem; Lord Radnor became a Brigadier General and Director of Agriculture. Shorncliffe Army Camp was full (as it was to be in the Second World War), while 2,000 Kaffirs and Chinese were encamped near Cherry Garden Avenue to help with loading and unloading supplies. Folkestone itself was an armed camp. Later in the war the town was said to be 'Canadianised', as tens of thousands of young men arrived from Canada to help the Mother country in her hour of need; their distinctive accent being heard everywhere. The Americans were to arrive later.

A boy called Walter Tull was born in Folkestone in 1888, the son of a slave from Barbados. He went to Mundella School, but after both his parents died he was sent to an orphanage. At the outbreak of war he was making a career as a professional footballer, but joined the Army and fought in the 1916 battle of the Somme. At the time officers had to be of pure European descent, but he was chosen as the first black officer to serve in the British Army. Recommended for the Military Cross, he died at Favreuil before he could receive his award; his body was never recovered .

WALTER TULL

Accommodation for the wounded was necessary. The Grand became a military hospital and the formerly derelict Bevan nursing home in Sandgate had eight doctors and a good record of cures. Hotels were taken for convalescents and there were two Canadian military hospitals. It was a common sight to see men in military uniform hobbling about the Leas on crutches. The YMCA provided canteens and sports – there had to be some entertainment - but too much was on offer according to Mrs. Grundy and the Social Purity League; they particularly disapproved of the baseball matches played on Sundays and the local politicians who endorsed the events. There was female company, as the Metropole was given over to the Women's Army Auxiliary Corps, many of whom went to France as drivers.

Life changed for the townspeople. Lists of the missing appeared in the press, gradually becoming longer and longer. Martin Winser advertised a fleet of hire cars for those who wished to escape in the event of an invasion. The department store Plummer Roddis found its business disorganised. Even the horses which pulled the Sandgate trams were sent to the front and had to be replaced by frequently disobedient mules, while the Leas became a sea of mud. Food was controlled until well after the war and a blackout enforced with fines for those who allowed lights to be seen. There were many spy scares and gossip about those who attempted to evade the military call-up on health or conscientious grounds. But on the whole everyone contributed what they could in money or services; civilians gave their time unstintingly and toiled long hours in hospitals or canteens.

TROOPS ON THE SLOPE ROAD, NOW CALLED THE ROAD OF REMEMBRANCE

During the War Folkestone was the port from which men and supplies were sent to France as Dover was blockaded. Houses on the Leas were commandeered and huts put up for temporary accommodation. The town was continually busy and it is estimated that eight million young men marched down the Slope Road, obeying the command *"Step Short"* as they reached the top of the hill, on their way to the brutal battlefields of France. How many returned it is impossible to calculate - so many young men were killed that a headmistress told her class that only one in ten of them could expect to get married. The Slope Road is now the Road of Remembrance and there are plans for a museum, involving a European campaign for fundraising. The anniversary in 2014 of the war's beginning will be a momentous one for the town.

As always through the centuries, there was great confidence in the Navy to keep the enemy at bay. However, on one fine Friday evening, the 25th of May 1917 - when the townspeople were out doing their weekend shopping - the war suddenly and shockingly came to Folkestone. Sixteen aeroplanes dropped 51 bombs, of which 31 exploded, one

BOMB DAMAGE IN TONTINE STREET MAY 25TH 1917

landing directly on Tontine Street. This attack was all the more galling as in 1878 when two German battleships had collided on a fine morning in full view of the Leas, and over a hundred lives were lost, the British had extended help and sympathy and had been thanked by the German Emperor. No doubt the bombing was the aftermath of a raid on London and an attempt to hit the station. It was carnage, the dead and dying being strewn all over the street in front of Messrs. Stokes' grocery shop. The Fire Brigade saved whom they could in the ruins of several shops, but 71 were killed - the bodies being laid out in the mortuary for identification - and 100 were injured. This is a memory never to be forgotten. There were to be later warnings but no further bombs.

Between the two wars 'Floral Folkestone' was a peaceful, prosperous and attractive town. It was now middle class rather than aristocratic and the town had to attract a new public. The smart set such as Noel Coward and Ian Fleming were to desert East Kent and go to live in the West Indies. Families resorted to the East Cliff sands (in spite of inadequate sewage disposal causing unwanted debris) and the East Cliff Pavilion provided food and entertainment. In 1927 the Leas Cliff Hall was opened. The whole area was landscaped, to incorporate an undercliff path, the Coronation Parade, cliff top lawns, shelters, rock garden and steps next to the sea at Bakers Gap. In spite of cliff falls, the railway

FLORAL DISPLAYS ON THE LEAS ARE STILL POPULAR

line to Dover was kept open. There was a campsite on the Warren, affording views of the two harbours, dazzling sunsets and unique chalk vegetation. The remains of the large

Roman villa were discovered; they could have been preserved and made a feature of the town, but most of the site has now disappeared over the cliff. House prices had gone up to £500 for a small house in the East end to £1,500 for a double fronted villa. The wages of Corporation workmen were one shilling and four pence an hour. A car driver was prosecuted for driving down Sandgate Hill at the dangerous speed of 25-30 mph.

The Leas and the Victorian houses were saved from commercial development thanks to the Radnor Estate, and the Leas was later leased to the Council together with the East Cliff. Many centuries of stewardship were brought to an end. 'Spacious and gracious', the town may well be thankful to the Lords of the Manor. The Leas was well known for its flower beds, including a floral clock and the name of whichever conference was in session displayed in plants. There were many such conferences, large and small, from the Folkestone Grocers' Association to the National Union of Teachers; the hotels and boarding houses profited accordingly. A colony of elderly and well-to-do residents occupied the tall-ceilinged

THE LEAS CLIFF HALL IN CONSTRUCTION, AS IT LOOKED WHEN FIRST OPENED IN 1927 AND TODAY FOLLOWING ITS 1984 REVAMP

houses (now flats), which were crammed with oversized furniture from their previous dwellings. These were people who could afford the good shops. You could buy a Rolls from Martin Walters, groceries from Jacksons of Piccadilly and expensive jewellery from Oclee's. Bobby's had moved up from Rendezvous Street to the Sandgate Road, part of a general shift from the narrow crowded shops of the High Street and Rendezvous Street to larger, more convenient premises. The zig-zag path and the lifts provided convenient access down to the sea, the pier, the new open-air swimming and boating pools and the

Rotunda, crammed with every sort of amusement machine. There was plenty of entertainment, from music hall turns at the Pier Pavilion and the Marine Pavilion to the excellent plays with famous actors, often pre-London productions, at the Pleasure Gardens Theatre.

A variety of festivals was held - music, cricket and hockey, and later, international folklore. Cricket had shifted from the polo field on the Leas to a new ground donated by Lord Radnor,

CHANGING ON THE BEACH WAS FORBIDDEN,TENTS WERE PROVIDED,1930

formerly part of Broad Mead Farm. The first County match was played there in 1928 with the support of Lord Harris, himself an England player, Kent captain and president. Don Bradman scored 149 not out against an England XI in 1934.

Jocelyn Brooke was another literary figure in Sandgate, the son of the owner of the well-known Folkestone wine firm, J.H. and J. Brooke. He was born in Radnor Cliff in 1908, shortly before H.G. Wells left in 1911. His three volumes of autobiography - 'A Military Orchid', 'A Mine of Serpents' and 'The Goose Cathedral' - have been recently reprinted in Penguin Modern Classics. They depict his experiences in the Army combined with memories of Sandgate, the local countryside and his boyhood, written with a delicate precision reminiscent of Proust. His best novel is 'The Dog at Clambercrown' and he wrote also a book on orchids.

The Second World War brought upon the people of Folkestone an ordeal from bombs and shells which can be compared with the experience of those living in the centre of

large cities. None of this had been foreseen, so that in the early months of the war, 13,000 evacuees had been sent to Folkestone from London and Cllr Wood was berating those who fled the town, as being the cause of economic ruin. Within a few months, however, Folkestone's schoolchildren had to be sent to Wales and reports emphasised the warm welcome they received in the homes of Merthyr Tydfil. Meanwhile the Folkestone population dropped from 47,000 to 12,000 The town had been chosen by Hitler as part of 'Operation Sealion'- his invasion plan –

CHRIST CHURCHFOLLOWING THE HIGH EXPLOSIVE BOMB SUNDAY17TH MARCH1942

with Sandgate Esplanade being the designated landing site for the 17th infantry division.

Sandgate Esplanade was guarded by a few mines and rolls of barbed wire. Invasion precautions in the rest of the town included pill boxes and gun emplacements all the way along the Leas, tank traps and concrete blocks. So far as German plans were concerned, however, August, 1940 was a turning point of the war, when invasion plans were averted. The RAF, at tremendous cost in pilots' lives, proved its superiority to the Luftwaffe in air battles which could be followed from the Leas. The struggle in the air continued, however, and many planes were shot down over the cliffs and sea. Tip-and-run raids went on until

BOMB DAMAGE IN ROSSENDALE ROAD18TH NOVEMBER 1940

1942, with parachute mines proving to be the worst, causing devastation over a large area. One mine in Beach Street caused 14 deaths and 60 casualties, with 200 houses damaged or demolished. There were many instances of outstanding bravery from the Fire Service and the Home Guard, which earned four George Medals. During the exodus from Dunkirk, the 35,000 troops who were landed in Folkestone had to be given food and helped on their way into special trains.

In August 1940 the shelling began. Anderson shelters were issued and families had to spend their nights in them. The shelling was unannounced and spasmodic, centred on the railway station. It was a constant menace throughout most of the war and caused a great deal of damage to buildings. There were 24 gun batteries between Boulogne and Calais, of which the Lindemann at Sangatte was the most

THE RESULTS OF A PARACHUTE MINELANDING ON BEACH STREET 18TH NOVEMBER 1940

powerful. In reply there were large ex-naval guns firing from Folkestone: one on Copt Point, near St. Andrews Hospital and four at the end of Clifton Crescent. It was indeed 'Front Line Folkestone' and 'Hell Fire Corner' which of course included Dover.

The fishermen went on doggedly, though their fishing grounds were circumscribed by minefields and they occasionally caught mines in their nets; they were subject to a curfew at dusk. Folkestone became a ghost town - children gone; many shops and 35 pubs shut; a permit needed to bring a car in; ruined houses and broken windows everywhere. Christ Church was bombed and only the tower remained. The blackout was enforced with special vigilance by the air-raid wardens. When the flying bombs or V1s started, every effort was made to shoot them down over the sea before they reached

London. Yet life and entertainment went on, thanks to the cinemas and dances at the

Leas Cliff Hall and Bobby's. By means of the local paper enough money was collected to buy three Lancaster bombers and two Spitfires.

Every effort was made to persuade the Germans that the invasion of France was to be launched from East Kent. Large houses were taken over by American and Canadian troops; there were lights, explosions and many radio signals. On September 25th, 1944 the last shell arrived. The Canadians had taken over the gun positions in France. At last the exhausted townspeople could sleep peacefully in their beds. The King and Queen visited to pay tribute to the Civil Defence services. There had been some four thousand air raid warnings, 123 people killed and ten thousand houses demolished or damaged.

CHRISTCHURCH, SANDGATE ROAD AS IT STANDS TODAY,

Gradually the population started to return. Many elderly residents stayed in hotels, afraid even to visit their homes as there had been rumours of looting. 'Picture Post' the most popular illustrated magazine of the period, published an article, 'Is Folkestone Dying?' which seemed at the time as if it could be only too true. But the shops opened, Bobby's (later Debenhams) prospered and there was renewed employment in the building trade as houses were repaired. Coffee at the Cocker or Frogmore cafes was popular with residents in the mornings. But many of the visitors did not return, as the popularity of cheap package holidays abroad increased, with their guaranteed good weather. Boarding houses were converted into flats as were even more of the large houses - no longer the preserve of large families with the staff housed in the attics or basements. Many hotels closed, while the Grand and the Metropole were converted into apartments (as the Grand had originally been). The ground floor of the Metropole became an Arts Centre, financed by a millionaire, Gerald Glover. It held many good exhibitions, small concerts and talks.

The Council did its best to clear in record time all the obstacles and tank traps that had been put in the way of possible invaders, so that normal life might be resumed. Some old landmarks went: the pier was destroyed by fire in 1945; the Pleasure Gardens Theatre, becoming shabbier and emptier, closed in 1960. However, the Leas Pavilion - originally a tea room - had many successful seasons under the ownership of Arthur Brough; during the summer for several years there was a new play every week, many of which rivalled London productions.

Dover was to keep its commanding position as regards the cross-channel traffic, but Folkestone had its car ferries, Boulogne being actually a more attractive destination than Calais. By the sixties, however, the town was fading. The Majestic and the Queens Hotels closed, leaving the Motel Burstin, which principally takes coach parties, as the only large hotel. Perhaps equally disadvantageous for those of more limited means was the gradual disappearance of the boarding houses. There were high hopes at the opening of the Channel Tunnel, but most travellers preferred to journey on to their destination without an overnight stay.

THE DEVELOPMENT AREA BELOW THE LEAS

Folkestone's decline is now being reversed and there are signs of a new beginning. Sydney de Haan came to Folkestone in the 1950s as proprietor of the Rhodesia Hotel, where his son Roger was brought up. The Old People's Holiday Bureau for the over 60s followed, with many patrons from the Midlands. Its name was changed to Saga, the age limit lowered to 50 and the firm expanded into insurance. Roger further built up the business and sold it for 1.3 billion pounds. It has now 2,500 employees, an economic benefit for the town. He decided to devote a considerable part of the proceeds to charitable purposes. The Roger de Haan Charitable Trust gives large sums to varied good causes, including hospices, the relief of aids in Africa and the Canterbury Cathedral appeal. A primary concern is the rehabilitation of Folkestone, to make it once more a pleasant place to live and work, To this end a master plan was prepared by Norman Foster, a world famous architect. The most-run down area of the town - the old High Street, Tontine Street and the area round the Harbour - is now the Creative Quarter. Shops have been repaired and let at reasonable rents to galleries and new businesses. There is an adult education centre; a University extension under the joint patronage of the University of Greenwich and the University of Christ Church, Canterbury; a jazz and pop centre, the Quarterhouse; a triennial art exhibition and the possibility of sculpture on the Leas. The Harbour is owned by Roger de Haan, along with 35 acres of development land in its vicinity to be used for housing and leisure.

All this will take years to come to fruition. Some of the businesses have struggled and it may be that some sort of transport up-and-down the steep side of the Pent Valley is advisable. Tontine Street, where once the favourite merchandise was, *"Hamburger, chips and beer, £5"* is already greatly improved. In scale and imagination the schemes can be compared with the great leap forward in the mid-nineteenth century facilitated by the fifth Earl of Radnor and the arrival of the railway. New high-speed trains to London are being introduced, cutting the journey time to under one hour.

With these relatively brief references to the present, we conclude our retrospective view of Folkestone over its long and varied history. We have seen something of the nature and extent of its importance, the changing fortunes of the inhabitants, rich and poor. Who can anticipate what the future will bring?"

BIBLIOGRAPHY

CHAPTER 1
THE PAST UNEARTHED

Course of lectures given at the University Centre, Folkestone, October-December 2008
Life of St. Eanswythe, John Capgrove. 1393-1464
Archaeology and the Channel Tunnel, Paul Bennett. Arch. Cant. Vol. cvi, 1988
The Folkestone Roman Villa 1989, B. Phelps, 50 Years of Kent Rescue
Roman Folkestone, S.E. Winbolt, Methuen, 1925
Brittannia, Sheppard Frere, Routledge, 1967
The Endinig of Roman Britain, A.S. Esmonde Cleary, 1989
Britannia, the Failed State, Stuart Laycock 2008

CHAPTER 2
MEDIEVAL FOLKESTONE

Domesday Book, Kent, compiled by direction of King William I, Winchester 1086, ed. Philip Morgan, Chichester 1983, Phillimore & Co.Ltd.
Copy of the Folkestone Customal, 1327, Peter Davies Heritage Room, FRL
The Medieval Buildings of Folkestone and the Pent Stream, information provided by the Canterbury Archaological Trust
Medieval Will Transcripts, Dr. E. Pole Stewart, 1451-1588, Peter Davies Heritage Room, FRL
Medieval Folkestone, Canon Scott Robinson, Arch. Cant., Vol. X, CIV-CXXVII

CHAPTERS 3 AND 4
THE TUDORS AND STUARTS

Henry VIII King and Court, Alison Weir, Pimlico 2002
Chamberlain's Accounts, 1515, 1541-1545, Town Clerk's bills, Town Dyke etc.
FC1 series. The cesses were on land,i.e. tenanted properties and on 'abilities' FC2 series
General Sessions of the Peace and Gaol Delivery which met once a year, records from 1604, held before the Mayor and some Jurats, juries empanelled by the Water Bailiff, JQ series
Common Assembly Minute Book, 1605-1715, Peter Davies Heritage Room, FRL
The Oxford History of England, The Seventeenth Century, Jenny Wormald, Oxford University Press

CHAPTER 5
THE EIGHTEENTH CENTURY

Common Assembly Minute Books,1715-1812
Chamberlain's Accounts, Peter Davies Heritage Room, FRL
Sir John Moore, Carola Oman, Hodder & Stoughton, 1953
The French are Coming, Peter Lloyd, Spellman
Coast of Conflict, Michael and Martin George, S & B Publications, 2004
Kent and the Napoleonic Wars, Peter Bloomfield, Kentish Sources, Kent Archives Office,1987
Smuggling in Folkestone, ed. Nicholas Reed, Lilburne Press, 2005
Borough Records, Lieutancy Papers, Cpm series, give details of male inhabitants liable for service, barges, boats, horses and arms available, precautions in the event of invasion, loaves to be provided, number of bakers etc. etc

CHAPTER 6
THE MAKING OF THE MODERN TOWN
THE COUNCIL

Borough Records: Legal. A mixed collection of documents covering subjects as various as flooding in Tontine Streeet, demolition of the medieval house in the Bayle 1915, rights of way concerning the harbour 1861, the Corporation's opposition to the Gas Company's bill, the Local Government

Boundaries Act 1887, building of a washhouse in Cambridge Gardens, the Folkestone Improvement
Act 1855 and its consequences
Common Assembly Minutes,
Council Minutes, Peter Davies Heritage Room, FRL

THE MANOR

Manor documents in the Peter Davies Heritage Room, FRL
Burke's Peerage, Baronetage and Knightage, 1999
There is a series of manor rolls, rents and leases, from 1402 onwards
Notebook of Jacob des Bouverie, 1696, U270 E1,
History of the Manor and Lordship of Folkestone, E. Hasted, 1790
Radnor Papers, mixed subjects in including the dispute over the Sandgate Railway
A Huguenot Family, 1536-1899, Jacob, Earl of Radnor, Foxbury Press, 2001

PARLIAMENT

The Barons of the Cinque Ports and the Parliamentary Representation of Hythe, George Wilks,
Folkestone, 1892, Hythe Library
The Rothschilds, F. Norton, Secker & Warburg, 1962
The Sassoons, S. Jackson, Heinemann, 1968
Reports in the Folkestone Chronicle, Express and Herald

CHAPTER 7
THE HARBOUR

Newspapers: Folkestone Herald, Folkestone Chronicle, Dover Telegraph
"Shipping, Cross Channel, Harbour" boxes, Peter Davies Heritage Room, FRL
Harbour Street, Folkestone, John Willson, CAT
Report on the state of Folkestone Harbour made to the Board of Admiralty, March 23, 1810
The Monthly Magazine, April 1, April 1, 1810
Captain Boxer's list of ships belonging to Folkestone 1860s from his pocket book
Captain Boxer s papers, F 1978 13/F 2,3,7
Jettee vouchers 1841, FO/Fuj 2/13, Treasurer's account books, coal dues, 1786-1845, FO/Fuj 1/1,
List of subscribers to the Folkestone Harbour Company, Auj 1/1 Peter Davies Heritage Room, FRL
Who's Who in Folkestone, Dr. E. Pole Stuart
Report of Captain Tyler on the new Harbour works, 7.8.69
The Select Committee to enquire into Railway Bill information 1836, House of Lords Library
Boat trains and Channel packets, Rixon Bucknall
Seafarers and their records, Robin Craig
An Act for the Support and Preservation of the Parish Church of Folkestone
Cross Channel packet services, R.J. Croft, University of Kent post-graduate thesis
Wilberforce's letter to Joseph Marryat, F 1981 3/C1

CHAPTERS 8 AND 9
THE ARRIVAL OF THE NAVVIES
RAILWAY PROGRESS AND CONSOLIDATION

Newspapers: Folkestone Chronicle, Folkestone Herald, Dover Express, Daily Telegraph,
Kentish Gazette
Herapath's Railway (and Commercial) Journal, Newspaper Library, Colindale
"Railway" boxes, Peter Davies Heritage Room, FRL
A History of English Railways, J.A. Francis, 1851
The Select Committee to enquire into Railway Bill Information, 1836, House of Lords Library
The Select Committee on Railways, Joseph Baxendale's Evidence, Hansard,March 8, 1844, p. 285
The Minutes of the Directors of the South Eastern Railway Company, Rail 635, Public Record Office
History of the Southern Railway, C. Dendy Marshall, Altan, 1968
The South Eastern and Chatham Railway, D.S. Nock
The Elham Valley Line, Brian Hart, Wild Swan Publications, 1984

Folkestone's Railways, Brian Hart, Wild Swan Publications, 2002
Pupils' Roll, Mill Bay Sunday School, 1839, Peter Davies Heritage Room, FRL
The Illustrated London News, 'To Boulogne and back in a day', July 1, 1843

CHAPTER 10
TRADES AND SERVICES

Newspapers: Folkestone Chronicle; Folkestone Herald, Folkestone Up-to-Date
Library boxes, 'Guide books'
There are a great number of trade directories which ran into many editions: The Universal British
Directory 1798, Kelly's Directories from 1845,;Pigot 1839, English's Advertising Sheets, English's
Handbook of Folkestone 1893; Views and Reviews of Folkestone. Pike, 1896;Goulden's Handbook,
1892
Census Returns
Holbein's Visitors' List, 1890
The Bradstone, Millfield and Cheriton Mills, Folkestone Herald, November, 1960

CHAPTER 11
BUILDERS AND ARCHITECTS

Victorian Architecture in Folkestone, Rev. Alan Gibson, Peter Davies Heritage Room, FRL
The Builders of Victorian Folkestone, Rev. Alan Gibson, Peter Davies Heritage Room, FRL
The Wear Bay Estate, Folkestone New Town, Peter Davies Heritage Room, FRL
Victorian Architecture, Dixon and Muthesis, Thames and Hudson, 1978
Maps, Directories, Advertisements, Folkestone Chronicle, Folkestone Herald
Buildings of England series, East Kent, Ed. Pevsner

CHAPTER 12
CHURCH AND CHAPEL

Newspapers, The Folkestone Chronicle, Express and Herald
The Parish Church of Folkestone, Matthew Woodward, Skeffington & Son, 1892
A Kentish Parson, Dame Eanswythe Evans, Folkestone Parish Church, 1980
Letters and Papers, foreign and domestic of the reign of Henry VIII, Index Vol.IX,
October 23, 1935
A Kentish Parson, ed. G. Ditchfield and B. Keith Jones, Kent Arts and Libraries, 1991
Much information on Woodward comes from an unpublished biography by the Rev. Tony Shepherd
Kent and the Oxford Movement, N. Yates, Kentish Sources VII, Kent Archives Office
Law Reports, Probate Division, 1876-7 Vol.I, pp. 316-63, 383-92, Vol. II pp.276-353
The Folkestone Ritual Case, Sir James Steven and others, Peter Davies Heritage Room, FRL
The Story of the Baptists, Rev. J.C. Carlile
A Tale of two Churches, Christ Church and Holy Trinity, Hilary Tolputt
Methodism in Folkestone, Rev. W. Brimmell

CHAPTER 13
THE SCHOOLS

The Kentish Pocket Companion, 1831
The Watering Places of Great Britain, 1831
Directories: Universal British, 1831;Finch, 1803;Holden, 1813; Pigot, 1823; Robson, 1828; Kelly,
1845; Bagshaw 1847; Williams, 1849; Melville, 1848; Kelly, 1882
School logs: St. Mary's; Sandgate School; Sydney Street, North Board School
John Constable, J.L Foster, Hutchinson, 1976
"Schools" boxes, Heritage Room, FRL
The Clarke family and Grove House School, Dr. J. Anderson, Bygone Kent, Vol. 5, No.9
Census returns, 1871
A History of Harvey Grammar School, the Rev. J. Howard Brown, Old Harveians Assn., 1962
The Castle Hill Magazine, K.Fol.70
There is a large collection of Harvey Grammar School documents; clerk's correspondence, minutes

of the trustees, FO QHA I/1-22 vouchers, 2/ 1-95
The Folkestone Chronicle and Folkestone Herald; advertisements, correspondence and editorials, particularly from 1870 onwards on the question of school boards

CHAPTER 14
THE LABOURING CLASS AND THE POOR

Newspapers: Folkestone Chronicle, Folkestone Herald, Folkestone Up-to-Date. Peter Davies Heritage Room, FRL
"Shops" box, Peter Davies Heritage Room, FRL
Crompton House, Sandgate Archives, Fire Station
Census returns
Charitable East London, The Victorian Society, Toynbee Hall, 1988
The Workhouse, Norman Longmate
Folkestone Abilities 1704-1735
The Poor, Kentish Sources, E. Melling
Archives in the Public Record Office: Folkestone Poor Books; Folkestone Overseers Accounts; The Poor Law Letter Book, The Elham Union Minute Book
Instructions to the Guardians of the Poor to be given to the Officers, the Clerk the Relieving Office and the Master

CHAPTERS 15 AND 16
THE RESORT
OH, I DO LIKE TO BE BESIDE THE SEASIDE

Bathing machine licenses, FO/ARC/1/1, Minute Book of Bathing Machine Company, F/1954/2/8, Peter Davies Heritage Room, FRL
HVL, September 23, 1891
The Folkestone Cliff Lifts, Brian Hart, Hillgate Publishing Company, 1983
HVL. December 1, 1886
Folkestone Town Football Club History, L. Barlow, 1950
Lemuel Wale's Cycling, F/193, Peter Davies Heritage Room, FRL
Folkestone Almanac, Thorpe & Co., 1895
Castle Hill Magazine, Vol.II, No. 4
Short histories of race courses, R. Greaves, Field Sports, 1939
Chronicles of the old theatres of Eastern England, Bavey MSS
Bayle Theatre correspondence
The Folkestone Fiery Serpent ed. A. Nevill
There are almost weekly descriptions of the progress and fate of the Exhibition from the end of May, 1885 to February 1887 in all local newspapers
Kent bibliography, 1977
Illustrations: Maidstone Central Reference Library; 'Leas', box, postcards
The Early Kentish Seaside, John Whyman , Kentish Sources VIII, Alan Sutton, Kent Archives Office
The Sandgate, Hythe and Folkestone Guide, Purday and Son, Sandgate, 1823
Rise and Progress of a Village, Linda Rene Martin
Sandgate Cholera Book, Peter Davies Heritage Room, FRL
Dickens in Folkestone, Ann Nevill
H.G. Wells, Reg Turnill
A Guide to all the Watering and Seabathing Places and Fashionable Directory,1831
The English Seaside Resort, J.K. Walton, Leicester University Press, St. Martins Press, New York, 1963
The Radnor Estate and Victorian Development of Folkestone', file, Peter Davies Heritage Room, FRL
Report to the General Board of Health into the sewerage, drainage and main supply of water by T. R. Rammell under the powers of the Public Health Act, K San/614 FRL
Post card collection, Dennis Vorley

INDEX

FitzWilliam Hugh, 6
Fleming Ian, 193
Folkestone Girls' School, 134, 141
Folkestone Herald, 10, 40, 41, 96, 98, 135, 147, 179, 181, 184
Folkestone Advanced Liberal Association, 45
Folkestone Arms, 63
Folkestone Central, 84, 85
Folkestone Charitable Organisation The, 153
Folkestone Chronicle The 36, 41, 45, 55, 56, 80, 96, 97, 112, 114, 133, 149, 152, 157, 160, 162, 165, 167, 168, 173, 174, 179, 180, 181
Folkestone Corresponding Committee, 66
Folkestone Cricket Club, 166
Folkestone Executive Committee, 171
Folkestone Express The, 167, 169, 174
Folkestone Fiery Serpent, 169
Folkestone Fishing Boat Insurance Company, 145
Folkestone Football Club, 154, 167
Folkestone Free Library, 156
Folkestone Grocers' Association, 193
Folkestone Lift Company,162
Folkestone Lord, 38, 39, 48, 79
Folkestone Museum, 4, 173
Folkestone Piscatorial Society, 168
Folkestone Sandgate Hythe Tramway Company, 163
Folkestone Savings Bank, 92, 142, 151
Folkestone Society, 155
Folkestone Society for Friendless Girls, 149
Folkestone Town Band, 166
Folkestone Waterworks, 38, 67, 105, 180
Folly Fields, 170
Foord Lane, 35
Foord, 7, 54, 91, 99, 100, 109, 121, 133, 136, 140, 153
Forbes Staats James, 82
Ford Madox Ford, 135
Foren William, 9
Foresters Arms The, 152
Forster W.E. 132, 133
Fosters Laundry, 90
Foster's Temperance Hotel, 187
Fox Augustus Lane, 9
Fox Charles James, 42
Francis Anderson & Co
Frederick Hotels, 186
Friendly Societies, 77, 142, 151

Gambrill John, 94, 100, 161
Gardner Joseph, 91, 108, 109, 123, 161, 171
Gas, 41, 46, 61, 83, 84, 86, 93, 98, 99, 103, 105, 114, 115, 137, 138, 139
Gebon John, 8, 9
George Lloyd, 47
George The, 63
George Lane, 92
George IV, 34
Gibson Alan Rev. 9, 182
Gilbert & Sullivan, 164, 172
Gildas, 3, 4
Gill Captain RN, 37, 78
Gironimo's Restaurant, 91
Glanfield William, 173
Glee Club Magdalen College Oxford, 162
Glover Gerald, 196
Goddard Fr. 123
Godfrey Thomas, 16
Godwin Earl, 5. 6
Golder Charles, 61, 65, 71, 72
Gordon Hotels, 40, 189
Gosling W.F. 90
Gostling William, 25
Gotto Edward, 137

Gough John, 27, 63
Grace Hill, 14, 35, 93, 98, 108, 149, 151, 153
Grand Hotel The, 91, 104, 110, 145, 165, 166, 190, 191, 196
Granville Lord, 170
Gravesend, 51, 66, 151
Great Train Robbery, 76, 102
Great Chart, 93
Grimston Gardens, 104, 105, 180
Grimston Avenue, 135
Gubbay Hannah, 47
Guestling, 11, 34
Guildhall, 17, 34, 37, 155
Guildhall Street, 35, 87, 90, 105, 109, 117, 136, 137, 149, 185
Gybbe William, 8

Hall & King, 89
Hambrook & Johns, 105
Hammond William, 146
Hankey Claude Rev, 121
Hankey General 42, 78, 79, 81
Haan de Sydney, 197
Haan de Roger, 197
Harbour Way, 27
Harbour Company The, 34, 37, 48
Harbour Street, 27, 35, 92, 106
Hardwick P.C. 107
Harris Lord, 167
Harrison T. 138, 173
Hart Elizabeth, 150
Hart George, 179, 188
Hart Isreal Sir. 47
Hart Philip, 88
Hart Richard, 35, 79, 81, 100, 116
Hart Simeon, 88
Harveian Institute, 155
Harveian Literary Institute, 38, 182
Harvey Eliab, 18, 19
Harvey Grammar School, 86, 126, 131, 136, 137, 139, 140, 141
Harvey Joan, 17
Harvey John, 17
Harvey Thomas, 17
Harvey William, 18. 101
Hasted, 9, 15, 16, 21, 24, 25, 143
Hastings, 63, 66, 87, 144
Hauereng Henry Sir, 7
Haverstock House, 186
Hawkinge, 7, 8, 9, 36, 91, 112
Hawkshaw John Sir, 58
Hawksworth Wheeler, 92
Hayward & Paramour, 172
Head Edward Rev. 138
Head Francis Rev, 138
Henry VIII, 12, 17
Henry II, 9
Henry VII, 11
Herapath Railway Journal, 50, 51, 64
Herdson Henry, 14
Herdson John, 36
Herdson Thomas, 14
Herne Bay, 66, 72, 159
High Church Union, 114
Hoare Samuel Sir, 47
Hobday Richard, 26
Hodgmen Richard, 37
Holbein's Visitor List, 35, 58, 70, 96, 98, 102, 145
Holden John, 161
Holden E.J. 105
Holden & Powell, 161
Holliday Robert, 15
Holy Trinity Church, 109, 120, 176

John and Ann Nevill enjoy a boat trip, Ischia, 2007